P9-DML-010

FRANK McCOURT taught for thirty years in various New York City high schools and in city colleges. *Angela's Ashes*, his first book, won the 1997 Pulitzer Prize, the National Book Critics' Circle Award, the *Los Angeles Times* Award and the Royal Society of Literature Award amongst others, and rapidly became a bestseller, topping all charts worldwide for over three years. *'Tis*, the sequel, continued its predecessor's huge success and the books have been published in more than twenty countries and languages. He lives in Connecticut and New York.

Visit www.AuthorTracker.co.uk for exclusive information on your favourite HarperCollins authors.

From the reviews of *Teacher Man*:

'McCourt has a compulsion to tell us the story of his life, but he does it so well – modulating beautifully from ventriloquistically exact repro teen-speak to rhapsodic meditations on his midlife crisis – that one couldn't possibly want him to stop. I wish I could have been in one of his classes'
LUCY HUGHES-HALLETT, *Sunday Times*

'This book is charming, and it relies heavily and success-fully on the lilting style and phonetic writing that marked out his last two books ... a really good read'
Observer

'This memoir about teaching is unlike any other I have read: relatively mundane events and incidents shine against that backdrop of that pathetic, abused child'
FRANCIS GILBERT, *Sunday Telegraph*

'Mightily entertaining ... sometimes hilarious ... but always engaging and humorous. *Teacher Man* is a full frontal depiction of the challenge, the comedy, the frustration, the failure, the pain, the drudgery and the pure unadulterated joy of teaching that makes it all worthwhile ... It's powerful writing. Overall a wonderfully told story, readable and entertaining'

SENATOR JOE O'TOOLE, Irish Independent

'This book brings laughter bubbling to the surface even as it tries to create an air of depression. McCourt cannot disguise the fact that his pupils love him, miserable Irish childhood and all, and (whisper it) that he loves them, too. McCourt taught his classes to drive out their fears. Inspiring stuff, and a book that every education bureaucrat should read'   FRAN ABRAMS, *New Statesman*

'The classroom tales are ... described with self-deprecating humour and a piercing insight into the psyche of the teenager. Despite his protestations otherwise, McCourt was clearly an inspiring figure, "I think of the 12,000 and wonder what I did for them." What they did for him was inspire this masterful memoir'

ANDREW SHIELDS, TimeOut

'Funny, insightful and affecting ... Thirty years teaching in New York City has provided McCourt with a mine of rich anecdotal material'   *Irish Times*

'A delightful memoir ... This book's freshness, its charm, comes from McCourt's observations of the teenagers he taught. It should be compulsory for anyone who ever underestimated a teacher's task. Here, brilliantly captured, is the horror and the humour of facing disruptive disengaged teenagers so streetwise that they can smell you out even before you enter the room'

Glasgow Herald

'McCourt's many fans will of course love this book, but it also should be mandatory reading for every teacher in America. And it wouldn't hurt some politicians to read it, too'

Publishers Weekly (starred review)

'Told in McCourt's inimitable style, this is a celebration of the joy of teaching which is wildly funny, acutely observant and painfully honest. It is also full of his affection for the kids he taught, without being too sentimental' *Irish Independent*

Also by Frank McCourt

Angela's Ashes
'Tis

AMERICA'S TEACHERS OF THE YEAR

Mr. Frank McCourt, a dedicated and serious creative writing
teacher at Stuyvesant High School, is Teacher Of The Year
1976

FRANK McCOURT

Teacher Man

A MEMOIR

HARPER PERENNIAL
London, New York, Toronto and Sydney

Harper Perennial
An imprint of HarperCollins*Publishers*
77–85 Fulham Palace Road
Hammersmith, London W6 8JB

www.harperperennial.co.uk

This edition published by Harper Perennial 2006

1

First published in Great Britain in 2005 by Fourth Estate

A catalogue record for this book is available from the British Library

ISBN-13 978-0-00-722802-7
ISBN-10 0-00-722802-3

Set in Bembo

Printed and bound in Great Britain by Clays Ltd, St Ives plc

Acknowledgments

Thanks to the American Academy in Rome for three months of scholarship, splendor and merriment.

Thanks to Pam Carter of the Savoy Hotel in London for a three-month pampering in a river suite.

Thanks to my agent, Molly Friedrich, for bright words on dim days.

For my editor, Nan Graham, bring up the trumpets and drums. I strung words together but, as I watched in wonder, she hinted and sculpted till a book emerged.

And love to you, Ellen, wonder wife, always merry and bright, always ready for the next adventure, always kind.

Prologue

If I knew anything about Sigmund Freud and psychoanalysis I'd be able to trace all my troubles to my miserable childhood in Ireland. That miserable childhood deprived me of self-esteem, triggered spasms of self pity, paralyzed my emotions, made me cranky, envious and disrespectful of authority, retarded my development, crippled my doings with the opposite sex, kept me from rising in the world and made me unfit, almost, for human society. How I became a teacher at all and remained one is a miracle and I have to give myself full marks for surviving all those years in the classrooms of New York. There should be a medal for people who survive miserable childhoods and become teachers, and I should be first in line for the medal and whatever bars might be appended for ensuing miseries.

I could lay blame. The miserable childhood doesn't simply happen. It is brought about. There are dark forces. If I am to lay blame it is in a spirit of forgiveness. Therefore, I forgive the following: Pope Pius XII; the English in general and King George VI in particular; Cardinal MacRory, who ruled Ireland when I was a child; the bishop of Limerick, who seemed to think everything was sinful; Eamonn De Valera, former prime minister (Taoiseach) and president of Ireland. Mr. De Valera was a half-Spanish Gaelic fanatic (Spanish onion in an Irish stew) who directed teachers all over Ireland to beat the native tongue into us and natural curiosity out of us. He caused us hours of misery. He was aloof and indifferent to the black and blue welts raised by schoolmaster sticks on various parts of our young bodies. I forgive, also, the priest who drove me from the confessional when I admitted to sins of self-abuse and self-pollution and penny thieveries from my mother's purse. He said I did not show a proper spirit of repentance, especially in the matter of the flesh. And even though he had hit that nail right on the head, his refusal to grant me absolution put my soul in such peril that if I had been flattened by a truck outside the church he would have been responsible for my eternal damnation. I forgive various bullying schoolmasters for pulling me out of my seat by the sideburns, for walloping me regularly with stick, strap and cane when I stumbled over answers in the catechism or when in my head I couldn't divide 937 by 739. I was told by my parents and other adults it was all for my own good. I forgive them for those whopping hypocrisies and wonder where they are at this moment. Heaven? Hell? Purgatory (if it still exists)?

I can even forgive myself, though when I look back at various stages of my life, I groan. What an ass. What timidities. What stupidities. What indecisions and flounderings.

But then I take another look. I had spent childhood and adolescence examining my conscience and finding myself in a perpetual state of sin. That was the training, the brainwashing, the conditioning and it discouraged smugness, especially among the sinning class.

Now I think it time to give myself credit for at least one virtue: doggedness. Not as glamorous as ambition or talent or intellect or charm, but still the one thing that got me through the days and nights.

F. Scott Fitzgerald said that in American lives there are no second acts. He simply did not live long enough. In my case he was wrong.

When I taught in New York City high schools for thirty years no one but my students paid me a scrap of attention. In the world outside the school I was invisible. Then I wrote a book about my childhood and became mick of the moment. I hoped the book would explain family history to McCourt children and grandchildren. I hoped it might sell a few hundred copies and I might be invited to have discussions with book clubs. Instead it jumped onto the best-seller list and was translated into thirty languages and I was dazzled. The book was my second act.

In the world of books I am a late bloomer, a johnny-come-lately, new kid on the block. My first book, *Angela's Ashes,* was published in 1996 when I was sixty-six, the second, *'Tis,* in 1999 when I was sixty-nine. At that age it's a wonder I was able to lift the pen at all. New friends of mine (recently acquired because of my ascension to the best-seller lists) had published books in their twenties. Striplings.

So, what took you so long?

I was teaching, that's what took me so long. Not in college or university, where you have all the time in the world for writing and other diversions, but in four different New York City public high schools. (I have read novels about the lives of university professors where they seemed to be so busy with adultery and academic in-fighting you wonder where they found time to squeeze in a little teaching.) When you teach five high school classes a day, five days a week, you're not inclined to go home to clear your head and fashion deathless prose. After a day of five classes your head is filled with the clamor of the classroom.

I never expected *Angela's Ashes* to attract any attention, but when it hit the best-seller lists I became a media darling. I had my picture taken hundreds of times. I was a geriatric novelty with an Irish accent. I was interviewed for dozens of publications. I met governors, mayors, actors. I met the first President Bush and his son the governor of Texas. I met President Clinton and Hillary Rodham Clinton. I met Gregory Peck. I met the Pope and kissed his ring. Sarah, Duchess of York, interviewed me. She said I was her first Pulitzer Prize winner. I said she was my first duchess. She said, Ooh, and asked the cameraman, Did you get that? Did you get that? I was nominated for a Grammy for the spoken word and nearly met Elton John. People looked at me in a different way. They said, Oh, you wrote that book, This way, please, Mr. McCourt, or Is there anything you'd like, anything? A woman in a coffee shop squinted and said, I seen you on TV. You must be important. Who are you? Could I have your autograph? I was listened to. I was asked for my opinion on Ireland, conjunctivitis, drinking, teeth, education, religion, adolescent angst, William Butler Yeats, literature in general. What books are you reading this summer? What books have you read this year? Catholicism, writing, hunger. I spoke to gatherings of dentists, lawyers, ophthalmologists and, of course, teachers. I traveled the world being Irish, being a teacher, an authority on misery of all kinds, a beacon of hope to senior citizens everywhere who always wanted to tell their stories.

They made a movie of *Angela's Ashes*. No matter what you write in America there is always talk of The Movie. You could write the Manhattan telephone directory, and they'd say, So, when is the movie?

If I hadn't written *Angela's Ashes* I would have died begging, Just one more year, God, just one more year because this book is the one thing I want to do in my life, what's left of it. I never dreamed it would be a best-seller. I hoped it would sit on booksellers' shelves while I lurked in the bookshop and watched beautiful women turn pages and shed the occasional tear. They'd buy the book, of course, take it home, loll on divans and read my story while sipping herbal tea or a fine sherry. They'd order copies for all their friends.

In *'Tis* I wrote about my life in America and how I became a teacher. After it was published I had the nagging feeling I'd given teaching short shrift. In America, doctors, lawyers, generals, actors, television people and politicians are admired and rewarded. Not teachers. Teaching is the downstairs maid of professions. Teachers are told to use the service door or go around the back. They are congratulated on having ATTO (All That Time Off). They are spoken of patronizingly and patted, retroactively, on their silvery locks. Oh, yes, I had an English teacher, Miss Smith, who really inspired me. I'll never forget dear old Miss Smith. She used to say that if she reached one child in her forty years of teaching it would make it all worthwhile. She'd die happy. The inspiring English teacher then fades into gray shadows to eke out her days on a penny-pinching pension, dreaming of the one child she might have reached. Dream on, teacher. You will not be celebrated.

You think you'll walk into the classroom, stand a moment, wait for silence, watch while they open notebooks and click pens, tell them your name, write it on the board, proceed to teach.

On your desk you have the English course of study provided by the school. You'll teach spelling, vocabulary, grammar, reading comprehension, composition, literature.

You can't wait to get to the literature. You'll have lively discussions about poems, plays, essays, novels, short stories. The hands of one hundred and seventy students will quiver in the air and they'll call out, Mr. McCourt, me, me, I wanna say something.

You hope they'll want to say something. You don't want them to sit gawking while you struggle to keep a lesson alive.

You'll feast on the bodies of English and American literature. What a time you'll have with Carlyle and Arnold, Emerson and Thoreau. You can't wait to get to Shelley, Keats and Byron and good old Walt Whitman. Your classes will love all that romanticism and rebellion, all that defiance. You'll love it yourself, because, deep down and in your dreams, you're a wild romantic. You see yourself on the barricades.

Principals and other figures of authority passing in the hallways will hear sounds of excitement from your room. They'll peer through the door window in wonder at all the raised hands, the eagerness and excitement on the faces of these boys and girls, these plumbers, electricians, beauticians, carpenters, mechanics, typists, machinists.

You'll be nominated for awards: Teacher of the Year, Teacher of the Century. You'll be invited to Washington. Eisenhower will shake your hand. Newspapers will ask you, a mere teacher, for your opinion on education. This will be big news: A teacher asked for his opinion on education. Wow. You'll be on television.

Television.

Imagine: A teacher on television.

They'll fly you to Hollywood, where you'll star in movies about your own life. Humble beginnings, miserable childhood, problems with the church (which you bravely defied), images of you solitary in a corner, reading by candlelight: Chaucer, Shakespeare, Austen, Dickens. You there in the corner blinking with your poor diseased eyes, bravely reading till your mother pulls the candle away from you, tells you if you don't stop the two eyes will fall out of your head entirely. You plead for the candle back, you have only a hundred pages left in *Dombey and Son,* and she says, No, I don't want to be leading you around Limerick with people asking how you went blind when a year ago you were kicking a ball with the best of them.

You say yes to your mother because you know the song:

> *A mother's love is a blessing*
> *No matter where you go*
> *Keep her while you have her*
> *You'll miss her when she's gone.*

Besides, you could never talk back to a movie mother played by one of those old Irish actresses, Sarah Allgood or Una O'Connor, with their sharp tongues and their suffering faces. Your own mother had a powerful hurt look, too, but there's nothing like seeing it on the big screen in black and white or living color.

Your father could be played by Clark Gable except that a) he might not be able to handle your father's North of Ireland accent and b) it would be a terrible comedown from *Gone With the Wind,* which, you remember, was banned in Ireland because, it is said, Rhett Butler carried his own wife, Scarlett, up the stairs and into bed, which upset the film censors in Dublin and caused them to ban the film entirely. No, you'd need someone else as your father because the Irish censors would be watching closely and you'd be badly disappointed if the people in Limerick, your city, and the rest of Ireland were denied the opportunity of seeing the story of your miserable childhood and subsequent triumph as teacher and movie star.

But that would not be the end of the story. The real story would be how you eventually resisted the siren call of Hollywood, how after nights of being dined, wined, feted and lured to the beds of female stars, established and aspiring, you discovered the hollowness of their lives, how they poured out their hearts to you on various satin pillows, how you listened, with twinges of guilt, while they expressed their admiration for you, that you, because of your devotion to your students, had become an idol and an icon in Hollywood, how they, the ravishing female stars, established and aspiring, regretted how they had gone astray, embracing the emptiness of their Hollywood lives when, if they gave it all up, they could rejoice daily in the integrity of teaching the future craftsmen, tradesmen and clerk-typists of America. How it must feel, they would say, to wake up in the morning, to leap gladly from the bed, knowing that before you stretched a day in which you'd do God's work with the youth of America, content with your meager remuneration, your real reward the glow of gratitude in the eager eyes of your students as they bear gifts from their grateful and admiring parents: cookies, bread, home-made pasta and the occasional bottle of wine from the backyard vines of Italian families, the mothers and fathers of your one hundred and seventy students at McKee Vocational and Technical High School, Borough of Staten Island, in the City of New York.

PART I

It's a Long Road to Pedagogy

1

Here they come.

And I'm not ready.

How could I be?

I'm a new teacher and learning on the job.

On the first day of my teaching career, I was almost fired for eating the sandwich of a high school boy. On the second day I was almost fired for mentioning the possibility of friendship with a sheep. Otherwise, there was nothing remarkable about my thirty years in the high school classrooms of New York City. I often doubted if I should be there at all. At the end I wondered how I lasted that long.

It is March 1958. I sit at my desk in an empty classroom in McKee Vocational and Technical High School in the Borough of Staten Island, New York City. I toy with the implements of my new calling: five manila folders, one for each class; a clump of crumbling rubber bands; a block of brown wartime composition paper flecked with whatever went into the making of it; a worn blackboard eraser; a stack of white cards that I will insert row by row into slots in this tattered red Delaney book to help me remember the names of one hundred and sixty-odd boys and girls who will sit in rows every day in five different classes. On the cards I'll record their attendance and tardiness and make little marks when boys and girls do bad things. I'm told I should keep a red pen to record the bad things, but the school hasn't supplied one, and now I have to request it on a form or buy one in a shop because the red pen for the bad things is the teacher's most powerful weapon. There are many things I will have to buy in a shop. In Eisenhower's America there is prosperity but it does not trickle down to schools, especially to new teachers who need supplies for their classes. There is a note from an assistant principal in charge of administration reminding all teachers of the city's financial plight and to please use these supplies sparingly. This morning I have to make decisions. In a minute the bell will ring. They'll swarm in and what will they say if they see me at the desk? Hey, look. He's hiding out. They are experts on teachers. Sitting at the desk means you're scared or lazy. You're using the desk as a barrier. Best thing is to get out there and stand. Face the music. Be a man. Make one mistake your first day and it takes months to recover.

The kids arriving are juniors, sixteen years old, eleven years in school from kindergarten to today. So, teachers come, teachers go, all kinds, old, young, tough, kind. Kids watch, scrutinize, judge. They know body language, tone of voice, demeanor in general. It's not as if they sit around in toilets or cafeterias discussing these things. They just absorb it over eleven years, pass it on to coming generations. Watch out for Miss Boyd, they'll say. Homework, man, homework, and she corrects it. Corrects it. She ain't married so she's got nothing else to do. Always try to get married teachers with kids. They don't have time for sitting around with papers and books. If Miss Boyd got laid regular she wouldn't give so much homework. She sits there at home with her cat listening to classical music, correcting our homework, bothering us. Not like some teachers. They give you a pile of homework, check it off, never even look at it. You could copy a page of the Bible and they'd write at the top, "Very nice." Not Miss Boyd. She's on to you right off. Excuse me, Charlie. Did you write this yourself? And you have to admit, no, you didn't and now you're up shit creek, man.

It's a mistake to arrive early, gives you too much time to think of what you're facing. Where did I get the nerve to think I could handle American teenagers? Ignorance. That's where I got the nerve. It is the Eisenhower era and newspapers report the great unhappiness of American adolescents. These are the "Lost Children of the Lost Children of the Lost Generation." Movies, musicals, books tell us of their unhappiness: *Rebel Without a Cause, The Blackboard Jungle, West Side Story, The Catcher in the Rye.* They make despairing speeches. Life is meaningless. All adults are phonies. What's the use of living at all? They have nothing to look forward to, not even a war of their own where they can kill natives in distant places and march up ticker-tape Broadway with medals and limps for the girls to admire. No use complaining to their fathers, who just fought a war, or their mothers, who waited while the fathers fought. Fathers say, Oh, shaddup. Don't bodder me. I got a pounda shrapnel up my ass an' I don't have time for you bitchin' an' moanin' wid your belly full an' your closet stuffed with clothes. F'Christ's sakes, when I was your age I was out woikin' in a junkyard before I went on the docks so I could send your sorry ass to school. Go squeeze your goddam pimples an' lemme read my paper.

There's so much teen unhappiness they form gangs and fight other gangs, not rumbles like the ones you see in movies with star-crossed romances and dramatic music in the background, but mean fights where they grunt and curse one another, where Italians, Blacks, Irish, Puerto Ricans attack with knives, chains, baseball bats in Central Park and Prospect Park and stain the grass with their blood, which is always red no matter where it came from. Then if there's a killing there's public outrage and accusations that if the schools and teachers were doing their jobs these terrible things wouldn't happen. There are patriots who say, If these kids have the time and energy to be fighting one another why can't we just ship them overseas to fight the goddam Communists and settle that problem for once and for all?

Vocational schools were seen by many as dumping grounds for students ill-equipped for academic high schools. That was snobbery. It didn't matter to the public that thousands of young people wanted to be auto mechanics, beauticians, machinists, electricians, plumbers, carpenters. They didn't want to be bothered with the Reformation, the War of 1812, Walt Whitman, art appreciation, the sex life of the fruit fly.

But, man, if we have to do it we'll do it. We'll sit in those classes that have nothing to do with our lives. We'll work in our shops where we learn about the real world and we'll try to be nice to the teachers and get outa here in four years. Whew!

Here they are. The door slams against the shelf that runs along the base of the blackboard, stirs a cloud of chalk dust. Entering a room is a big deal. Why couldn't they simply walk into the room, say, Good morning, and sit? Oh, no. They have to push and jostle. One says, Hey, in a mock threatening way and another one says, Hey, right back. They insult one another, ignore the late bell, take their time sitting. That's cool, baby. Look, there's a new teacher up there and new teachers don't know shit. So? Bell? Teacher? New guy. Who is he? Who cares? They talk to friends across the room, lounge in desks too small for them, stick out their legs, laugh if someone trips. They stare out the window, over my head at the American flag or the pictures taped to the walls by Miss Mudd, now retired, pictures of Emerson, Thoreau, Whitman, Emily Dickinson and—how did he get here?— Ernest Hemingway. It's the *Life* magazine cover and that picture is everywhere. They gouge their initials on desk tops with penknives, declarations of love with hearts and arrows alongside the long-ago gougings of their fathers and brothers. Some old desks are gouged so deep you can see your knees through holes where hearts and names used to be. Couples sit together, hold hands, whisper and gaze into each other's eyes while three boys against the back closets sing doo-wop, bass, baritone and high notes, man, snap fingers, tell the world they're just teenagers in love.

Five times a day they push into the room. Five classes, thirty to thirty-five in each class. Teenagers? In Ireland we saw them in American movies, moody, surly, driving around in cars, and we wondered why they were moody and surly. They had food and clothes and money and still they were mean to their parents. There were no teenagers in Ireland, not in my world. You were a child. You went to school till you were fourteen. If you were mean to your parents they'd give you a good belt in the gob and send you flying across the room. You grew up, got a laboring job, got married, drank your pint on a Friday night, jumped on the wife that same night and kept her pregnant forever. In a few years you emigrated to England to work on the building sites or to enlist in His Majesty's forces and fight for the Empire.

The problem of the sandwich started when a boy named Petey called out, Anyone wan' a baloney sandwich?

You kiddin'? Your mom must hate you, givin' you sandwiches like that.

Petey threw his brown-paper sandwich bag at the critic, Andy, and the class cheered. Fight, fight, they said. Fight, fight. The bag landed on the floor between the blackboard and Andy's front-row desk.

I came from behind my desk and made the first sound of my teaching career: Hey. Four years of higher education at New York University and all I could think of was Hey.

I said it again. Hey.

They ignored me. They were busy promoting the fight that would kill time and divert me from any lesson I might be planning. I moved toward Petey and made my first teacher statement, Stop throwing sandwiches. Petey and the class looked startled. This teacher, new teacher, just stopped a good fight. New teachers are supposed to mind their own business or send for the principal or a dean and everyone knows it's years before they come. Which means you can have a good fight while waiting. Besides, what are you gonna do with a teacher who tells you stop throwing sandwiches when you already threw the sandwich?

Benny called out from the back of the room. Hey, teach, he awredy threw the sangwidge. No use tellin' him now don't throw the sangwidge. They's the sangwidge there on the floor.

The class laughed. There's nothing sillier in the world than a teacher telling you don't do it after you already did it. One boy covered his mouth and said, Stoopid, and I knew he was referring to me. I wanted to knock him out of his seat, but that would have been the end of my teaching career. Besides, the hand that covered his mouth was huge, and his desk was too small for his body.

Someone said, Yo, Benny, you a lawyer, man? and the class laughed again. Yeah, yeah, they said, and waited for my move. What will this new teacher do?

Professors of education at New York University never lectured on how to handle flying-sandwich situations. They talked about theories and philosophies of education, about moral and ethical imperatives, about the necessity of dealing with the whole child, the gestalt, if you don't mind, the child's felt needs, but never about critical moments in the classroom.

Should I say, Hey, Petey, get up here and pick up that sandwich, or else? Should I pick it up myself and throw it into the wastepaper basket to show my contempt for people who throw sandwiches while millions starve all over the world?

They had to recognize I was boss, that I was tough, that I'd take none of their shit.

The sandwich, in wax paper, lay halfway out of the bag and the aroma told me there was more to this than baloney. I picked it up and slid it from its wrapping. It was not any ordinary sandwich where meat is slapped between slices of tasteless white American bread. This bread was dark and thick, baked by an Italian mother in Brooklyn, bread firm enough to hold slices of a rich baloney, layered with slices of tomato, onions and peppers, drizzled with olive oil and charged with a tongue-dazzling relish.

I ate the sandwich.

It was my first act of classroom management. My mouth, clogged with sandwich, attracted the attention of the class. They gawked up at me, thirty-four boys and girls, average age sixteen. I could see the admiration in their eyes, first teacher in their lives to pick up a sandwich from the floor and eat it in full view. Sandwich man. In my boyhood in Ireland we admired one schoolmaster who peeled and ate an apple every day and rewarded good boys with the long peel. These kids watched the oil dribble down my chin to my two-dollar tie from Klein-on-the-Square.

Petey said, Yo, teacher, that's my sandwich you et.

Class told him, Shaddap. Can't you see the teacher is eating?

I licked my fingers. I said, Yum, made a ball of paper bag and wax paper and flipped it into the trash basket. The class cheered. Wow, they said, and Yo, baby, and M-a-a-a-n. Look at dat. He eats the sandwich. He hits the basket. Wow.

So this is teaching? Yeah, wow. I felt like a champion. I ate the sandwich. I hit the basket. I felt I could do anything with this class. I thought I had them in the palm of my hand. Fine, except I didn't know what to do next. I was there to teach, and wondered how I should move from a sandwich situation to spelling or grammar or the structure of a paragraph or anything related to the subject I was supposed to teach, English.

My students smiled till they saw the principal's face framed in the door window. Bushy black eyebrows halfway up his forehead shaped a question. He opened the door and beckoned me out. A word, Mr. McCourt?

Petey whispered, Hey, mister. Don't worry about the sandwich. I didn't want it anyway.

The class said, Yeah, yeah, in a way that showed they were on my side if I had trouble with the principal, my first experience of teacher-student solidarity. In the classroom your students might stall and complain but when a principal or any other outsider appeared there was immediate unity, a solid front.

Out in the hallway, he said, I'm sure you understand, Mr. McCourt, it isn't seemly to have teachers eating their lunch at nine a.m. in their classrooms in the presence of these boys and girls. Your first teacher experience and you choose to begin it by eating a sandwich? Is that proper procedure, young man? It's not our practice here, gives children the wrong idea. You can see the reasoning, eh? Think of the problems we'd have if teachers just dropped everything and began to eat their lunches in class, especially in the morning when it's still breakfast time. We have enough trouble with kids sneaking little nibbles during morning classes and attracting cockroaches and various rodents. Squirrels have been chased from these rooms, and I won't even mention rats. If we're not vigilant these kids, and some teachers, your colleagues, young man, will turn the school into one big cafeteria.

I wanted to tell him the truth about the sandwich and how well I handled the situation, but if I did it might be the end of my teaching job. I wanted to say, Sir, it was not my lunch. That was the sandwich of a boy who threw it at another boy and I picked it up because I'm new here and this thing happened in my class and there was nothing in the courses at college on sandwiches, the throwing and retrieving of. I know I ate the sandwich but I did it out of desperation or I did it to teach the class a lesson about waste and to show them who was in charge or, Jesus, I ate it because I was hungry and I promise never to do it again for fear I might lose my good job though you must admit the class was quiet. If that's the way to capture the attention of kids in a vocational high school you ought to send out for a pile of baloney sandwiches for the four classes I still have to meet today.

I said nothing.

The principal said he was there to help me because, Ha, ha, I looked like I might need a lot of help. I'll admit, he said, you had their full attention. OK, but see if you can do it in a less dramatic way. Try teaching. That's what you're here for, young man. Teaching. Now you have ground to recover. That's all. No eating in class for teacher or student.

I said, Yes, sir, and he waved me back to the classroom.

The class said, What'd he say?

He said I shouldn't eat my lunch in the classroom at nine a.m.

You wasn't eatin' no lunch.

I know, but he saw me with the sandwich and told me not to do it again.

Man, that's unfair.

Petey said, I'll tell my mom you liked her sandwich. I'll tell her you got in a lot of trouble over her sandwich.

All right, Petey, but don't tell her you threw it away.

Naw, naw. She'd kill me. She's from Sicily. They get excited over there in Sicily.

Tell her it was the most delicious sandwich I ever had in my life, Petey.

OK.

Mea culpa.

Instead of teaching, I told stories.

Anything to keep them quiet and in their seats.

They thought I was teaching.

I thought I was teaching.

I was learning.

And you called yourself a teacher?

I didn't call myself anything. I was more than a teacher. And less. In the high school classroom you are a drill sergeant, a rabbi, a shoulder to cry on, a disciplinarian, a singer, a low-level scholar, a clerk, a referee, a clown, a counselor, a dress-code enforcer, a conductor, an apologist, a philosopher, a collaborator, a tap dancer, a politician, a therapist, a fool, a traffic cop, a priest, a mother-father-brother-sister-uncle-aunt, a bookkeeper, a critic, a psychologist, the last straw.

In the teachers' cafeteria veterans warned me, Son, tell 'em nothing about yourself. They're kids, goddam it. You're the teacher. You have a right to privacy. You know the game, don't you? The little buggers are diabolical. They are not, repeat not, your natural friends. They can smell it when you're going to teach a real lesson on grammar or something, and they'll head you off at the pass, baby. Watch 'em. Those kids have been at this for years, eleven or twelve, and they have teachers all figured out. They'll know if you're even thinking about grammar or spelling, and they'll raise their little hands and put on that interested expression and ask you what games you played as a kid or who do you like for the goddam World Series. Oh, yeah. And you'll fall for it. Next thing is you're spilling your guts and they go home not knowing one end of a sentence from the other, but telling the moms and dads about your life. Not that they care. They'll get by, but where does that leave you? You can never get back the bits and pieces of your life that stick in their little heads. Your life, man. It's all you have. Tell 'em nothing.

The advice was wasted. I learned through trial and error and paid a price for it. I had to find my own way of being a man and a teacher and that is what I struggled with for thirty years in and out of the classrooms of New York. My students didn't know there was a man up there escaping a cocoon of Irish history and Catholicism, leaving bits of that cocoon everywhere.

My life saved my life. On my second day at McKee a boy asks a question that sends me into the past and colors the way I teach for the next thirty years. I am nudged into the past, the materials of my life.

Joey Santos calls out, Yo, teach. . . .

You are not to call out. You are to raise your hand.

Yeah, yeah, said Joey, but . . .

They have a way of saying yeah yeah that tells you they're barely tolerating you. In the yeah yeah they're saying, We're trying to be patient, man, giving you a break because you're just a new teacher.

Joey raises his hand. Yo, teacher man. . . .

Call me Mr. McCourt.

Yeah. OK. So, you Scotch or somethin'?

Joey is the mouth. There's one in every class along with the complainer, the clown, the goody-goody, the beauty queen, the volunteer for everything, the jock, the intellectual, the momma's boy, the mystic, the sissy, the lover, the critic, the jerk, the religious fanatic who sees sin everywhere, the brooding one who sits in the back staring at the desk, the happy one, the saint who finds good in all creatures. It's the job of the mouth to ask questions, anything to keep the teacher from the boring lesson. I may be a new teacher but I'm on to Joey's delaying game. It's universal. I played the same game in Ireland. I was the mouth in my class in Leamy's National School. The master would write an algebra question or an Irish conjugation on the board and the boys would hiss, Ask him a question, McCourt. Get him away from the bloody lesson. Go on, go on.

I'd say, Sir, did they have algebra in olden times in Ireland?

Mr. O'Halloran liked me, good boy, neat handwriting, always polite and obedient. He would put the chalk down, and from the way he sat at his desk and took his time before speaking you could see how happy he was to escape from algebra and Irish syntax. He'd say, Boys, you have every right to be proud of your ancestors. Long before the Greeks, even the Egyptians, your forefathers in this lovely land could capture the rays of the sun in the heart of winter and direct them to dark inner chambers for a few golden moments. They knew the ways of the heavenly bodies and that took them beyond algebra, beyond calculus, beyond, boys, oh, beyond beyond.

Sometimes, in the warm days of spring, he dozed off in his chair and we sat quietly, forty of us, waiting for him to wake, not even daring to leave the room if he slept past going-home time.

No. I'm not Scotch. I'm Irish.

Joey looks sincere. Oh, yeah? What's Irish?

Irish is whatever comes out of Ireland.

Like St. Patrick, right?

Well, no, not exactly. This leads to the telling of the story of St. Patrick, which keeps us away from the b-o-r-i-n-g English lesson, which leads to other questions.

Hey, mister. Everyone talk English over there in Ireland?

What kinda sports didja play?

You all Catlics in Ireland?

Don't let them take over the classroom. Stand up to them. Show them who's in charge. Be firm or be dead. Take no shit. Tell them, Open your notebooks. Time for the spelling list.

Aw, teacher, aw, Gawd, aw man. Spelling. Spelling. Spelling. Do we haveta? They moan, B-o-r-i-n-g spelling list. They pretend to bang their foreheads on desks, bury their faces in their folded arms. They beg for the pass. Gotta go. Gotta go. Man, we thought you were a nice guy, young and all. Why do all these English teachers have to do the same old thing? Same old spelling lessons, same old vocabulary lessons, same old shit, excuse the language? Can't you tell us more about Ireland?

Yo, teacher man. . . . Joey again. Mouth to the rescue.

Joey, I told you my name is Mr. McCourt, Mr. McCourt, Mr. McCourt.

Yeah, yeah. So, mister, did you go out with girls in Ireland?

No, dammit. Sheep. We went out with sheep. What do you think we went out with?

The class explodes. They laugh, clutch their chests, nudge, elbow one another, pretend to fall out of their desks. This teacher. Crazy, man. Talks funny. Goes out with sheep. Lock up your sheep.

Excuse me. Open your notebooks, please. We have a spelling list to cover.

Hysterics. Will sheep be on the list? Oh, man.

That smart-ass response was a mistake. There will be trouble. The goody-goody, the saint and the critic will surely report me: Oh, Mom, oh, Dad, oh, Mr. Principal, guess what teacher said in class today. Bad things about sheep.

I'm not prepared, trained or ready for this. It's not teaching. It has nothing to do with English literature, grammar, writing. When will I be strong enough to walk into the room, get their immediate attention and teach? Around this school there are quiet industrious classes where teachers are in command. In the cafeteria older teachers tell me, Yeah, it takes at least five years.

Next day the principal sends for me. He sits behind his desk, talking into the telephone, smoking a cigarette. He keeps saying, I'm sorry. It won't happen again. I'll speak to the person involved. New teacher, I'm afraid.

He puts the phone down. Sheep. What is this about sheep? Sheep?

I dunno what I'm gonna do with you. There's a complaint you said "dammit" in class. I know you're just off the boat from an agricultural country and don't know the ropes, but you should have some common sense.

No, sir. Not off the boat. I've been here eight and a half years, including my two years in the army, not counting years of infancy in Brooklyn.

Well, look. First the sandwich, now the sheep. Damn phone ringing off the hook. Parents up in arms. I have to cover my ass. You're two days in the building and two days you're in the soup. How do you do it? If you'll excuse the expression you're inclined to screw up a bit. Why the hell did you have to tell these kids about the sheep?

I'm sorry. They kept asking me questions, and I was exasperated. They were only trying to keep me away from the spelling list.

That's it?

I thought the sheep thing was a bit funny at the time.

Oh, yeah, indeed. You standing there advocating bestiality. Thirteen parents are demanding you be fired. There are righteous people on Staten Island.

I was only joking.

No, young man. No jokes here. There's a time and place. When you say something in class they take you seriously. You're the teacher. You say you went out with sheep and they're going to swallow every word. They don't know the mating habits of the Irish.

I'm sorry.

This time I'll let it go. I'll tell the parents you're just an Irish immigrant off the boat.

But I was born here.

Could you be quiet for one minute and listen while I save your life, huh? This time I'll let it go. I won't put a letter in your file. You don't realize how serious it is to get a letter in your file. If you've got any ambition to rise in this system, principal, assistant principal, guidance counselor, the letter in the file will hold you back. It's the start of the long downward slide.

Sir, I don't want to be principal. I just want to teach.

Yeah, yeah. That's what they all say. You'll get over it. These kids will give you gray hair before you're thirty.

It was clear I was not cut out to be the purposeful kind of teacher who brushed aside all questions, requests, complaints, to get on with the well-planned lesson. That would have reminded me of that school in Limerick where the lesson was king and we were nothing. I was already dreaming of a school where teachers were guides and mentors, not taskmasters. I didn't have any particular philosophy of education except that I was uncomfortable with the bureaucrats, the higher-ups, who had escaped classrooms only to turn and bother the occupants of those classrooms, teachers and students. I never wanted to fill out their forms, follow their guidelines, administer their examinations, tolerate their snooping, adjust myself to their programs and courses of study.

If a principal had ever said, The class is yours, teacher. Do with it what you like, I would have said to my students, Push the chairs aside. Sit on the floor. Go to sleep.

What?

I said, Go to sleep.

Why?

Figure it out for yourself while you're lying there on the floor.

They'd lie on the floor and some would drift off. There would be giggling as boy wriggled closer to girl. Sleepers would snore sweetly. I'd stretch out with them on the floor and ask if anyone knew a lullaby. I know a girl would start and others would join. A boy might say, Man, what if the principal walked in. Yeah. The lullaby continues, a murmur around the room. Mr. McCourt, when are we getting up? He's told, Shush, man, and he shushes. The bell rings and they're slow off the floor. They leave the room, relaxed and puzzled. Please don't ask me why I'd have such a session. It must be the spirit that moves.

2

If you were in my classes in the early McKee days you would have seen a scrawny young man in his late twenties with unruly black hair, eyes that flared with a chronic infection, bad teeth and the hangdog look you see on immigrants in Ellis Island photographs or on pick-pockets being arrested.

There were reasons for the hangdog look:

I was born in New York and taken to Ireland before I was four. I had three brothers. My father, an alcoholic, wild man, great patriot, ready always to die for Ireland, abandoned us when I was ten going on eleven. A baby sister died, twin boys died, two boys were born. My mother begged for food, clothing, and coal to boil water for the tea. Neighbors told her to place us in an orphanage, me and my brothers. No, no, never. The shame of it. She hung on. We grew. My brothers and I left school at fourteen, worked, dreamed of America and, one by one, sailed away. My mother followed with the youngest, expecting to live happily ever after. That's what you're supposed to do in America, but she never had a moment of happy-ever-after.

In New York I worked at menial and laboring jobs till I was drafted into the United States Army. After two years in Germany I went to college on the GI Bill to become a teacher. In college there were courses on literature and composition. There were courses on how to teach by professors who did not know how to teach.

So, Mr. McCourt, what was it like growing up in, you know, Ireland?

I'm twenty-seven years old, a new teacher, dipping into my past to satisfy these American teenagers, to keep them quiet and in their seats. I never thought my past would be so useful. Why would anyone want to know about my miserable life? Then I realize this is what my father did when he told us stories by the fire. He told us about men called seanachies who traveled the country telling the hundreds of stories they carried in their heads. People would let them warm themselves by the fire, offer them a drop, feed them whatever they were having themselves, listen to hours of story and song that seemed endless, give them a blanket or a sack to cover themselves on the bed of straw in the corner. If the seanachie needed love there might be an aging daughter available.

I argue with myself, You're telling stories and you're supposed to be teaching.

I am teaching. Storytelling is teaching.

Storytelling is a waste of time.

I can't help it. I'm not good at lecturing.

You're a fraud. You're cheating our children.

They don't seem to think so.

The poor kids don't know.

I'm a teacher in an American school telling stories of my school days in Ireland. It's a routine that softens them up in the unlikely event I might teach something solid from the curriculum.

One day, my schoolmaster joked that I looked like something the cat brought in. The class laughed. The master smiled with his great yellow horsey teeth and gobs of phlegm stirred and rattled in his gullet. My classmates took that as a laugh, and when they laughed with him I hated them. I hated the master, too, because I knew that for days to come I'd be known in the school yard as the one the cat brought in. If the master had made that remark about another boy I would have laughed, too, because I was as great a coward as the next one, terrified of the stick.

There was one boy in the class who did not laugh with everyone else: Billy Campbell. When the class laughed, Billy would stare straight ahead and the master would stare at him, waiting for him to be like everyone else. We waited for him to drag Billy from his seat, but he never did. I think the master admired him for his independence. I admired him, too, and wished I had his courage. It never came to me.

Boys in that Irish school mocked the American accent I had from New York. You can't go away and leave your accent behind, and when they mock your accent you don't know what to do or think or feel till pushing starts and you know they're trying to get a rise out of you. It's you against forty boys from the lanes of Limerick and you can't run, for if you do, you'll be known as a sissy or a nancy boy the rest of your life. They call you gangster or redskin and then you fight and fight till someone hits you on the nose and you're pumping blood all over your one shirt, which will get you into terrible trouble with your mother, who will leave her chair by the fire and give you a good clitther on the head for fighting at all. There's no use trying to explain to your mother that you got all this blood from defending your American accent, which you have because of her in the first place. No, she'll say, now she has to boil water and wash your bloody shirt and see if she can dry it before the fire so that you can have it for school tomorrow. She says nothing about the American accent that got you into trouble in the first place. But it's all right because in a few months that accent will disappear to be replaced, thank God, with a Limerick accent anyone but my father would be proud of.

Because of my father, my troubles were not over. You'd think with my perfect Limerick accent at the age of four the boys would stop tormenting me but, no, they start mimicking my father's North of Ireland accent and saying he's some class of a Protestant and now I have to defend him and once more it's home to my mother with the bloody shirt and my mother yells if she has to wash this shirt one more time it will surely fall apart in her hands. The worst part was the time when she couldn't get the shirt dry by morning and I had to wear it damp to school. When I came home my nose was stuffed and my whole body shivered with the damp again, this time from sweat. My mother was distracted and cried all over me for being

27

mean to me and sending me to school with that damp shirt that was getting redder and redder from all the fights. She put me to bed and buried me under old overcoats and the blanket from her own bed till the shivering stopped and I drifted off to sleep listening to her downstairs talking to my father and saying it was a sad day they left Brooklyn to have the children tormented in the school yards of Limerick.

After two days in bed I returned to school in the shirt that was now a pale shade of pink. The boys said pink was a color for sissies and was I a girl?

Billy Campbell stood up to the biggest of them. Leave the Yank alone, he said.

Oh, said the big boy. Who's goin' to make me?

I am, said Billy, and the big boy went to the other side of the yard to play. Billy understood my problem because his father was from Dublin and sometimes the boys sneered even at that.

I told stories about Billy because he had the kind of courage I admired. Then one of my McKee students raised his hand and said it was all right to admire Billy but didn't I stand up to a whole group over my American accent and shouldn't I admire myself? I said no, I did only what I had to do with everyone in that Irish school pushing and taunting me, but this fifteen-year-old McKee boy insisted you have to give yourself credit, not too much because that would be bragging. I said, OK, I'd give myself credit for fighting back except that I wasn't as brave as Billy, who would fight not for himself but for others. He owed me nothing but he still defended me and that was a kind of courage I hoped to have some day.

My students ask about my family and bits of my past drift into my head. I realize I'm making discoveries about myself and I tell this story the way my mother told a neighbor:

I was pushing the pram with Malachy in it and him a little fella barely two. Frank was walking along beside me. Outside Todd's store on O'Connell Street a long black motorcar pulled up to the pavement and out got this rich woman all dressed up in furs and jewelry. Well, didn't she look into the pram and didn't she offer to buy

Malachy on the spot. You can imagine what a shock that was to me, a woman wanting to buy Malachy with his golden blond hair, his pink cheeks, his lovely little pearly white teeth. He was so lovely there in the pram, and I knew parting with him would break my heart. Besides, what would my husband say if I came home and told him I sold the child? So I told the woman no and she looked so sad my heart went out to her.

When I grew older and heard her tell that story for the hundredth time, I said she should have sold Malachy and there would have been more food for the rest of us. She said, Well, I offered you but the woman wasn't a bit interested.

Girls in the class said, Aw, gee, Mr. McCourt, your mother shouldn't have done that to you. People shouldn't offer to sell their children. You ain't so ugly.

Boys in the class said, Well, he ain't no Clark Gable. Just kiddin', Mr. McCourt.

Mea culpa.

When I was six, the schoolmaster in Ireland told me I was a bad boy. You're a very bad boy. He said all the boys in the class were very bad boys. He reminded us that he was using the word very, a word he would use only on special occasions like this. If we ever used that word answering a question or writing a composition he'd have our scalps. On this occasion, it was allowed. That's how bad we were. He had never seen such a collection and wondered what was the use of teaching urchins and amadauns. Our heads were filled with American trash from the Lyric Cinema. We were to bow those heads, pound our chests and say, *Mea culpa, mea culpa, mea maxima culpa.* I thought it meant, I am sorry, till he wrote on the board, "*Mea culpa.* I am guilty." He said we were born in Original Sin, which was supposed to be washed away with the waters of baptism. He said it was clear that rivers of baptismal water had been wasted on the likes of us. One look at our darting little eyes was proof of our wickedness.

He was there to prepare us for First Confession and First Communion, to save our worthless souls. He taught us Examination of Conscience. We were to look inward, to search the landscape of our souls. We were born with Original Sin, which was a nasty oozing thing marring the dazzling whiteness of our souls. Baptism restored their white perfection. But now we were older and there were the sins: sores, gashes, abscesses. We were to drag them wriggling, squirming, putrid, into God's glorious light. Examination of Conscience, boys, followed by the *mea culpa*. Powerful laxative, boys. Cleans you out better than a dose of salts.

Every day we practiced Examination of Conscience and confessed our sins to him and the class. The master said nothing, sat at his desk, nodded, fondled the slim stick he used to keep us in a state of grace. We confessed to all the Seven Deadly Sins: Pride, Covetousness, Lust, Anger, Gluttony, Envy, Sloth. He would point the stick and say, Madigan, confess to us how you committed the Deadly Sin, Envy. Our favorite Deadly Sin for confessing was Gluttony, and when he pointed the stick at Paddy Clohessy and told him, Clohessy, the Gluttony, Paddy described a meal you could only dream about: pig's head with potatoes and cabbage and mustard, no end of lemonade to wash it down, followed by ice cream and biscuits and tea with loads of milk and sugar and, if you liked, you could rest awhile and have more of the same, your mother not a bit put out by your appetite, because there was enough for everyone and more where that came from.

The master said, Clohessy, you are a poet of the palate. No one knew what palate meant till three of us went around the corner to see if the Andrew Carnegie librarian might let us look at the big dictionary near her desk. She said, What do ye want to know palate for? and when we told her that's what Paddy Clohessy was a poet of she looked up the word and said our teacher must be losing his wits. Paddy was stubborn. He asked her what palate was and when she said it was the center of taste sensation he looked delighted with himself and made clucking noises with his tongue. He even did it going through the streets till Billy Campbell asked him to stop as it was making him hungry.

We confessed to breaking all the Ten Commandments. If you said you committed adultery or coveted your neighbor's wife the master knew you didn't know what you were talking about, Don't get above yourself, boy, and moved on to the next penitent.

After First Communion we continued Examination of Conscience for the next sacrament: Confirmation. The priest said Examination of Conscience and confession would save us from hell. His name was Father White and we were interested in him because one of the boys said he never wanted to be a priest at all. His mother forced him into the priesthood. We doubted that boy, but he said he knew one of the maids at the priests' house and she said Father White got drunk at dinner and told the other priests his only dream was to grow up and drive the bus that went from Limerick to Galway and back but his mother wouldn't let him. It was strange to be examined by someone who became a priest because his mother made him. I wondered if the dream of the bus was in his head while he stood at the altar saying Mass. It was strange, also, to think of a priest getting drunk, because everyone knows they're not supposed to. I used to look at buses passing by and picture him up there, smiling away and no priestly collar choking the life out of him.

When you get into the habit of examining your conscience it's hard to stop, especially when you're an Irish Catholic boy. If you do bad things you look into your soul, and there are the sins, festering. Everything is either a sin or not a sin and that's an idea you might carry in your head the rest of your life. Then when you grow up and drift away from the church, *Mea culpa* is a faint whisper in your past. It's still there, but now you're older and not so easily frightened.

When you're in a state of grace the soul is a pure dazzling white surface, but your sins create abscesses that ooze and stink. You try to save yourself with *Mea culpa*, the only Latin words that mean anything to you or God.

If I could travel to my twenty-seventh year, my first teaching year, I'd take me out for a steak, a baked potato, a pint of stout. I'd give myself a good talking to. For Christ's sake, kid, straighten up.

Throw back those miserable bony shoulders. Stop mumbling. Speak up. Stop putting yourself down. In that department the world will be happy to oblige. You're starting your teaching career, and it isn't an easy life. I know. I did it. You'd be better off as a cop. At least you'd have a gun or a stick to defend yourself. A teacher has nothing but his mouth. If you don't learn to love it, you'll wriggle in a corner of hell.

Somebody should have told me, Hey, Mac, your life, Mac, thirty years of it, Mac, is gonna be school, school, school, kids, kids, kids, papers, papers, papers, read and correct, read and correct, mountains of papers piling up at school, at home, days, nights reading stories, poems, diaries, suicide notes, diatribes, excuses, plays, essays, even novels, the work of thousands—thousands—of New York teenagers over the years, a few hundred working men and women, and you get no time for reading Graham Greene or Dashiell Hammett, F. Scott Fitzgerald or good old P. G. Wodehouse, or your main man, Mr. Jonathan Swift. You'll go blind reading Joey and Sandra, Tony and Michelle, little agonies and passions and ecstasies. Mountains of kid stuff, Mac. If they opened your head they'd find a thousand teenagers clambering all over your brain. Every June they graduate, grow up, work and move on. They'll have kids, Mac, who will come to you someday for English, and you're left facing another term of Joeys and Sandras, Tonys and Michelles, and you'll want to know: Is this what it's all about? Is this to be your world for twenty/thirty years? Remember, if this is your world, you're one of them, a teenager. You live in two worlds. You're with them, day in, day out, and you'll never know, Mac, what that does to your mind. Teenager forever. June will come and it's bye-bye, teacher, nice knowin' you, my sister's gonna be in your class in September. But there's something else, Mac. In any classroom, something is always happening. They keep you on your toes. They keep you fresh. You'll never grow old, but the danger is you might have the mind of an adolescent forever. That's a real problem, Mac. You get used to talking to those kids on their level. Then when you go to a bar for a beer you forget how to talk to your friends and they look at you. They look at you like you just arrived from another planet and they're right. Day after day in the classroom means you're in another world, Mac.

So, teacher, how did you come to America and all that?

I tell them about my arrival in America at nineteen years of age, that there was nothing about me, on me, in my head or suitcase, to suggest that in a few years I'd be facing five classes a day of New York teenagers.

Teacher? I never dreamed I could rise so high in the world.

Except for the book in the suitcase, everything I wore or carried off the ship was secondhand. Everything in my head was second-hand, too: Catholicism; Ireland's sad history, a litany of suffering and martyrdom drummed into me by priests, schoolmasters and parents who knew no better.

The brown suit I wore came from Nosey Parker's pawnshop, Parnell Street, Limerick. My mother bargained for it. The Nose said that suit would be four pounds, and she said, Is it coddin' me you are, Mr. Parker?

No, I'm not coddin' you, he said. That suit was wore wanst be a cousin of the Earl of Dunraven himself and anything worn be the aristocracy has higher value.

My mother said she wouldn't care if it was worn by the earl himself for all the good he and his ilk ever did for Ireland with their castles and servants and never a thought for the sufferings of the people. She'd offer three pounds and not a penny more.

The Nose snapped that a pawnshop was no place for patriotism and she snapped back that if patriotism was something you could show on the shelf he'd be polishing it and overcharging the poor. He said, Mother o' God, missus. You were never like this before. What came over you?

What came over her was that this was like Custer's last stand, her last chance. This was her son, Frank, going to America and she couldn't send him off looking like this, wearing the relics of oul'

33

decency, this one's shirt, that one's trousers. Then she showed how clever she could be. She had very little money left, but if Mr. Parker could see his way to throwing in a pair of shoes, two shirts, two pairs of socks and that lovely green tie with the golden harps she wouldn't forget the favor. It wouldn't be long before Frank would be sending home dollars from America and when she needed pots, pans and an alarm clock she'd think immediately of The Nose. Indeed, she could see half a dozen items there on the shelves she couldn't live without once the dollars came pouring in.

The Nose was no daw. From years behind the counter he knew the tricks of his customers. He knew, also, my mother was so honest she hated owing anybody anything. He said he valued her future custom, and he himself wouldn't want to see that lad there landing shabby in America. What would the Yanks say? So for another pound, oh, take off another shilling, she could have the extra items.

My mother said he was a decent man, that he'd get a bed in heaven and she wouldn't forget him, and it was strange seeing the respect passing between them. The lane people of Limerick had no use for pawnbrokers, but where would they be without them?

The Nose had no suitcases. His customers were not known for traveling the world, and he had a good laugh over that with my mother. He said, World travelers, how are you. She looked at me as if to say, Take a good look at The Nose for it isn't every day you'll see him laugh.

Feathery Burke, in Irishtown, had suitcases for sale. He sold anything old, secondhand, stuffed, useless or ready for the fire. Ah, yes, he had the very thing for the young fella going to America, God bless him, that would be sending money home to his poor old mother.

I'm hardly old, said my mother, so none of your plamas. How much for the suitcase?

Yerra, missus, I'll give it away to you for two pounds because I don't want to be standing between the boy and his fortune in America.

My mother said that before she'd pay two pounds for that worn-out piece of cardboard held together by a spit and a prayer she'd wrap my things in brown paper and twine and send me off to New York like that.

Feathery looked shocked. Women from the back lanes of Limerick were not supposed to carry on like that. They were supposed to be respectful of their betters and not rise above their station, and I was surprised myself to see my mother in that pick-quarrel mood.

She won, told Feathery what he was charging was pure robbery, we were better off under the English, and if he didn't come down in his price she'd go to that decent man Nosey Parker. Feathery gave in.

God above, missus. A good thing I didn't have children for if I did and I had to deal with the likes of you every day they'd be standing in the corner whimpering with the hunger.

She said, Pity about you and the children you never had.

She folded the clothes into the suitcase and said she'd take the whole lot home so that I could go and buy the book. She walked away from me, up Parnell Street, puffing on a cigarette. She walked with energy that day, as if the clothes and the suitcase and my going away would open doors.

I went to O'Mahony's Bookshop to buy the first book in my life, the one I brought to America in the suitcase.

It was *The Works of William Shakespeare: Gathered into One Volume,* published by the Shakespeare Head Press, Oldhams Press Ltd. and Basil Blackwood, MCMXLVII. Here it is, cover crumbling, separating from the book, hanging on through the kindness of tape. A well-thumbed book, well marked. There are passages underlined that once meant something to me though I look at them now and hardly know why. Along the margins notes, remarks, appreciative comments, congratulations to Shakespeare on his genius, exclamation marks indicating my appreciation and befuddlement. Inside the cover I wrote, "Oh, that this too, too solid flesh, etc." It proves I was a gloomy youth.

When I was thirteen/fourteen I listened to Shakespeare plays on the radio of Mrs. Purcell, the blind woman next door. She told me

Shakespeare was an Irishman ashamed of what he came from. A fuse blew the night we listened to *Julius Caesar* and I was so eager to find out what happened to Brutus and Mark Antony I went to O'Mahony's Bookshop to get the rest of the story. A sales clerk in the shop asked me in a superior way if it was my intention to buy that book and I told him I was thinking about it but first I'd have to find out what happened to everyone in the end, especially the one I liked, Brutus. The man said never mind Brutus, pulled the book away from me and said this was not a library and would I kindly leave. I backed into the street embarrassed and blushing and wondering at the same time why people won't stop bothering people. Even when I was small, eight or nine, I wondered why people won't stop bothering people and I've been wondering ever since.

The book was nineteen shillings, half a week's wages. I wish I could say I bought it because of my profound interest in Shakespeare. It wasn't that way at all. I had to have it because of a film I saw where an American soldier in England went around spouting Shakespeare and all the girls fell madly in love with him. Also, if you even hint that you read Shakespeare, people give you that look of respect. I thought if I learned long passages I'd impress the girls of New York. I already knew "Friends, Romans, countrymen," but when I said it to a girl in Limerick she gave me a curious look as if I were coming down with something.

Going up O'Connell Street I wanted to unwrap my package and let the world see me with Shakespeare in my oxter but I didn't have the nerve. I passed the small theater where I once saw a traveling company perform *Hamlet* and remembered how I felt sorry for myself for the way I'd suffered like him. At the end of the play that night Hamlet himself returned to the stage to tell the audience how grateful he and the cast were for our attendance and how weary he was, he and the cast, and how much they'd appreciate our help in the form of small change, which we could deposit in the lard tin by the door. I was so moved by the play because so much of it was about me and my gloomy life that I dropped sixpence into the lard tin and wished I could have attached a note to let Hamlet know who I was and how my suffering was real and not just in a play.

Next day I delivered a telegram to Hanratty's Hotel and there was the cast from *Hamlet,* drinking and singing in the bar while a porter ran back and forth loading a van with their luggage. Hamlet himself sat alone at the end of the bar, sipping his glass of whiskey, and I don't know where the courage came from but I said hello to him. After all, we both had been betrayed by our mothers and our suffering was great. The world would never know about mine and I envied him for the way he was able to express his anguish every night. Hello, I said, and he stared at me with two black eyes under black eyebrows in a white face. He had all those words from Shakespeare in his head but now he kept them there and I blushed like a fool and tripped over my feet.

I rode my bicycle up O'Connell Street in a state of shame. Then I remembered the sixpence dropped into the lard tin, sixpence that paid for their whiskey and singing at Hanratty's Bar, and I wanted to go back and confront the whole cast and Hamlet himself and tell them what I thought of them with their false stories of weariness and the way they drank the money of poor people.

Let the sixpence go. If I went back they'd surely throw Shakespeare words at me and Hamlet would stare at me again with his cold black eyes. I'd have no words for that and I'd look foolish if I tried staring back at him with my red eyes.

My students said spending all that money on a Shakespeare book was dumb, no disrespect intended, and if I wanted to make an impression on people why didn't I go to the library and copy down all the quotes? Also, you'd have to be pretty dumb to be impressed with a guy just because he quoted this old writer that no one could read anyway. Sometimes they have these Shakespeare plays on TV and you can't understand a word, so what's the use? The money I paid for the book could have been spent on something cool like shoes or a nice jacket or, you know, taking a girl to the movies.

Some girls said that was real cool the way I used Shakespeare to make an impression on people though they wouldn't know what I was talking about. Why did Shakespeare have to write in that old language nobody could understand? Why?

I couldn't answer. They said again, Why? I felt trapped but all I could do was to tell them I didn't know. If they waited I'd try to find out. They looked at one another. The teacher doesn't know? How could that be? Is he for real? Wow. How did he get to be a teacher?

Hey, teacher man, you got any more stories?

No, no, no.

You keep saying no, no, no.

That's it. No more stories. This is an English class. Parents are complaining.

Aw, man. Mr. McCourt, you ever in the army? You fight in Korea?

I never thought much of my life but I went on doling out bits and pieces of it, my father's drinking, days in Limerick slums when I dreamed of America, Catholicism, drab days in New York, and I was surprised that New York teenagers asked for more.

3

I told them that after my two years in the army the GI Bill helped me doze through four years at New York University. I worked nights to supplement my allowance from the government. I could have attended part time, but I was eager to graduate and impress the world and women with my degree and my college knowledge. I was expert at making excuses for late papers and missed exams. I shuffled and mumbled the mishaps of my life to patient professors, hinted at great sadnesses. The Irish accent helped. I lived on the edge of faith and begorrah.

University librarians poked me when I snored behind a stack of books. One librarian told me snoozing was strictly forbidden. She was kind enough to suggest that out in Washington Square Park there was no end of benches where I could stretch till the cops came. I thanked her and told her how I'd always admired librarians, not only for their mastery of the Dewey Decimal System, but for their helpfulness in other areas of daily living.

The professor of education at New York University warned us about our teaching days ahead. He said first impressions are crucial. He said, The way you meet and greet your first class might determine the course of your whole career. Your whole career. They're watching you. You're watching them. You're dealing with American teenagers, a dangerous species, and they'll show you no mercy. They'll take your measure and they'll decide what to do with you. You think you're in control? Think again. They're like heat-seeking missiles. When they go after you they're following a primal instinct. It is the function of the young to get rid of their elders, to make room on the planet. You know that, don't you? The Greeks knew it. Read the Greeks.

The professor said that before your students enter the room you must have decided where you'll be—"posture and placement"—and who you'll be—"identity and image." I never knew teaching could be that complicated. He said, You simply cannot teach unless you know where to position yourself physically. That classroom can be your battleground or your playground. And you have to know who you are. Remember Pope: "Know thyself, presume not God to scan / The proper study of mankind is man." First day of your teaching you are to stand at your classroom door and let your students know how happy you are to see them. Stand, I say. Any playwright will tell you that when the actor sits down the play sits down. The best move of all is to establish yourself as a presence and to do it outside in the hall-way. Outside, I say. That's your territory and when you're out there you'll be seen as a strong teacher, fearless, ready to face the swarm. That's what a class is, a swarm. And you're a warrior teacher. It's something people don't think about. Your territory is like your aura, it goes with you everywhere, in the hallways, on the stairs and, assuredly, in the classroom. Never let them invade your territory. Never. And remember: teachers who sit or even stand behind their desks are essentially insecure and should try another line of work.

I liked the way he said assuredly, the first time I ever heard it used outside of a Victorian novel. I promised myself that when I became a teacher I'd use the word, too. It had an important sound to it that would make people sit up and pay attention.

I thought it was terrific the way you could stand up there on that little platform with your podium and your desk and talk for an hour with everyone before you making notes and if you had any kind of good looks or personality the girls would be tripping over themselves to see you afterward in your office or anywhere else. That's what I thought at the time.

The professor said he had made an informal study of teenage behavior in high school and if we were sensitive observant teachers we'd notice certain phenomena moments before class bells rang. We'd notice how adolescent temperatures rose, blood raced and there was enough adrenaline to power a battleship. He smiled and you could see how pleased he was with his ideas. We smiled back because professors have the power. He said teachers must observe how students present themselves. He said, So much—so much, I say—depends on how they enter a room. Observe their entrances. They amble, they strut, they shuffle, they collide, they joke, they show off. You, yourself, might think nothing of entering a room, but for a teenager it can be everything. To enter a room is to move from one environment to another and that, for the teenager, can be traumatic. There be dragons, daily horrors from acne to zit.

I could barely understand what the professor was talking about but I was very impressed. I never thought there was so much involved in stepping into a room. I thought teaching was a simple matter of telling the class what you knew and then testing them and giving them grades. Now I was learning how complicated the life of a teacher could be, and I admired this professor for knowing all about it.

The student next to me in the professor's class whispered, This guy is so full of crap. He never taught a high school class in his life. The student's name was Seymour. He wore a yarmulke, so it was no wonder he said wise things from time to time, or he could have been showing off for the red-haired girl sitting in front of him. When she looked over her shoulder to smile at Seymour's remarks you could see she was beautiful. I wished I could have shown off myself, but I rarely knew what to say, whereas Seymour had an opinion on everything. The red-haired girl told Seymour if he felt that strongly he should speak up.

Hell, no, said Seymour. I'd be out on my ass.

She smiled at him and when she smiled at me I thought I'd float out of my seat. She said her name was June and then raised her hand for the professor's attention.

Yes?

Professor, how many high school classes have you taught?

Oh, I've observed dozens of classes over the years.

But have you ever actually taught in a high school?

What's your name, young lady?

June Somers.

Haven't I just told you I've observed and supervised dozens of student teachers?

My father is a high school teacher, professor, and he says you know nothing about high school teaching till you've done it.

He said he didn't know what she was getting at. She was wasting the time of this class and if she wanted to continue the discussion she could make an appointment with his secretary to meet in his office.

She stood and slung her bag strap on her shoulder. No, she would not make an appointment to see him and saw no reason why he couldn't simply answer her question about his teaching experience.

That's enough, Miss Somers.

She turned and looked at Seymour, glanced at me and walked toward the door. The professor stared and dropped the piece of chalk in his hand. By the time he retrieved it she was gone.

What would he do now about Miss June Somers?

Nothing. He said the hour was nearly over, he'd see us next week, picked up his bag and walked out. Seymour said June Somers had screwed herself royally. Royally. He said, One thing I'll tell you. Don't mess around with professors. You can't win. Ever.

The following week he said, Did you see that? Jesus.

I didn't think someone wearing a yarmulke should say Jesus like that. How would he like it if Yahweh or G dash D were a curse and I blasted him with it? But I said nothing for fear he might laugh at me.

He said, They're going out. I saw them in a Macdougal Street café all lovey-dovey drinking coffee, holding hands and looking into each other's eyes. Goddam. I guess she had a little chat in his office and moved on.

My mouth was dry. I thought some day I'd run into June and find my tongue and we'd go to a movie together. I'd choose something foreign with subtitles to show how sophisticated I was and she'd admire me and let me kiss her in the dark, missing a dozen subtitles and the thread of the story. That wouldn't matter because we'd have plenty to talk about in a cozy Italian restaurant where candles flickered and her red hair twinkled back and who knows what that would lead to because that was as far as my dreams would go. Who did I think I was anyway? What made me think she'd look at me for one second?

I prowled the coffee shops of Macdougal Street hoping she might see me and smile and I'd smile back and sip my coffee so casually she'd be impressed, take a second look. I'd make sure she could see the cover of my book, something by Nietzsche or Schopenhauer, and she'd wonder why she was wasting her time with the professor when she could be with that sensitive Irishman sunk in German philosophy. She'd excuse herself and on her way to the ladies' toilet drop a scrap of paper on my table with her phone number.

Which is what she did the day I saw her at the Café Figaro. When she left the table the professor looked after her with such an air of ownership and pride I could have knocked him from his chair. Then he glanced at me and I knew he didn't even recognize me as a student from his class.

He called for his bill, and while the waitress stood at his table obscuring his view, June was able to drop that scrap of paper on my table. I waited till they left. "Frank, call me tomorrow." The telephone number was scrawled in lipstick.

God. She noticed me, a dockside laborer fumbling my way toward a teaching career, and the professor was, Jesus, a professor. But she knew my name. I was weak in the head from happiness. There was my name on a paper napkin with lipstick that had touched her lips and I knew I'd keep that piece of paper forever. I'd be buried with it.

I called her and she asked if I knew where we could have a quiet drink.

Chumley's.

OK.

What would I do? How would I sit? What would I say? I was having a drink with the most beautiful girl in Manhattan, who probably slept every night with that professor. That was my Calvary, thinking of her with him. Men in Chumley's looked at me and envied me and I knew what they were thinking. Who is that miserable specimen with that beautiful girl, that knockout, that stunner? Yeah, maybe I was her brother or cousin. No, even that was unlikely. I wasn't good-looking enough even to be her third or fourth cousin.

She ordered a drink. Norm's away, she said. He teaches a course in Vermont two days a week. I suppose bigmouth Seymour told you everything.

No.

So, why are you here?

You . . . you invited me.

What do you think of yourself?

What?

Simple question. What do you think of yourself?

I don't know. I . . .

She looked disapproving. You call when you're told to call. You appear when you're told to appear and you don't know what you think of yourself. For Christ's sakes, say one good thing about yourself. Go ahead.

I felt blood rushing to my face. I had to say something or she might get up and walk away.

A platform boss on the piers once said I was a tough little mick.

Oh, well. Take that remark and a dime and you can ride the subway two stops. You're a lost soul. That's easy to see. Norm likes lost souls.

Words jumped from my mouth: I don't care what Norm likes.

Oh, God. She'll get up and walk away. No. She laughed so hard she nearly choked on her wine. Then everything was different. She smiled at me and smiled and smiled. I felt so happy I could barely stay in my skin.

She reached across the table and put her hand on mine and my heart was a mad animal in my chest. Let's go, she said.

We walked to her apartment on Barrow Street. Inside, she turned and kissed me. She moved her head in a circular way so that her tongue traveled clockwise in my mouth and I thought, Lord, I am not worthy. Why didn't God tell me about this before my twenty-sixth year?

She said I was a healthy peasant and obviously starved for affection. I didn't like being called a peasant—Jesus, hadn't I read books, every word of E. Laurie Long, P. G. Wodehouse, Mark Twain, E. Philips Oppenheim, Edgar Wallace and good old Dickens—and I thought what we were doing here was more than showing affection. I said nothing because I had no experience of activities like this. She asked me if I liked monkfish and I said I didn't know because I'd never heard of it before. She said everything depended on how you cooked it. Her secret was shallots. Not everyone agrees with that, she said, but it worked for her. It's a delicate whitefish best cooked with a good white wine. Not an ordinary cooking wine, but a good one. Norm cooked fish once but he made a mess of it, used some piss from California that turned the fish into an old shoe. The poor dear knew his literature and his lecturing, but nothing about wine or fish.

It's strange to be with a woman who takes your face in her hands and tells you to have faith in yourself. She said, My father came from Liverpool and he drank himself to death because he was afraid of the world. He said he wished he was a Catholic so he could join a monastery and never have to see a human being again, and it was my mother who tried to get him to say good things about himself. He couldn't, so he drank and died. Do you drink?

Not much.

Be careful. You're Irish.

Your father wasn't Irish.

No, but he could have been. Everyone in Liverpool is Irish. Let's cook that monkfish.

She handed me a kimono. It's OK. Change in the bedroom. If

it's good enough for a samurai it's good enough for a tough little mick who ain't so tough.

She changed into a silver dressing gown that seemed to have a life of its own. One moment it clung to her, then hung in a way that let her move freely inside. I preferred the clinging part and it kept me alive inside my kimono.

She asked if I liked white wine and I said yes because I was learning that yes was the best answer to every question, at least with June. I said yes to the monkfish and the asparagus and the two flickering candles on the table. I said yes to the way she raised her wineglass and touched it against mine till they went *ping*. I told her this was the most delicious dinner I'd ever had in my life. I wanted to go on and say I was in heaven but that might sound forced and she might give me the kind of strange look that would ruin the whole night and my life beyond.

Norm was never mentioned in the six nights that followed the night of the monkfish except that there were twelve fresh roses in a vase in her bedroom with a card that said love from Norm. I drank extra wine to boost my courage enough to ask, How the hell can you lie in this bed with me in the presence of Norm's fresh roses? but I never did. I couldn't afford roses so I brought her carnations, which she put in a large glass jar beside the roses. There was no competition. Beside Norm's roses my carnations looked so sad I bought her a dozen roses with my last few dollars. She sniffed them and said, Oh, they're beautiful. I didn't know what to say to that as I hadn't grown them, just bought them. Norm's roses in the glass jar looked dry and it made me happy to think my roses would replace them, but what she did then gave me the greatest pain I ever had in my heart.

From my chair in the kitchen I could see what she was doing in the bedroom, taking my roses one by one and placing them delicately among, between and around Norm's roses, standing back, looking at them, using my fresh roses to prop up the roses of Norm that were going limp, stroking the roses, his and mine, and smiling as if one set of roses was as good as the other.

She must have known I was watching. She turned and smiled at me, suffering, nearly blubbering, in the kitchen. They're beautiful, she said again. I knew she was talking about twenty-four roses, not just my dozen, and I wanted to yell something at her and storm out like a real man.

I didn't. I stayed. She made stuffed pork chops with applesauce and mashed potatoes and it tasted like cardboard. We went to bed and all I could think of was my roses mingled with his, that son-of-a-bitch in Vermont. She said I seemed low in energy and I wanted to tell her I wished I was dead. It's OK, she said. People just get used to each other. You have to keep it fresh.

Was this her way of keeping it fresh? Juggling two of us at one time, stuffing her vase with flowers from different men?

Near the end of that spring term I met Seymour on Washington Square. How's it going? he said, and laughed as if he knew something. How's the gorgeous June?

I stammered and shifted from one foot to the other. He said, Don't worry. She did it to me, too, but she had me only two weeks. I knew what she was up to and I told her to go to hell.

Up to?

It's all for old Norm. She has me up, she has you up and Christ knows who else she has up, and she tells Norm all about it.

But he goes to Vermont.

Vermont, my ass. The minute you leave her place he's in there lapping up the details.

How do you know?

He told me. He likes me. He tells her about me, she tells him about you, and they know I'm telling you about them, and they have a hell of a time. They talk about you and how you don't know your ass from your elbow about anything.

I walked away and he called after me, Anytime, man, anytime.

I scraped through the teacher's license examination. I scraped through everything. Passing score on the teacher examination was sixty-five; mine was sixty-nine. The passing points came, I think, through the kindness of an English chairman at Eastern District High School in Brooklyn who judged my demonstration lesson and my good luck in having a skimpy knowledge of the poetry of the Great War. An alcoholic professor at NYU told me in a friendly way that I was a half-assed student. I was offended till I thought about it and realized he was right. I was half-assed all around, but promised that someday I'd pull myself together, focus, concentrate, make something of myself, snap out of it, get my act together, all in the good old American way.

We sat on chairs in the corridors of Brooklyn Technical High School waiting for interviews, filling out forms, signing statements declaring our loyalty to America, assuring the world we were not now, nor had we ever been, members of the Communist Party.

I saw her long before she sat beside me. She wore a green scarf and dark glasses and when she pulled off the scarf there was a dazzle of red hair. I had the yearning ache for her but I wouldn't give her the satisfaction of turning to look.

Hi, Frank.

If I were a character in a novel or movie I would have stood and walked away, proud. She said hi again. She said, You look tired.

I snapped at her to show her I was not going to be polite after what she did to me. No, I am not tired, I said. But then she touched my face with her fingers.

That fictional character would have pulled his head back to show he hadn't forgotten, was not going to soften because of two greetings and a few fingertips. She smiled and touched my cheek again.

Everyone in the hallway was looking at her and I thought they were wondering what she was doing with me: she was that gorgeous and I was hardly a prize. They saw her hand on mine.

How are you anyway?

Fine, I croaked. I looked at that hand and thought of it roaming across Norm's body.

She said, Are you nervous about the interview?

I snapped again. No, I'm not.

You'll be a fine teacher.

I don't care.

You don't care? So why are you going through this?

There's nothing else to do.

Oh. She said she was getting a teacher's license to teach for a year and write a book about it. This was Norm's suggestion. Norm the big expert. He said education in America was a mess and a muck-raking book from inside the school system would be a best-seller. Teach a year or two, complain about the terrible state of the schools, and you have a big seller.

My name was called for the interview. She said, How about coffee afterwards?

If I'd had any pride or self-esteem I would have told her no and walked away but I said, OK, and went to my interview with my heart pounding.

I said good morning to the three examiners, but they're trained not to look at teacher candidates. Man in the middle said, You have a couple of minutes to read the poem on the desk before you. After you've read it we'll ask you to analyze it and tell us how you'd teach it to a high school class.

The title of the poem described how I felt at that interview: "I Would I Might Forget That I Am I."

Bald man on the right asked if I knew the form of the poem.

Yes, oh, yes. It's a sonata.

A what?

Oh, I'm sorry. A sonnet. Fourteen lines.

And the rhyme?

Ah . . . ah . . . abbaabbacdcdc.

They looked at one another and I didn't know if I was right or wrong.

And the poet?

Ah, I think it's Shakespeare. No, no, Wordsworth.

Neither, young man. It's Santayana.

The bald man glared at me as if I had offended him. Santayana, he said, Santayana, and I almost felt ashamed of my ignorance.

They looked grim and I wanted to declare that asking questions about Santayana was unfair and unjust due to the fact he was in no textbook or anthology I ever looked at in my four dozing years at New York University. They did not ask but I volunteered the only knowledge I had of Santayana, that if we don't learn from history we're bound to repeat our mistakes. They looked unimpressed, even when I told them I knew Santayana's first name, George.

So, said the man in the middle. How would you teach this poem?

I babbled. Well . . . I think . . . I think . . . it's partly about suicide and how Santayana is fed up, and I'd talk about James Dean because teenagers admire him and how he probably killed himself subconsciously on a motorbike, and I'd bring in Hamlet's suicide soliloquy, "To be or not to be," and let them talk about their own feelings about suicide if they ever had any.

Man on the right said, What would you do for reinforcement?

I don't know, sir. What is reinforcement?

He raised his eyebrows and looked at the others as if trying to be patient. He said, Reinforcement is an activity, enrichment, follow-up, some kind of assignment where you clinch the learning so that it's embedded in the student's memory. You can't teach in a vacuum. A good teacher relates the material to real life. You understand that, don't you?

Oh. I felt desperate. I blurted, I'd tell them to write a hundred-and-fifty-word suicide note. That would be a good way of encouraging them to think about life itself, because Samuel Johnson said the prospect of hanging in the morning focuses the mind wonderfully.

Man in the middle exploded. What?

Man on the right shook his head. We're not here to talk about Samuel Johnson.

Man on the left hissed. Suicide note? You would do no such thing. Do you hear me? You are dealing with tender minds. Jesus Christ! You are excused.

I said, Thank you, but what was the use? I was sure that was the end of me. Easy to see they didn't like me, my ignorance of Santayana and reinforcement, and I was sure the suicide-note idea was the last straw. They were high school department heads or had other important jobs and I disliked them the way I disliked anyone with power over me, bosses, bishops, college professors, tax examiners, foremen in general. Even so, I wondered why people like these examiners are so impolite they make you feel unworthy. I thought if I were sitting in their place I'd try to help candidates overcome their nervousness. If young people want to become teachers they should be encouraged and not intimidated by examiners who seemed to think Santayana was the center of the universe.

That is what I felt at the time but I didn't know the ways of the world. I didn't know that people up there have to protect themselves against people down here. I didn't know that older people have to protect themselves against younger people who want to push them off the face of the earth.

After my interview she was already in the hallway, knotting her scarf under her chin, telling me, That was a breeze.

It was no such thing. They asked me about Santayana.

Really? Norm adores Santayana.

Did this woman have any sense at all, ruining my day with Norm and that damn Santayana?

I don't give a shit about Norm. Santayana, too.

My, my. Such eloquence. Is the Irishman having a little tantrum?

I wanted to hold my chest to calm my rage. Instead, I walked away and kept walking even when she called, Frank, Frank, we could be serious.

I walked across the Brooklyn Bridge, repeating, We could be serious, all the way to McSorley's on East Seventh Street. What did she mean?

I drank beer after beer, ate liverwurst and onion on crackers, pissed mightily in McSorley's massive urinals, called her from the public phone, hung up when Norm answered, felt sorry for myself, wanted to call Norm again, invite him to a showdown on the sidewalk, picked up the phone, put it down, went home, whimpered into my pillow, despised myself, called myself an ass till I fell into a boozy sleep.

Next day, hungover and suffering, I traveled to Eastern District High School in Brooklyn for my teaching test, the last hurdle for the license. I was supposed to arrive an hour before the lesson, but took the wrong subway train and arrived half an hour late. The English department chairman said I could come back another time, but I wanted to get it over with, especially since I knew I was on the road to failure anyway.

The chairman handed me sheets of paper with the subject of my lesson: War Poems. I knew the poems by heart, Siegfried Sassoon's "Does it Matter?" and Wilfred Owen's "Anthem for Doomed Youth."

When you teach in New York you're required to follow a lesson plan. First, you are to state your aim. Then you are to motivate the class because, as everyone knows, those kids don't want to learn anything.

I motivate this class by telling them about my aunt's husband, who was gassed in World War I and when he came home the only job he could find was shoveling coal, coke and slack at the Limerick Gas Works. The class laughs and the chairman smiles slightly, a good sign.

It isn't enough to teach the poem. You are to "elicit and evoke," involve your students in the material. Excite them. That is the word from the Board of Education. You are to ask pivotal questions to encourage participation. A good teacher should launch enough pivotal questions to keep the class hopping for forty-five minutes.

A few kids talk about war and their family members who survived World War II and Korea. They say it wasn't fair the way some came home with no faces and no legs. Losing an arm wasn't that bad because you always had another. Losing two arms was a real pain because someone had to feed you. Losing a face was something else. You only had one and when that was gone, that was it, baby. One girl with a lovely figure and wearing a lacy pink blouse said her sister was married to a guy who was wounded at Pyongyang and he had no arms at all, not even stubs where you could stick on the false arms. So her sister had to feed him and shave him and do everything and all he ever wanted was sex. Sex, sex, sex, that's all he ever wanted, and her sister was getting all worn out.

The chairman in the back of the room says, Helen, in a warning voice, and she says to the whole class, Well, it's true. How would you like to have someone you have to give a bath to and feed and then go to bed with three times a day. Some of the boys snicker but stop when Helen says, I'm sorry. I get so sad over my sister and Roger because she said she can't go on. She'd leave him but he'd have to go to the veterans' hospital. He said if that ever happened he'd kill himself. She turns around to speak to the chairman in the back of the room. I'm sorry over what I said about sex but that's what happened and I didn't mean to be disrespectful.

I admired Helen so much for her maturity and courage and her lovely breasts I could hardly go on with the lesson. I thought I wouldn't mind being an amputee myself if I had her near me all day, swabbing me, drying me, giving me the daily massage. Of course, teachers were not supposed to think like that but what are you to do when you're twenty-seven and someone like Helen is sitting there in front of you bringing up topics like sex and looking the way she did?

One boy will not let go. He says Helen's sister shouldn't worry about her brother-in-law committing suicide because that would be impossible when you didn't have arms. If you didn't have arms you didn't have a way of dying.

Two boys say you shouldn't have to face life without a face or legs when you're only twenty-two. Oh, sure, you could always get false legs, but you could never get a false face and who would ever go out with you? That'd be the end and you'd never have children or anything. Your own mother wouldn't want to look at you and all your food would have to come through a straw. It was very sad knowing you'd never want to look in the bathroom mirror anymore for fear of what you might see or what you might not see, a face gone. Imagine how hard it was for the poor mom when she had to decide to throw out her son's razor and shaving cream knowing he'd never use them again. Never ever again. She could never actually go into his room and say, Son, you're never gonna use these shaving things anymore and a lotta stuff is piling up here so I'm gonna throw them out. Can you imagine how he'd feel, sitting there with no face, and his own mother telling him, in a way, it was all over? You'd only do that to someone you didn't like and it was hard to think a mother wouldn't like her son even if he had no face. No matter what condition you're in your mother is supposed to like you and stand behind you. If she doesn't, where are you and what's the use of living at all?

Some boys in the class wish they had their own war so they could go over there and get even. One boy says, Oh, bullshit, you can never get even, and they boo him and shout him down. His name is Richard and they say it's well known around the school what a Communist he is. The chairman makes notes, probably on how I've lost control of the class by allowing more than one voice in the room. I feel desperate. I raise my voice, Anyone here ever see a movie about German soldiers called *All Quiet on the Western Front*? No, they never saw it and why should they pay money to see movies about Germans after what they did to us? Goddam krauts.

How many of you are Italian? Half the class.

Does this mean you'd never see an Italian movie after they fought against America in the war?

No, it has nothing to do with war. They just don't want to watch those movies with all those dumb subtitles that move so fast you can never catch up with the story and when there is snow in the movie and the subtitles are white how the hell are you supposed to read anything? A lot of these Italian movies come with snow and dogs taking a leak against a wall, and they're depressing anyhow with people standing in streets waiting for something to happen.

The Board of Education ruled that a lesson must have a summary that pulls everything together and leads to a homework assignment or reinforcement or some kind of outcome, but I forget, and when the bell rings there's an argument going on between two boys, one defending John Wayne, the other saying he was a big phony who never went to war. I try to pull everything together in one grand summary but the discussion dribbles away. I tell them, Thank you, but no one is listening and the chairman scratches his forehead and makes notes.

I walked toward the subway, berating myself. What was the use? Teacher, my arse. I should have stayed in the army with the dogs. I'd be better off on the docks and the warehouses, lifting, hauling, cursing, eating hero sandwiches, drinking beer, chasing waterfront floozies. At least I'd be with my own kind, my own class of people, not getting above meself, acushla. I should have listened to the priests and the respectable people in Ireland who told us beware of vanity, accept our lot, there's a bed in heaven for the meek of heart, the humble of soul.

Mr. McCourt, Mr. McCourt, wait up.

That was the chairman calling from a half block away. Wait up. I walked back toward him. He had a kind face. I thought he was there to console me with a Too bad, young man.

He was out of breath. Look, I'm not supposed to even talk to you but I just want to say you'll be getting your exam results in a few weeks. You have the makings of a fine teacher. I mean, for Christ's sakes, you actually knew Sassoon and Owen. I mean, half the people walking in here can't tell the difference between Emerson and Mickey Spillane. So, when you get your results and you're looking for a job, just call me. OK?

Oh, yes, sure, yes, I will. Thanks.

I danced along the street, walked on air. Birds chirped on the elevated subway platform. People looked at me with smiles and respect. They could see I was a man with a teaching job. I wasn't such an idiot after all. Oh, Lord. Oh, God. What would my family say? A teacher. The word will go around Limerick. Did you hear about Frankie McCourt? Jaysus, he's a teacher over there in America. What was he when he left? Nothing. That's what he was. Poor miserable bugger that looked like something the cat brought in. I'd call June.

Tell her I was offered a teaching job already. In a high school. Not as high up as Norman the professor, but still . . . I stuck a dime into the phone box. It dropped. I put the phone down again. Calling her meant I needed to call her, and I didn't need to need. I could live without her in the tub and the monkfish and the white wine. The train rumbled in. I wanted to tell people, sitting and standing, I was offered a teaching job. They'd smile up from their newspapers. No, no call to June. Let her stay with Norm, who destroyed monkfish and knew nothing about wine, depraved Norm who couldn't take June as she was. No, I'd make my way downtown to Port Warehouses, ready to work till my teacher's license arrived. My teacher's license. I'd like to wave it from the top of the Empire State Building.

When I called about the teaching job the school said sorry, the kindly chairman had passed away and, sorry, no positions were available and good luck in my search. Everyone said as long as I had the license I'd have no trouble finding a job. Who the hell would want a lousy job like that? Long hours, low pay and what gratitude do you get for dealing with the brats of America? Which is why the country was crying out for teachers.

School after school told me, Sorry, your accent's gonna be a problem. Kids, you know, like to mimic, and we'd have Irish brogues all over the school. What would parents say when their kids come home sounding like, you know, like Barry Fitzgerald? You unnerstand our position? Assistant principals wondered how I managed to get a license with that brogue. Didn't the Board of Education have any standards anymore?

I was disheartened. No room for me in the great American Dream. I returned to the waterfront, where I felt more comfortable.

4

Hey, Mr. McCourt, did you ever do real work, not teaching, but, you know, real work?

Are you joking? What do you call teaching? Look around this room and ask yourself if you'd like to get up here and face you every day. You. Teaching is harder than working on docks and warehouses. How many of you have relatives working along the waterfront?

Half the class, mostly Italian, a few Irish.

Before I came to this school I worked on Manhattan, Hoboken and Brooklyn piers, I said. One boy said his father knew me from Hoboken.

I told them, After college I passed the exams for the teacher's license but I didn't think I was cut out for the life of a teacher. I knew nothing about American teenagers. Wouldn't know what to say to you. Dockside work was easier. Trucks backed in. We swung our hooks. Haul, hoist, pull, push. Stack on pallets. Forklift slides in, lifts the load, reverses, stacks the load in the warehouse, and back to the platform. You worked with your body and your brain had a day off. You worked eight to noon, had a foot-long sandwich and a quart of beer for lunch, sweated it off from one to five, headed home, hungry for dinner, ready for a movie and a few beers in a Third Avenue bar.

Once you got the hang of it you moved like a robot. You kept up with the strongest man on the platform and size didn't matter. You used your knees to save your back. If you forgot, platform men would bark, Chrissakes, you got a rubber spine or sumpin'? You learned to use the hook different ways with different loads: boxes, sacks, crates, furniture, great chunks of greasy machinery. A sack of beans or peppers has a mind of its own. It can change shape one way or another and you have to go with it. You looked at the size, shape and weight of an item and you knew in a second how to lift and swing it. You learned the ways of truckers and their helpers. Independent truckers were easy. They worked for themselves, set their own pace. Corporation truckers prodded you to hurry up, man, lift the damn load, let's go, I wanna get outa heah. Truckers' helpers were surly no matter who they worked for. They played little games to test you and throw you off, especially if they thought you were just off the boat. If you worked close to the edge of pier or platform they'd suddenly drop their side of the sack or crate hard enough to pull an arm from its socket and you learned to stay away from the edge of anything. Then they'd laugh and say, Faith an' begorrah, Paddy, or Top o' the mornin' with a fake Irish accent. You'd never complain to a boss about any of this. He'd say, Whassa matter, kid? Can't you take a little joke? Complaining only made matters worse. The word might get to a trucker or a helper and he might accidentally bump you off the platform or even the pier. A big new man from Mayo took offense when someone put a rat's tail in his sandwich and when he threatened to kill whoever did it he was accidentally toppled into the Hudson and everyone laughed before they threw him a line and hauled him out dripping with river scum. He learned to laugh and they stopped bothering him. You can't work the piers with a long face. After a while they stop picking on you and the word goes around that you know how to take your lumps. Eddie Lynch, the platform boss, told me I was a tough little mick and that meant more to me than the day I was promoted to corporal in the United States Army because I knew I wasn't that tough, just desperate.

I told my classes I was so uncertain about teaching I thought of simply spending my life at Port Warehouses, big fish, small pond. My bosses would be so impressed with my college degree they'd hire me as checker and promote me to an office job where I'd surely rise in the world. I might become boss of all checkers. I knew how it was with warehouse office workers or office workers anywhere. They pushed papers around, yawned, looked out the window at us slaving away on the platform.

I did not tell my classes about Helena, the telephone woman who offered more than doughnuts in the back of the warehouse. I was tempted till Eddie said if you even brushed against her you'd wind up in St. Vincent's Hospital with a dripping dick.

What I missed about the piers was the way people spoke their minds and didn't give a shit. Not like the college professors who would tell you, On the one hand, yes, on the other hand, no, and you didn't know what to think. It was important to know what professors thought so you could give it back to them at exam time. In the warehouses everyone insulted everyone else in a joking way till someone stepped over the line and the hooks came out. It was remarkable when that happened. You could see from the way the laughs faded and the smiles got tighter that some bigmouth was getting too close to the bone and you knew the next thing was the hook or the fist.

Work stopped when fights broke out on piers and loading docks. Eddie told me men got tired of lifting and hauling and stacking, same damn thing year in year out, and that's why they insulted and pushed one another to the edge of a real fight. They had to do something to break the routine and the long silent hours. I told him I didn't mind working all day and not saying a word and he said, Yeah, but you're peculiar. You're only here a year an' a half. If you did this fifteen years your mouth would be goin' too. Some of these guys fought in Normandy and the Pacific and what are they now? Donkeys. Donkeys with purple hearts already. Pathetic donkeys in a dead end. They get drunk over on Hudson Street and brag about their medals as if the world gives a shit. They'll tell you they're working for the kids, the kids, the kids. A better life for the kids. Jesus! I'm glad I never got married.

If Eddie hadn't been there the fights would have been worse. He was the man with eye and ear on everything and he could sniff trouble in the wind. If two men started to go at it Eddie would stick his great belly between them and tell them get the hell off his platform and finish their fight in the street. Which they never did because they were really grateful for the excuse to avoid the fist and especially the hook. You can handle a fist but you never know where a hook is coming from. Still, they'd keep on muttering and giving each other the finger, but it was all gas now because the moment had passed, the challenge was over, the rest of us were back at work and what's the use of a fight if there's no one to see what a killer you are?

Helena came from the office to watch the fights and when they were over she'd whisper to the winners and invite them to a dark place in the warehouse for a nice time.

Eddie said some of those rotten bastards pretended to fight so Helena would be nice to them, and if he ever saw me in the back with her after a fight he'd throw my ass in the river. He said that because of the time I had a fight or nearly had a fight with the driver Fat Dominic, who was dangerous because of rumors he was connected to the mob. Eddie said that was bullshit. If you were really connected you weren't driving and breaking your ass unloading rigs. The rest of us believed Dominic probably knew people who were connected, or even made, so it was a good idea to cooperate with him. But how could you cooperate when he sneered, Whassa madda, Paddy? Can't talk? Maybe a dummy humped your momma, huh?

Everyone knows that on the docks or the platforms, or anywhere, you are never to let anyone insult your mother. Kids know it from the time they're able to talk. You might not even like your mother, but that doesn't matter. They can say anything they like about you, but insulting your mother is pushing it and if you let it go you lose all respect. If you need someone to help with a load on the platform or the pier they'll turn their backs. You don't exist. They won't even share a liverwurst sandwich with you at lunchtime. If you wander round the docks and the warehouses and you see men eating alone, you'll know they're in deep shit, men who tolerated insults to their mothers or once scabbed across a picket line. A scab can be forgiven in a year but never a man who allowed an insult to his mother.

I got back at Dominic with an army insult. Hey, Dominic, you're such a fat slob, when was the last time you saw your dick and how do you know it's really there?

He swung around and knocked me off the platform with the flat of his fist and when I hit the street I lost control and jumped back on the platform, clawing at him with my hook. He had the smile now, the one that says, You poor miserable shit, you're gonna die, and when I lunged at him he pushed my face away with the palm of his hand and knocked me to the street again. The palm of the hand is the most insulting thing in a fight. A punch with a closed fist is a straightforward honorable thing. It's what boxers do. But the palm in the face says you're beneath contempt and you'd rather have two black eyes than sink beneath contempt. The black eyes will clear up, but the other thing is there forever.

Then he added insult to insult. When I grabbed the edge of the platform to pull myself back up he stepped on my hand and spat on my head and that sent me into such a white rage I swung my hook and caught him in the back of the leg and pulled till he yelled, You little shit. I see blood on my leg you're dead.

There was no sign of blood. The hook was deflected by the thick leather of his work boots, but I was ready to keep swiping for flesh till Eddie rushed down the steps and pulled me away. Gimme that hook. You are one crazy mick. Get on the bad side of Dominic and you're shit in the street.

He told me get inside, change my clothes, leave by another door, go home, get the hell outa here.

Will I be fired?

No, you won't, goddammit. We can't fire everyone who has a fight here, but you'll lose half a day's pay we'll have to slip to Dominic.

But why should I lose money to Dominic? He started it.

Dominic brings us business and you're passing through. You'll be graduating from college and he'll still be driving in loads. You're lucky to be alive, kid, so take your lumps and go home. Think about it.

On my way out I looked back to see if Helena was there and she was, with that little come-hither smile, but Eddie was there, too, and I knew there was no hope of going to the dark place with her with Eddie glaring.

Some day when it was my turn on the forklift I'd get revenge on Fat Dominic. I'd hit the pedal and jam the fat one against a wall and listen to him scream. That was my dream.

But it never happened and that's because everything changed between him and me the day he backed in his rig and called to Eddie from the cab, Hey, Eddie, who you got unloadin' today?

Durkin.

Nah. Don't gimme Durkin. Gimme bigmouth mick with the hook.

Dominic, are you crazy? Let it go.

Nah. Just gimme bigmouth.

Eddie asked me if I could handle it. If I didn't want to I didn't have to. He said, Dominic's not the boss around here. I said I could handle any fat slob and Eddie told me cut it out. Chrissakes, watch your mouth. We're not gonna bail you out again. Get to work and watch the mouth.

Dominic was up on the platform, unsmiling. He said this was a real job, cases of Irish whiskey, and there might be a dropped case along the way. One or two bottles might be broken, but the rest were for us and he was sure we could handle it. There was a fast little smile and I felt too embarrassed to smile back. How could a man smile after he used the palm of his hand on me instead of his fist?

Christ, you're one gloomy mick, he said.

I was going to call him a wop, but I didn't want the palm of his hand again.

He talked in a cheerful way as if nothing had ever happened between us. That puzzled me because whenever I had a quarrel or fight with someone I turned away from them for a long time. We loaded pallets with the cases and he told me in a normal way his first wife was Irish but she died of TB.

Can you imagine that? T damn B. Lousy cook, my first wife, like the rest of the Irish. Don't get offended, kid. Don't gimme the look. But, boy, could she sing. Opera stuff, too. Now I'm married to an Italian. Don't have a note in her head but, boy, can she cook.

He stared at me. She feeds me. That's why I'm a fat slob can't see his knees.

I smiled and he called to Eddie, Hey, asshole. You owe me ten. I made the little mick smile.

We finished unloading and stacked the pallets inside and it was time to drop a case of whiskey for breakage and sit on bags of peppers in the fumigation room with truckers and warehousemen and make sure nothing from that case was wasted.

Eddie was the kind of man you'd like to have for a father. He explained things to me when we sat on the platform bench between loads. When he explained things to me I was puzzled I didn't know these things already. I was supposed to be the college boy but he knew more and I had more respect for him than I had for any professor.

His own life was a dead end. He took care of his father who came out of World War I shellshocked. Eddie could have put him in a veterans' hospital but he said they were hellholes. While Eddie worked a woman came in every day and fed his father and cleaned him. In the evening Eddie wheeled him to the park, then home to watch the news on television, and that was Eddie's life. He didn't complain. He just said it was always his dream to have children but it wasn't in the cards. His father was gone in the head but his body was sound. He'd live forever and Eddie would never have the place to himself.

He chain-smoked on the platform and ate huge meatball sandwiches washed down with pints of chocolate malted. The cigarette cough got him one day when he was yelling at Fat Dominic to straighten out that damn rig and back it in, You drive like a Hoboken hoor, and when the cough came it tangled with the laugh and he couldn't catch his breath and collapsed on the platform with a cigarette still in his mouth, Fat Dominic in the cab of his rig yelling insults at him till he saw Eddie turning whiter than white and gasping for air. By the time Fat Dominic had heaved out of the cab and up the platform, Eddie was gone and instead of coming over to him and talking the way they talk to the dead in the movies Fat Dominic backed away and waddled down the steps to his truck weeping like a great fat whale and driving away forgetting he had a load to deliver.

I stayed with Eddie till the ambulance took him away. Helena came from the office and told me I looked terrible and sympathized with me as if Eddie were my father. I told her I was ashamed of myself because no sooner was Eddie out of sight than I thought I might apply for his job. I said, I could do it, couldn't I? I was a college graduate. She told me the boss would hire me in a minute. He'd be proud to say Port Warehouses had the only college-graduate checker and platform boss on the waterfront. She said sit there at Eddie's desk to get used to it and write a note to the boss saying I was interested in the job.

Eddie's clipboard was on the desk. It still held the manifest from Fat Dominic. A red pencil hung by a string from the clip. A coffee mug half filled with black coffee sat on the desk. The coffee mug said EDDIE on the side. I thought I'd have to get a mug like that with FRANK printed on it. Helena would know where to buy it. It gave me a feeling of comfort to think she might be there to help. She said, What are you waiting for? Write the note. I looked at Eddie's coffee mug again. I looked out at the platform where he had fallen and died and I could not write the note. Helena said this was the opportunity of a lifetime. I'd make a hundred dollars a week, f'Gawd's sakes, up from the lousy seventy-seven I made now.

No, I could never take Eddie's place on that platform, didn't have his generosity of belly and heart. Helena said, OK, OK, you're right. What's the use of a college education you just gonna stand on the platform checking off sacks of peppers? Any dropout can do that, no offense to Eddie. You wanna be another Eddie? Spend your life checking Fat Dominic? You just go be a teacher, honey. You'll get more respect.

Was it the coffee mug and the little push from Helena that got me off the waterfront and into the classroom or was it my conscience telling me, Face it, stop hiding and teach, man?

When I told stories about the docks they looked at me in a different way. One boy said it was funny to think you had a teacher up there that worked like real people and didn't come from college just talking about books and all. He used to think he'd like to work on the piers, too, because of all the money you make on overtime and little deals here and there with the dropped broken goods but his father said he'd break his ass, ha ha, and you didn't talk back to your father in an Italian family. His father said, If this Irishman can get to be a teacher, so can you, Ronnie, so can you. So forget the docks. You might make money but what good is that when you can't straighten your back?

5

Long after my teaching days I scribble numbers on pieces of paper, and I'm impressed by what they mean. In New York I taught in five different high schools and one college: McKee Vocational and Technical High School, Staten Island; the High School of Fashion Industries in Manhattan; Seward Park High School in Manhattan; Stuyvesant High School in Manhattan; night classes at Washington Irving High School in Manhattan; New York Community College in Brooklyn. I taught by day, by night, and in summer school. My arithmetic tells me that about twelve thousand boys and girls, men and women, sat at desks and listened to me lecture, chant, encourage, ramble, sing, declaim, recite, preach, dry up. I think of the twelve thousand and wonder what I did for them. Then I think of what they did for me.

The arithmetic tells me I conducted at least thirty-three thousand classes.

Thirty-three thousand classes in thirty years: days, nights, summers.

In universities you can lecture from your old crumbling notes. In public high schools you'd never get away with it. American teenagers are experts in the tricks of teachers, and if you try to hoodwink them they'll bring you down.

So, yo, teacher man, what else happened in Ireland?

I can't talk about that now. We have to cover the vocabulary chapter in the textbook. Open to page seventy-two.

Aw, man, you tell the other classes stories. Can't you tell us just one little thing?

OK, one little thing. When I was a boy in Limerick I never thought I'd grow up to be a teacher in New York. We were poor.

Oh, yeah. We heard you didn't have no refrigerator.

Right, and we had no toilet paper.

What? No toilet paper? Everybody has toilet paper. Even in China where everybody's starving they have toilet paper. Even in Africa.

They think I'm exaggerating and they don't like it. There's a limit to hard-luck stories.

You tryin' to tell us you'd go an' pull up your pants and not wipe yourself?

Nancy Castigliano raises her hand. Excuse me, Mr. McCourt. It's nearly lunchtime, and I don't wanna hear no more about people having no toilet paper.

OK, Nancy, we'll move on.

Facing dozens of teenagers every day brings you down to earth. At eight a.m. they don't care how you feel. You think of the day ahead: five classes, up to one hundred and seventy-five American adolescents; moody, hungry, in love, anxious, horny, energetic, challenging. No escape. There they are and there you are with your headache, your indigestion, echoes of your quarrel with your spouse, lover, landlord, your pain-in-the-ass son who wants to be Elvis, who appreciates nothing you do for him. You couldn't sleep last night. You still have that bag filled with the papers of the one hundred and seventy-five students, their so-called compositions, careless scrawls. Oh, mister, did you read my paper? Not that they care. Writing compositions is not how they intend to spend the rest of their lives. That's something you do only in this boring class. They're looking at you. You cannot hide. They're waiting. What are we doing today, teacher? The paragraph? Oh, yeah. Hey, everybody, we gonna study the paragraph, the structure, topic sentence an' all. Can't wait to tell my mom tonight. She's always asking how was school today. Paragraphs, Mom. Teacher has a thing about paragraphs. Mom'll say, Very nice, and go back to her soap opera.

They straggle in from auto mechanics shop, the real world, where they break down and reassemble everything from Volkswagens to Cadillacs, and here's this teacher going on about the parts of a paragraph. Jesus, man. You don't need paragraphs in an auto shop.

If you bark or snap, you lose them. That's what they get from parents and the schools in general, the bark and the snap. If they strike back with the silent treatment, you're finished in the classroom. Their faces change and they have a way of deadening their eyes. Tell them open their notebooks. They stare. They take their time. Yeah, they'll open their notebooks. Yes, sir, here we go opening our notebooks nice and easy so nothing falls out. Tell them copy what's on the board. They stare. Oh, yeah, they tell one another. He wants us to copy what's on the board. Look at that. Man wrote something on the board and wants us to copy it. They shake their heads in slow motion. You ask, Are there any questions? and all around the room there is the innocent look. You stand and wait. They know it's a forty-minute showdown, you versus them, thirty-four New York teenagers, the future mechanics and craftsmen of America.

You're just another teacher, man, so what are you gonna do? Stare down the whole class? Fail the whole class? Get with it, baby. They have you by the balls and you created the situation, man. You didn't have to talk to them like that. They don't care about your mood, your headache, your troubles. They have their own problems, and you are one of them.

Watch your step, teacher. Don't make yourself a problem. They'll cut you down.

Rain changes the mood of the school, mutes everything. The first class comes in silently. One or two say good morning. They shake drops from their jackets. They're in a dream state. They sit and wait. No one talks. No requests for the pass. No complaints, no challenges, no back talk. Rain is magic. Rain is king. Go with it, teacher man. Take your time. Lower your voice. Don't even think about teaching English. Forget about taking attendance. This is the mood of a house after a funeral. No harsh headlines today, no cruel news from Vietnam. Outside the room a footfall, a laugh from a teacher. Rain clatters against windows. Sit at your desk and let the hour slip by. A girl raises her hand. She says, Aw, Mr. McCourt, you ever in love? You're new but you know already when they ask questions like that they're thinking of themselves. You say, Yes.

Did she give you up or did you give her up?

Both.

Oh, yeah? You mean you were in love more than once?

Yes.

Wow.

A boy raises his hand. He says, Why can't teachers treat us like human beings?

You don't know. Well, man, if you don't know, tell them, I don't know. Tell them about school in Ireland. You went to school in a state of terror. You hated it and dreamed of being fourteen and getting a job. You never thought about your own school days like this before, never talked about it. You wish this rain would never stop. They're in their seats. No one had to tell them hang up their jackets. They're looking at you as if they had just discovered you.

It should rain every day.

Or there are spring days when heavy clothing is discarded and each class is a vista of breasts and biceps. Little zephyrs wafting through the windows caress the cheeks of teachers and students, send smiles from desk to desk, from row to row till the room is all adazzle. Pigeon coo and sparrow chirp tell us be of good cheer, summer is a-comin' in. Those shameless pigeons, indifferent to the teen throb in my room, copulate on the windowsill and that is more seductive than the best lesson by the greatest teacher in the world.

On days like this I feel I could teach the toughest of the tough, the brightest of the bright. I could hug and cocker the saddest of the sad.

On days like this there is background music with hints of zephyr, breast, biceps, smile and summer.

And if my students ever wrote like that I'd send them to Simplicity School.

Twice a year at McKee we had Open School Day and Open School Night, when parents visited the school to see how their children were faring. Teachers sat in classrooms talking to parents or listening to their complaints. Most visiting parents were mothers because that was the job of the woman. If the mother found her son or daughter was misbehaving or not performing well then it would be up to the father to take steps. Of course the father would take steps only with the son. The daughter was a matter for the mother. It wouldn't be right for a father to knock his daughter around the kitchen or tell her she was grounded for a month. Certain problems belonged to the mother. Also, they had to decide on how much information to give the father. If the son was doing poorly and she had a violent husband she might soften her story so that her boy would not wind up on the floor with blood streaming from his nose.

Sometimes a whole family might come to visit the teacher and the room would be packed with fathers and mothers and small children running up and down the aisles. The women talked to one another in a friendly way, but the men sat quietly at desks that could barely accommodate their size.

No one ever told me how to handle parents on Open School Day. My first time at McKee, I had a student monitor, Norma, who gave out numbers so that parents would know who was next.

First, I had to deal with the problem of my accent, especially with the women. As soon as I opened my mouth they'd say, Oh, my God, what a cute brogue. Then they'd tell me how their grandparents came from the Old Country, how they came here with nothing and now owned their own gas station out in New Dorp. They wanted to know how long I was in this country and how I got into teaching. They said it was wunnerful I was a teacher because most of our people were cops and priests and they'd whisper there were too many Jews in the school. They'd send their kids to Catholic schools except that Catholic schools were not known for vocational or technical training. It was all history and prayers, which was all right for the next world, but their kids had to think about this world. No disrespect intended. Finally, they'd ask how was he doing, their little Harry?

I had to be careful if the dad was sitting there. If I made negative comments about Harry the dad might go home and punch him and word would get out to my other students that I was not to be trusted. I was learning that teachers and kids have to stick together in the face of parents, supervisors and the world in general.

I said positive things about all my students. They were attentive, punctual, considerate, eager to learn and every one of them had a bright future and the parents should be proud. Dad and Mom would look at each other and smile and say, See? or they'd be puzzled and say, You talkin' about our kid? Our Harry?

Oh, yes. Harry.

Does he behave himself in class? Is he respectful?

Oh, yes. He contributes to all our discussions.

Oh, yeah? That's not the Harry we know. He must be different in school because at home he's a regular little shit, excuse the language. Home we can't get a word out of him. Can't get him to do nothing. All he wants is to sit an' listen to that goddam rock 'n' roll day an' night, day an' goddam night.

The dad was vehement. It's the worst thing ever happened to this country with that Elvis shakin' his ass all over television, excuse the language. I'd hate to have a daughter in this day and age watching that crap. Got a good mind to throw that phonograph in the garbage. I'd dump the TV, too, but I gotta have a little relaxation the end of a day on the piers, know what I mean?

Other parents became impatient and inquired, sarcastically polite, if there was a possibility I could get away from discussions of Elvis Presley and talk to them about their sons and daughters. Harry's parents informed them it was their turn to see about their kid. It was a free country, last they'd heard, and they weren't gonna be cut off in the middle of their interview with this nice teacher from the Old Country.

But the other parents said, Yeah, yeah, teacher. Hurry it up. We don't got all night. We're working people, too.

I didn't know what to do. I thought if I said thank you to the parents at the desk they might get the hint and go but the vehement dad said, Hey, we're not finished.

Norma, my student monitor, understood my dilemma and took charge. She announced to the parents that if they wanted longer interviews with me they could make appointments to see me on a series of afternoons.

I never told Norma any such thing. I didn't want to spend my life in that classroom, day after day, with disgruntled parents, but she went calmly on, passed around a sheet of paper, told the disgruntled ones to print, please print, don't write, their names and phone numbers and Mr. McCourt would be in touch.

The rumbling subsided and everyone complimented Norma on her efficiency and told her she should be a teacher herself. She told them she had no intention of being a teacher. Her big dream was to work in a travel agency and get free tickets everywhere. One mother said, Oh, don't you wanna settle down and have kids? You'd be a great mother.

Then Norma said the wrong thing and tension was back in the room. No, she said, I don't want kids. Kids are a pain. You have to change their diapers and then come to school to see how they're doing and you're never free.

She wasn't supposed to talk like that and you could feel the hostility toward her rising in the room. A few minutes ago parents were complimenting her on her efficiency and now they felt insulted by her remarks on parenthood and kids. One father tore up the sheet of paper she'd handed out for names and phone numbers. He threw it toward the front of the room where I sat. Hey, he said, somebody dump that in the garbage. He picked up his coat and told his wife, Let's get outa here. This place is a nuthouse. His wife barked at me, Don't you have no control over these kids? This one was my daughter I'd break her face. She got no right to insult the mothers of America like that.

My face felt like a fire. I wanted to apologize to the parents in the room and the mothers of America. I wanted to tell Norma, Go away. You've ruined my first Open School Day. She stood by the door coolly saying goodnight to the parents who left, ignoring the way they glared at her. Now what was I supposed to do? Where was the book by a professor of education that would help? Fifteen parents still sat in the room waiting to hear about their sons and daughters. What should I say to them?

Norma spoke again and my heart began to sink. Ladies and gentlemen, that was a dumb thing I said and I'm so sorry. It wasn't Mr. McCourt's fault. He's a good teacher. He's new, you know, just here a few months, so he's just a learning teacher. I shoulda kept my mouth shut because I got him in trouble and I'm sorry.

Then she began to cry and a number of mothers rushed to comfort her while I sat at my desk. It was Norma's job to call the parents up, one by one, but she was surrounded by that group of comforting mothers and I didn't know if I should act independently and say, Next? The parents seemed more interested in Norma's plight than in the future of their own children, and when the bell rang to signal the end of the meetings, they smiled and left saying it was nice, this visit with me, and good luck in my teaching career.

Paulie's mother may have been right. On my second Open School Day she told me I was a fraud. She was proud of her Paulie, future plumber, nice kid who wanted to start his own business some day, marry a nice girl, raise a family and stay out of trouble.

I should have been indignant and asked her who the hell she thought she was talking to but, at the back of my head, there was always a nagging doubt I was teaching under false pretenses.

I ask my kid what he learned in school an' he tells me stories about Ireland an' you coming to New York. Stories, stories, stories. You know what you are? A fraud, a goddam fraud. And I'm saying that with the best intentions, trying to help.

I wanted to be a good teacher. I wanted the approval that would come when I sent my students home stuffed with spelling and vocabulary and all that would lead to a better life but, *mea culpa,* I didn't know how.

The mother said she was Irish, married to an Italian, and she could see right through me. Right off she knew my game. When I told her I agreed with her she said, Ooh, you agree with me? You actually know you're a fraud?

I'm just trying to make my way. They ask me questions about my life and I answer because they won't listen when I try to teach English. They look out the window. They doze. They nibble on sandwiches. They ask for the pass.

You could teach them what they're supposeta learn, spelling and the big words. My son, Paulie, hasta go out in the world and what's he gonna do when he can't spell an' use the big words, eh?

I told Paulie's mother that someday I hoped to be a master teacher, confident in the classroom. In the meantime I could only keep trying. That somehow made her emotional and brought on the tears. She rooted around in her handbag for a handkerchief and took so long I offered her mine. She shook her head. She said, Who does your laundry? That handkerchief. Jesus, I wouldn't wipe my ass with that handkerchief. You a bachelor or what?

I am.

I can tell from the look of that handkerchief, the saddest-lookin' gray handkerchief I ever seen in my life. That's bachelor gray, is what it is. Your shoes, too. I never seen such sad shoes. No woman would ever let you buy shoes like them. Easy to see you was never married.

She wiped her cheeks with the back of her hand. You think my Paulie can spell handkerchief?

I don't think so. It's not on the list.

See what I mean? You people are out of it. You don't have handkerchief on the list and he'll be blowing his nose the rest of his life. And you know what you got on the list? Usufruct, f'Christ's sakes, u-s-u-f-r-u-c-t. Who came up with that one? That one of those words you throw around at your fancy cocktail parties in Manhattan? Now what in hell is Paulie gonna do with a word like that? And here's another one, c-o-n-d-i-g-n. I asked six people if they knew what that meant. I even asked an assistant principal in the hallway. He pretended he knew but you could see he was talking through his ass. Plumber. My kid's gonna be a plumber and charge big money to make house calls, just like a doctor, so I don't see why he needs to clog his head with twenty-dollar words like usufruct and the other one, do you?

I said you have to be careful what you fill your head with. My own head was so packed with stuff from Ireland and the Vatican I could hardly think for myself.

She said she didn't care what was in my head. That was my own damn business, and I should really keep it to myself. Every day my Paulie comes home telling us these stories and we don't need to hear them. We got our own troubles. She said it was easy to see I was just off the boat, all innocent like a little sparrow that fell out of a nest.

No, I'm not just off the boat. I was in the army. How could I be innocent? I had all kinds of jobs. I worked on the docks. I graduated from New York University.

See? she said. That's what I mean. I ask you a simple question an' you give me the story of your life. That's what you wanna watch, Mr. McCurd. These kids don't need to know the life story of every teacher in the school. I went to the nuns. They wouldn't give you the time of day. You asked them about their lives they'd tell you mind your own business, pull you up by the ears, crack you across the knuckles. Stick to the spelling and the words, Mr. McCurd, and the parents of this school will thank you forever. Forget the storytelling. If we want stories we got a *TV Guide* and the *Reader's Digest* at home.

I struggled. I thought I'd like to be a tough no-nonsense English teacher, stern and scholarly, allowing an occasional laugh, but no more. Old-timers in the teachers' cafeteria told me, The little bastards have to be kept under control. Give 'em an inch, kid, and you'll never get it back.

Organization is everything. I would start all over. Draw up a plan for each class that would account for every minute left in the term. I was master of this vessel and I would set a course. They'd sense my purpose. They would know where they were going and what was expected of them . . . or else.

Or else. . . . Yeah, mister, that's what all the teachers say. Or else. We thought you were gonna be different being Irish an' all.

Time to take charge. Enough, I said. Forget this Irish thing. No more stories. No more nonsense. English teacher is going to teach English and won't be stopped by little teenage tricks.

Take out your notebooks. That's right, your notebooks.

I wrote on the board, "John went to the store."

A class groan traveled the room. What is he doing to us? English teachers. All the same. Here he goes again. Old John to the store. Grammar, for Chrissakes.

All right. What is the subject of this sentence? Does anyone know the subject of this sentence? Yes, Mario?

It's all about this guy wants to go to the store. Anyone can see that.

Yes, yes, that's what the sentence is about, but what is the subject? It's one word. Yes, Donna.

I think Mario is right. It's all about—

No, Donna. The subject here is one word.

How come?

What do you mean, How come? Aren't you taking Spanish? Don't you have grammar in Spanish? Doesn't Miss Grober tell you the parts of a sentence?

Yeah, but she's not always bothering us with John going to the store.

My head feels hot and I want to shout, Why are you so damn stupid? Didn't you ever have a grammar lesson before? Christ in heaven, even I had grammar lessons, and in Irish. Why do I have to struggle here this sunny morning while spring birds chirp outside? Why do I have to look at your sullen resentful faces? You sit here, your bellies stuffed. You're well-clothed and warm. You're getting a free high school education and you're not the slightest bit grateful. All you have to do is cooperate, participate a little. Learn the parts of a sentence. Jesus. Is that asking too much?

There are days I'd love to walk out of here, slam the door behind me, tell the principal shove this job up his arse, head down the hill to the ferry, sail to Manhattan, walk the streets, have a beer and a hamburger at the White Horse, sit in Washington Square, watch luscious NYU coeds saunter by, forget McKee Vocational and Technical High School forever. Forever. It's clear I can't teach the simplest thing without their objections. Their resistance. Simple sentence: subject, predicate and, maybe, if we get around to it someday, the object, direct and indirect. I don't know what to do with them. Try the old threats. Pay attention or you're going to fail. If you fail you won't graduate and if you don't graduate blah blah blah. All your friends will be out there in the big wide world pinning their high school diplomas to their office walls, successful, respected by one and all. Why can't you just look at this sentence and, for once in your miserable teenage existence, make an attempt to learn.

Every class has its chemistry. There are some classes you enjoy and look forward to. They know you like them and they like you in return. Sometimes they'll tell you that was a pretty good lesson and you're on top of the world. That somehow gives you energy and makes you want to sing on the way home.

There are some classes you wish would take the ferry to Manhattan and never return. There's something hostile about the way they enter and leave the room that tells you what they think of you. It could be your imagination and you try to figure out what will bring them over to your side. You try lessons that worked with other classes but even that doesn't help and it's because of that chemistry.

They know when they have you on the run. They have instincts that detect your frustrations. There were days I wanted to sit behind my desk and let them do whatever they damn well pleased. I just could not reach them. Four years on the job in 1962 and I didn't care anymore. I told myself I never cared in the first place. You entertain them with stories of your miserable childhood. They make all those phony sounds. Oh, poor Mr. McCourt, musta been awful growin' up in Ireland like that. As if they cared. No. They're never satisfied. I should have followed the advice of old-timer teachers to keep my big mouth shut. Tell 'em nothing. They just use you. They figure you out and move in on you like heat-seeking missiles. They find out where you're vulnerable. Could they possibly know that "John went to the store" is as far as I can go in grammar? Lead me not into gerunds, dangling participles, cognate objects. I will surely be lost.

I gave them the grim look and sat at my desk. Enough. I couldn't continue the charade of grammar teacher.

I said, Why did John go to the store?

They looked surprised. Yo, man, what's this? That has nothing to do with grammar.

I'm asking you a simple question. Nothing to do with grammar. Why did John go to the store? Can't you guess?

A hand in the back of the room. Yes, Ron?

I think John went to the store to get a book on English grammar.

And why did John go to the store to get a book on English grammar?

'Cause he wanted to know everything and come in here and impress good old Mr. McCourt.

And why would he want to impress good old Mr. McCourt?

'Cause John has a girlfriend name of Rose and she's a good girl knows all kindsa grammar and she's gonna graduate an' be a secretary in a big company in Manhattan and John don't wanna be no dumb ass trying to marry Rose. That's why he goes to the store to get the book on grammar. He's gonna be a good boy and study his book and when he don't understand something he's gonna ask Mr. McCourt because Mr. McCourt knows everything and when John marries Rose he's gonna invite Mr. McCourt to the wedding and ask

Mr. McCourt to be godfather to their first child, which will be called Frank after Mr. McCourt.

Thank you, Ron.

The class erupted, cheering, applauding, but Ron was not stopping. His hand went up again.

Yes, Ron?

When John got to the store he didn't have no money so he had to rob the book on grammar but when he tried to walk outa the store he was stopped and the cops were called and now he's in Sing Sing and poor old Rose is crying her eyes out.

They made sympathetic sounds. Poor Rose. The boys wanted to know where she could be found and they'd be willing to stand in for John. Girls dabbed at their eyes till Kenny Ball, class tough guy, said it was only a story and what was all this bullshit anyway? He said, Teacher writes a sentence on the board and next thing is the guy going to the store robs a book and winds up in Sing Sing. Who ever heard such bull and is this an English class or what?

Ron said, Well, I guess you can do better, right?

All these made-up stories don't mean nothing. Don't help you get a job.

The bell rang. They left and I erased from the board "John went to the store."

Next day Ron raised his hand again. Hey, teacher, what would happen if you fooled around with those words?

What do you mean?

OK. You write up there, "To the store John went." How about that?

Same thing. John is still the subject of the sentence.

OK. How about "Went John to the store"?

Same thing.

Or "John to the store went." Would that be OK?

Of course. It makes sense, doesn't it? But you could make nonsense of it. If you said to someone, John store to the went, they'd think it was gibberish.

What's gibberish?

Language that makes no sense.

I had a sudden idea, a flash. I said, Psychology is the study of the way people behave. Grammar is the study of the way language behaves.

Go on, teacher man. Tell them of your brilliant discovery, your great breakthrough. Ask, Who knows what psychology is?

Write the word on the board. They like big words. They take them home and intimidate their families.

Psychology. Who knows it?

It's when people go crazy and you have to find out what's wrong with them before you put them in the looney bin.

The class laughed. Yeah, yeah. Like this school, man.

I pushed it. If someone acts crazy, the psychologist studies them to find out what's wrong. If someone talks in a funny way and you can't understand them, then you're thinking about grammar. Like, John store to the went.

So it's gibberish, right?

They liked that word and I patted myself on the back for bringing it to them, news from the vast world of the English language. Teaching is bringing the news. Big breakthrough for new teacher. Gibberish. They said it to one another and laughed. But it was stuck in their heads. A few years into my teaching career, and I managed to make one word stick. Ten years from now they'd hear "gibberish" and think of me. Something was happening. They were beginning to understand what grammar was. If I kept at it I might understand it myself.

The study of the way language behaves.

No stopping me now. I said, Store the to went John. Does that make sense? Of course not. So you see, you have to have words in their proper order. Proper order means meaning and if you don't have meaning you're babbling and the men in white coats come and take you away. They stick you in the gibberish department of Bellevue. That's grammar.

Ron's girlfriend, Donna, raised her hand. What about John, the first boy ever to go to jail for stealing a book on grammar? You left him up in Sing Sing with all those mean people. And what became of Rose? Did she wait for John? Was she true to him?

Tough guy Ken said, Naw, they never wait for you.

Excuse me, said Donna, putting on a sarcastic air. I'd wait for Ron if he went to jail for robbing a grammar book.

Stealing, I said. The English teacher is instructed by superiors to correct these little errors.

What? said Donna.

Not robbing. The proper word is stealing.

Yeah. OK.

I told myself, Shut up. Stop interrupting them. Who gives a fiddler's fart about the difference between stealing and robbing. Let them talk.

Ken sneered at Donna. Yeah, sure. I bet you'd wait. All these guys got their asses shot off in France and Korea an' next thing they're gettin' Dear John letters from their girlfriends and their wives. Oh, yeah.

I had to step in. All right, all right. We're talking about John sentenced to Sing Sing for stealing a grammar book.

Ken sneered again. Yeah, they're big on grammar in Sing Sing. All these killers sit around Death Row talkin' grammar alla time.

Ken, I said. It's not Ron. It's John.

That's right, said Donna. It's John up there and he starts teaching everyone grammar and they all come out of Sing Sing talking like college professors and the government is so grateful to John they give him a job teaching grammar in McKee Vocational and Technical High School.

Ken wanted to respond but the class cheered and clapped and said, Right on, Donna, right on, and drowned him out.

English teachers say if you can teach grammar in a vocational high school you can teach anything anywhere. My classes listened. They participated. They didn't know I was teaching grammar.

Maybe they thought we were just making up stories about John in Sing Sing but when they left the classroom they looked at me in a different way. If teaching could be like this every day I might stay till I'm eighty. Old Silver Locks up there, a bit bent, but don't under-estimate him. Just ask him a question on the structure of the sentence and he'll straighten his spine and tell you that story of how he brought psychology and grammar together way back in the middle of the twentieth century.

6

Mikey Dolan handed me a note from his mother explaining his absence the day before:

Dear Mr. McCort, Mikey's grandmother who is my mother eighty years of age fell down the stairs from too much coffee and I kept Mikey at home to take care of her and his baby sister so I could go to my job at the coffee shop in the ferry terminal. Please excuse Mikey and he'll do his best in the future as he likes your class. Sincerely yours, Imelda Dolan. P.S. His grandmother is OK.

When Mikey handed me the note, so blatantly forged under my nose, I said nothing. I had seen him writing it at his desk with his left hand to disguise his own handwriting, which, because of his years in Catholic primary schools, was the best in the class. The nuns didn't care whether you went to heaven or hell or married a Protestant as long as your handwriting was clear and handsome and if you were weak in that department they'd bend your thumbs back till you screamed for mercy and promised a calligraphy that would open the doors of heaven. Also, if you wrote with the left hand, it was clear proof you were born with a Satanic streak and it was the business of the sisters to bend your thumbs, even here in America, land of the free and home of the brave.

So, there was Mikey, laboring with his left hand to disguise his exquisite Catholic calligraphy. This was not his first time forging a note but I said nothing because most of the parental-excuse notes in my desk drawer were written by the boys and girls of McKee Vocational and Technical High School and if I were to confront each forger I'd be busy twenty-four hours a day. It would also lead to indignation, hurt feelings and strained relations between them and me.

I said to one boy, Did your mother really write this note, Danny?

He was defensive, hostile. Yeah, my mother wrote it.

It's a nice note, Danny. She writes well.

McKee students were proud of their mothers and only a lout would let that compliment pass without thanks.

He said thanks, and returned to his seat.

I could have asked him if the note was his but I knew better. I liked him and didn't want him sullen in the third row. He'd tell classmates I suspected him and that might make them sullen, too, because they'd been forging excuse notes since they learned to write and years later they don't want to be bothered by teachers suddenly getting moral.

An excuse note is just a part of school life. Everyone knows they're fiction, so what's the big deal?

Parents getting kids out of the house in the morning have little time for writing notes that they know will wind up in the school garbage anyway. They're so harried they'll say, Oh, you need an excuse note for yesterday, honey? Write it yourself and I'll sign it. They sign it without even looking at it and the sad part is they don't know what they're missing. If they could read those notes they'd discover their kids are capable of the finest American prose: fluent, imaginative, clear, dramatic, fantastic, focused, persuasive, useful.

I threw Mikey's note into a desk drawer along with dozens of others: notes written on every size and color of paper, scrawled, scratched, stained. While my classes took a test that day I began to read notes I had only glanced at before. I made two piles, one for the genuine notes written by mothers, the other for forgeries. The second was the larger pile, with writing that ranged from imaginative to lunatic.

I was having an epiphany. I always wondered what an epiphany would be like and now I knew. I wondered also why I'd never had this particular epiphany before.

Next day everyone had excuse notes, not only from Adam and Eve but from God and Lucifer, some compassionate, some nasty. On behalf of Eve, Lisa Quinn defended her seduction of Adam on the grounds that she was tired of lying around Paradise doing nothing day in, day out. She was also tired of God sticking His nose into their business and never allowing them a moment of privacy. It was all right for Him. He could go off and hide behind a cloud somewhere and roar from time to time if He saw her or Adam go near his precious apple tree.

There are heated discussions about the relative guilt and sinfulness of Adam and Eve. It is agreed, unanimously, that Lucifer the snake is a bastard, a son of a bitch and no good. No one is so brave to say anything negative about God although there are hints and suggestions He could have been a little more understanding of the plight of the First Man and the First Woman.

Mikey Dolan says you could never talk like this in Catholic schools. Jesus (sorry), the nuns would pull you out of your seat by the ears and have your parents in to explain where you got ideas that were pure blasphemy.

Other boys in the class, non-Catholics, brag they'd never put up with that bullshit. They'd knock the nuns on their ass and how come the Catholic boys were such sissies?

The discussion was drifting and I worried that details might get to Catholic parents who would object to a mention of nuns treated roughly. I asked them to think about anyone in the past, present or in history who could use a good excuse note. I wrote the suggestions on the blackboard:

Eva Braun, Hitler's girlfriend.

Hey, How about Hitler himself?

Naw, never. No excuses there.

Maybe he had a miserable childhood.

I couldn't agree. An excuse note for Hitler might be a great for a writer but the excuse would never come from this

Isn't it remarkable, I thought, how they resist any kind of writing assignment in class or at home. They whine and say they're busy and it's hard putting two hundred words together on any subject. But when they forge these excuse notes they're brilliant. Why? I have a drawer full of excuse notes that could be turned into an anthology of Great American Excuses or Great American Lies.

The drawer was filled with samples of American talent never mentioned in song, story or scholarly study. How could I have ignored this treasure trove, these gems of fiction, fantasy, creativity, crawthumping, self-pity, family problems, boilers exploding, ceilings collapsing, fires sweeping whole blocks, babies and pets pissing on homework, unexpected births, heart attacks, strokes, miscarriages, robberies? Here was American high school writing at its best—raw, real, urgent, lucid, brief, lying:

The stove caught fire and the wallpaper went up and the fire department kept us out of the house all night.

The toilet was blocked and we had to go down the street to the Kilkenny Bar where my cousin works to use their toilet but that was blocked too from the night before and you can imagine how hard it was for my Ronnie to get ready for school. I hope you'll excuse him this one time and it won't happen again. The man at the Kilkenny Bar was very nice on account of how he knows your brother, Mr. McCord.

Arnold doesn't have his work today because he was getting off the train yesterday and the door closed on his school bag and the train took it away. He yelled to the conductor who said very vulgar things as the train drove away. Something should be done.

His sister's dog ate his homework and I hope it chokes him.

Her baby brother peed on her story when she was in the bathroom this morning.

A man died in the bathtub upstairs and it overflowed and messed up all Roberta's homework on the table.

Her big brother got mad at her and threw her essay out the window and it flew away all over Staten Island which is not a good thing because people will read it and get the wrong impression unless they read the ending which explains everything.

He had the composition you told him to write but he was going over it on the ferry and a big wind came and blowed it away.

We were evicted from our apartment and the mean sheriff said if my son kept yelling for his notebook he'd have us all arrested.

I imagined the writers of excuse notes on buses, trains, ferries, in coffee shops, on park benches, trying to discover new and logical excuses, trying to write as they thought their parents would.

They didn't know that honest excuse notes from parents were usually dull. "Peter was late because the alarm clock did not go off." A note like that didn't even merit a place in the trash can.

Toward the end of the term I typed a dozen excuse notes on a stencil and distributed them to my two senior classes. They read, silently and intently.

Yo, Mr. McCourt, what's this?

Excuse notes.

Whaddya mean, excuse notes? Who wrote them?

You did, or some of you did. I omitted the names to protect the guilty. They're supposed to be written by parents, but you and I know the real authors. Yes, Mikey?

So, what are we supposed to do with these excuse notes?

We'll read them aloud. I want you to realize this is the first class in the world ever to study the art of the excuse note, the first class, ever, to practice writing them. You are so lucky to have a teacher like me who has taken your best writing, the excuse note, and turned it into a subject worthy of study.

They're smiling. They know. We're in this together. Sinners.

Some of the notes on that sheet were written by people in this class. You know who you are. You used your imagination and didn't settle for the old alarm-clock story. You'll be making excuses the rest of your life and you'll want them to be believable and original. You might even wind up writing excuses for your own children when they're late or absent or up to some devilment. Try it now. Imagine

you have a fifteen-year-old son or daughter who needs an excuse for falling behind in English. Let it rip.

They didn't look around. They didn't chew on their pens. They didn't dawdle. They were eager, desperate to make up excuses for their fifteen-year-old sons and daughters. It was an act of loyalty and love and, you never know, some day they might need these notes.

They produced a rhapsody of excuses, ranging from a family epidemic of diarrhea to a sixteen-wheeler truck crashing into a h... to a severe case of food poisoning blamed on the McKee ... School cafeteria.

They said, More, more. Could we do more?

I was taken aback. How do I handle this enthusiasm?

There was another epiphany or a flash of inspiration o... tion or something. I went to the board and wrote: "For ... Tonight."

That was a mistake. The word homework carries ... notations. I erased it and they said, Yeah, yeah.

I told them, You can start it here in class and c... or on the other side of the moon. What I'd like yo...

I wrote it on the board: "An Excuse Note fro... or "An Excuse Note from Eve to God."

The heads went down. Pens raced across p... this with one hand tied behind their backs. W... Secret smiles around the room. Oh, this is a g... know what's coming, don't we? Adam bl... Adam. They both blame God or Lucifer. Bla... God, who has the upper hand and kicks ... their descendants wind up in McKee Voc... School writing excuse notes for the first ... God Himself needs an excuse note for ...

The bell rang, and for the first tim... of teaching, I saw high school stude... urged out of the room by friends h...

Yo, Lenny. Come on. Finish it...

On the board: Julius and Ethel Rosenberg, executed in 1953 for treason.

How about excuse notes for draft dodgers?

Oh, yeah, Mr. McCourt. These guys have big excuse notes. They don't wanna fight for their country but that's not us.

On the board: Judas, Attila the Hun, Lee Harvey Oswald, Al Capone, all the politicians in America.

Yo, Mr. McCourt, could you put teachers up there? Not you but all these pain-in-the-ass teachers that be giving us tests every other day.

Oh, I couldn't do that. They're my colleagues.

OK. OK, we can write excuse notes for them explaining why they have to be like that.

Mr. McCourt, the principal is at the door.

My heart sinks.

Into the room the principal escorts the Staten Island Superintendent of Schools, Mr. Martin Wolfson. They don't acknowledge my existence. They don't apologize for interrupting the class. They walk up and down the aisles, peering at student papers. They pick them up for a closer look. Superintendent shows one to the principal. Superintendent frowns and purses his lips. Principal purses his lips. Class understands these are significant and important people. To show loyalty and solidarity they refrain from asking for the pass.

On their way out the principal frowns at me and whispers that the superintendent would like to see me next period even if they have to send someone to cover my class. I know. I know. I've done something wrong again. The shit will hit the fan and I don't know why. There will be a negative letter in my file. You do your best. You take the ball on the hop. You try something that has never ever been done in the whole history of the world. You have your kids hopping with enthusiasm over the excuse notes. But now comes the reckoning, teacher man. Down the hallway to the principal's office.

He is sitting at his desk. The way the superintendent stands still in the middle of the room reminds me of a repentant high school kid.

Ah, Mr. . . . Mr. . . .

McCourt.

Come in. Come in. Only a minute. I just want to tell you that that lesson, that project, whatever the hell you were doing in there, was top-notch. Top-notch. That, young man, is what we need, that kind of down-to-earth teaching. Those kids were writing on a college level.

He turns to the principal and says, That kid writing an excuse note for Judas. Brilliant. But I have a reservation or two. I'm not sure if the writing of excuse notes for evil or criminal people is justifiable or wise, though on second thoughts, it's what lawyers do, isn't it? And from what I've seen in your class you might have some promising future attorneys in there. So, I just want to shake your hand and tell you don't be surprised if there's a letter in your file attesting to your energetic and imaginative teaching. Thank you and maybe you should divert them to more remote figures in history. An excuse note for Al Capone is a little risky. Thank you again.

God in heaven. High praise from the Superintendent of Schools in Staten Island. Shall I dance down the hallway or shall I lift and fly? Will the world object if I sing?

I sing. Next day, I tell the class I know a song they'll like, a tongue-twister of a song, and here it is:

O ro the rattlin' bog, the bog down in the valley O,
O ro the rattlin' bog, the bog down in the valley O.
And in that bog there was a tree, a rare tree, a rattlin' tree,
And the tree in the bog and the bog down in the valley O.

We sang verse after verse and they laughed as they tried to get their tongues around the words and wasn't it great to see that teacher up there singing. Man, school should be like this every day, us writing excuse notes and teachers singing all of a sudden for some reason.

The reason was I realized there was enough material in human history for millions of excuse notes. Sooner or later, everyone needs an excuse. Also, if we sang today we could sing tomorrow and why not? You don't need an excuse for singing.

7

Augie was a nuisance in class, talking back, bothering the girls. I called his mother. Next day the door is thrown open and a man in a black T-shirt with the muscles of a weightlifter yells, Hey, Augie, come 'ere.

You can hear Augie gasp.

Talkin' a yeh, Augie. I haveta go in there you gonna wish you was dead. Come 'ere.

Augie yelps, I didn't do nothin'.

The man lumbers into the room, down the aisle to Augie's seat, lifts Augie into the air, carries him over to the wall, bangs him, repeatedly, against the wall.

I told you—*bang*—never—*bang*—never give your teacher—*bang*—no trouble—*bang*. I hear you give your teacher trouble—*bang*—I'm gonna tear your goddam head off—*bang*—an' stick it up your ass—*bang*. You hear me—*bang*?

Hey. Hold on. This is my classroom. I am the teacher. I can't have the world barging in here like this. I'm supposed to be in charge.

Excuse me.

The man ignores me. He is busy banging his son so hard against the wall that Augie hangs limp in his hands.

I have to show who's in charge in this classroom. People can't just walk in here and reduce their sons to jelly. I repeat, Excuse me.

The man drags Augie back to his seat and turns to me. He gives you trouble again, mister, I kick his ass here to New Jersey. He was brought up to give respect.

He turns to the class. This teacher here to learn youse kids. Youse don't lissena the teacher youse don't graduate. Youse don't graduate youse wind up on the piers in some dead-end job. Youse don't lissena teacher youse doin' yourselves no favor. Unnerstand what I'm tellin' youse?

They say nothing.

Y'unnerstand what I'm tellin' youse or youse a bunch o' dummies? Or is there some tough guy here wants to say something?

They say they understand, and all the tough guys are silent.

OK, teacher, youse can go back to work now.

On the way out he slams the door so hard chalk dust slides down the blackboard, and windows rattle. There is a cold hostile silence in the room that says, We know you called Augie's father. We don't like teachers who call people's fathers.

No use saying, Oh, look. I didn't ask Augie's father to do that. I just spoke to his mother and thought they'd talk to him and tell him behave in class. It's too late. I've gone behind their backs, shown I can't handle the situation myself. There's no respect for teachers who send you to the office or call parents. If you can't handle it yourself you shouldn't even be a teacher. You should get a job sweeping the streets or picking up the garbage.

Sal Battaglia smiled every morning and said, Hi, teach. Sal sat with his girlfriend, Louise, and looked happy. When they held hands across the aisle everyone walked around them because it was understood this was the real thing. Someday Sal and Louise would be married and that was sacred.

Sal's Italian family and Louise's Irish family didn't approve, but at least the wedding would be Catholic and that was OK. Sal joked to the class his family worried he might starve to death with an Irish wife on account of how the Irish can't cook. He said his mother wondered how the Irish survived at all. Louise spoke up, said they could say what they liked, but the Irish had the most beautiful babies in the world. Sal blushed. Cool Italian, nearly eighteen, with the mass of black curly hair, actually blushed. Louise laughed and we all laughed when she reached across the aisle to touch the redness of his face with her delicate white hand.

The class went quiet when Sal took her hand and kept it against his face. You could see his eyes glistening with tears. What came over him? I stood with my back to the blackboard, not knowing what to say or do, not wanting to break the spell. At a time like this how could I go on with our discussion of *The Scarlet Letter*?

I went behind my desk, pretended to be busy, silently took the attendance again, filled out a form, waited for the bell to ring in ten minutes, watched Sal and Louise leave, hand in hand, and envied them the way everything was laid out. After graduation there would be an engagement. Sal would become a master plumber, Louise a legal stenographer, the highest you can go in the secretarial world unless you got the crazy notion to become a lawyer. I told Louise she was bright enough to be anything, but she said no no, what would her family say? She had to earn a living, get ready for her life with Sal. She'd learn Italian cooking so she wouldn't be beholden all the time to Sal's mother. A year after the wedding a baby would appear, a little round well-fed Italian-Irish-American baby and that would bring the two families together forever and who cared what countries their parents came from.

None of that happened because of an Irish kid who went after Sal in a Prospect Park gang rumble and clobbered him with a two-by-four. Sal didn't even belong to a gang. He was just passing through delivering an order from the restaurant where he worked nights and weekends. He and Louise knew these gang wars were stupid, especially with the Irish and Italians, who were all Catholic and white. So why? What was it all about? Something called turf, territory, even worse, girls. Hey, get your guinea hands off my girl. Get your fat mick ass out of our neighborhood. Sal and Louise could understand rumbling with the Puerto Ricans or the Negroes, but not one another, for Christ's sakes.

Sal returned wearing a bandage to cover his stitches. He swung over to the right side of the room, well away from Louise. He ignored the class and no one looked at him or spoke to him. Louise took her old seat, tried to catch his eye. She turned toward me as if I had answers or could fix things. I felt inadequate and indecisive. Should I go back there, squeeze her shoulder, whisper encouraging words about how Sal would get over this? Should I go to Sal, apologize for the Irish race, tell him you can't judge a whole people by the actions of one lout in Prospect Park, remind him Louise was still lovely, still loved him?

How are you supposed to discuss the conclusion of *The Scarlet Letter*, the happy end for Hester and Pearl, with Louise sitting a few rows back, her heart broken, Sal staring straight ahead ready to murder the first Irishman to cross his path?

Ray Brown raised his hand. Good old Ray, always stirring the pot. Hey, Mr. McCourt, how come no Negroes in this book?

I must have looked blank. Everyone but Louise and Sal laughed. I don't know, Ray. I don't think they had Negroes in old New England.

Sal jumped from his seat. Yeah, they had Negroes, Ray, but the Irish killed them all. Snuck up behind them and busted their heads.

Oh, yeah? said Ray.

Yeah, said Sal. He picked up his bag, walked out, made his way to the guidance office. The counselor told me Sal asked for a transfer to Mr. Campbell's class, who at least wasn't Irish, and didn't have that stupid accent. You could never imagine Mr. Campbell hitting you from behind with a two-by-four, but, That McCourt. He's Irish and you can never trust those sneaky bastards.

I did not know what to do about Sal. It was three months to graduation and I should have tried to talk to him but I was unsure of what to say. In the school hallways I often saw teachers comforting kids. Arm around the shoulder. The warm hug. Don't worry, everything will be OK. Boy or girl saying thank you, tears, teacher squeezing shoulder one last time. That's what I wanted to do. Should I have told Sal I was not a two-by-four-wielding lout? Should I have insisted on telling him how unfair it was to make Louise suffer for the actions of someone who was probably drunk? Oh, you know how the Irish are, Sal. And he would have laughed and said, OK, Irish have that problem, and made up with Louise.

Or should I have talked to Louise, trotted out a few platitudes like, Oh, you'll get over it in time or There's more than one fish in the ocean or You won't be single long, Louise. Boys are going to be knocking on your door.

I knew if I tried to talk to either one I would have fumbled and stammered. The best thing was to do nothing, which is all I was capable of anyway. Someday I'd comfort someone in the hall with the strong arm around the shoulder, the soft word, the hug.

Teachers refuse to have Kevin Dunne in their classes. The kid is just a royal pain in the ass, troublemaker, out of control. If the principal insists on sticking him in their classes they'll throw in their papers, demand their pensions, walk out. That kid belongs in a zoo, monkey section, not a school.

So they send him to the new teacher, the one who cannot say no: me. Also, you can see with that red hair, freckles all over, that name, the kid is Irish, and surely an Irish teacher with a genuine brogue can handle the little bastard. Guidance counselor says he is counting on something, you know, atavistic, something that might strike a chord. A real Irish teacher could surely stir something ethnic in Kevin's genes. Right? Guidance counselor says Kevin is going on nineteen and should be graduating this year but after being kept back two years there is no chance he'll ever wear cap and gown. No chance at all. The school is playing a waiting game, hoping he'll drop out, join the army or something. They'll take anyone in the army these days, the lame, the halt, the blind, the Kevins of the world. They say he'll never make it to my classroom alone, so would I please pick him up at the guidance office.

He sits in an office corner, lost in a parka too big for him, his face deep in the hood. The guidance counselor says, Here he is, Kevin. Here's your new teacher. Pull your hood down so he can see you.

Kevin doesn't move.

Oh, come on, Kevin. Drop the hood.

Kevin shakes his head. The head moves but the hood stays in place.

OK, you go with Mr. McCourt, and try to cooperate.

Guidance counselor whispers, He might, you know, identify with you a little.

He identifies with nothing. He sits at his desk drumming with his fingers, hidden inside his hood. The principal, on his rounds, sticks his head in the door and tells him, Son, take off that hood. Kevin ignores him. The principal turns to me. We having a little discipline problem here?

That's Kevin Dunne.

Oh, and he backs out.

I feel trapped in some kind of mystery. When I mention him to other teachers they roll their eyes and tell me new teachers are often stuck with the impossible cases. The guidance counselor tells me don't worry about it. Kevin is trouble but he's dysfunctional and won't be around long. Just be patient.

Next day, just before noon, he asks for the pass. He says, How come you give me the pass just like that? How come? You wanna get rid of me, right?

You said you wanted the pass. Here it is. Go.

Why you telling me go?

It's just an expression.

That's not fair. I didn't do nothing wrong. I don't like people saying go like I was some kind of dog.

I wish I could take him aside for a talk, but I know I'm no good at that. It's easier to talk to the whole class than to one boy. It isn't so intimate.

He disrupts the class with irrelevant remarks: English has more dirty words than any other language; If you wear your right shoe on

He touches my shoulder with his multicolored hand, tells me I'm the greatest teacher in the world and if anyone ever gives me trouble he'll take care of them because he has ways of dealing with people who bother teachers.

He takes home dozens of glass jars.

He does not return in September. Guidance people at the Board of Education send him to a special school for incorrigibles. He runs away and lives awhile with the white mice in his father's garage. Then the army takes him and his mother comes to the school to tell me he's missing in Vietnam and she shows me a picture from his room. On the table the glass jars are arranged in a series of letters that say MCCORT OK.

See, his mother says. He liked you for helping him, but the Communists got him, so tell me, what was the use? Look at all the moms have kids blown to bits. Jesus, you don't even have a finger to bury and will you tell me what's goin' on in that country over there nobody ever heard of? Will you tell me that? One war finishes, another one starts and you're lucky if you just have daughters won't be sent over there.

From a canvas bag she pulls the large pickle jar filled with Kevin's dried paints. She says, Look at that. Every color in the rainbow in that jar. And you know what? He cut off all his hair and you can see where he mixed it in with those paints. That's a work of art, right? And I know he'd want you to have it.

I could have been honest with Kevin's mother, told her I did little for her son. He seemed like a lost soul, floating around looking for a place to drop anchor, but I didn't know enough, or I was too shy to show affection.

I kept the jar on my desk, where it glowed, incandescent, and when looked at clumps of Kevin's hair I felt sorry over the way I let him drift out of the school and off to Vietnam.

My students, especially the girls, said the jar was beautiful, yeah, a work of art, and it must have taken a lot of work. I told them about Kevin and some of the girls cried.

A maintenance man cleaning the classroom thought the jar was junk and took it away to the trash in the basement.

I talked to teachers in the cafeteria about Kevin. They shook their heads. They said, Too bad. Some of these kids slip through the cracks but what the hell is the teacher supposed to do? We have huge classes, no time, and we're not psychologists.

8

At thirty I married Alberta Small and started courses at Brooklyn College for the Master of Arts in English Literature, a degree that would help me rise in the world, earn respect, increase my teacher salary.

To fulfill the requirements for the degree I wrote a thesis on Oliver St. John Gogarty, doctor, poet, playwright, novelist, wit, athlete, champion drinker at Oxford, memoirist, senator, friend (briefly) of James Joyce, who turned him into the Buck Mulligan of *Ulysses* and made him famous worldwide and forever.

My thesis title was "Oliver St. John Gogarty: A Critical Study." There was nothing critical about the thesis. I chose Gogarty because of my admiration for him. If I read him and wrote about him, some of his charm, talent and learning would surely rub off on me. I might develop some of his dash and flair, his flamboyant air. He was a Dublin character, and I hoped I might become a debonair, hard-drinking, poetic Irishman like him. I'd be a New York character. I'd set the table on a roar and dominate the bars of Greenwich Village with song and story. At the Lion's Head Bar I drank whiskey after whiskey to give myself the courage to be colorful. Bartenders suggested I slow down. Friends said they didn't understand a word coming out of my mouth. They lifted me out of the bar and into a taxi, paid the driver and told him to drive nonstop till I reached my door in Brooklyn. I tried to be Gogarty-witty with Alberta but she told me for God's sakes be quiet, and all I got for my efforts to be Gogartian was a hangover so agonizing I fell to my knees and asked God to take me.

Professor Julian Kaye accepted my thesis despite "a repetitiousness of style and a solemnity which conflicts with the subject, Gogarty."

My first and favorite professor at Brooklyn College was Morton Irving Seiden, Yeats scholar. He wore a bow tie, he could lecture three hours on the Anglo-Saxon Chronicles or Chaucer or Matthew Arnold, the material perfectly organized in his head. He was there to lecture, pour knowledge into empty vessels, and if you had any questions you could see him in his office. He would not waste class time.

He had written his doctoral dissertation at Columbia University on Yeats and a book, *Paradox of Hate,* in which he argued that fear of Jewish sexuality was a major cause of anti-Semitism in Germany.

I took his year-long course on the History of English Literature, from Beowulf to Virginia Woolf, from warrior to worrier. You could see he wanted us to know and understand how English literature had developed and the language along with it. He insisted we should know the literature the way a doctor knows the body.

Everything he said was news to me, one of the benefits of being innocent and ill-educated. I knew bits and pieces of English literature but it was thrilling with Seiden, rolling along from writer to writer, from century to century, pausing for a closer look at Chaucer, John Skelton, Christopher Marlowe, John Dryden, the Enlightenment, the Romantics, the Victorians and on into the twentieth century with Seiden reading passages to illustrate the development of English from Anglo-Saxon through Middle English through Modern English.

After those lectures I felt sorry for people on subway trains who didn't know what I knew and I was eager to get back to my own classroom and tell my students how the English language had changed down the centuries. I tried to prove it by reading passages from Beowulf but they said, Nah, that ain't English. You think we're stoopid?

I tried to imitate Seiden's elegant style with my classes of plumbers, electricians, auto mechanics, but they looked at me as if I had lost my wits.

Professors could get up there and lecture to their hearts' content with never a fear of contradiction or a quibble. That was a life to be envied. They never had to tell anyone sit down, open your notebook, no, you may not have the pass. They never had to break up fights. Assignments were to be completed on time. No excuses, sir or madam, this is not high school. If you find it difficult to keep up with the work you ought to drop the course. Excuses are for children.

I envied Seiden, and college professors in general, their weekly four or five classes. I taught twenty-five. They had complete authority. I had to earn it. I said to my wife, Why should I have to struggle with moody teenagers when I could live the easy life of a college professor? Wouldn't it be a pleasure to stroll into the classroom in that casual way, nod to acknowledge their mere existence, deliver the lecture to the back wall or a tree outside the window, scratch a few illegible notes on the board, announce the next paper to be written, seven hundred words on money symbolism in Dickens's *Bleak House*? No complaints, no challenges, no excuses.

Alberta said, Oh, stop the whining. Get off your ass and get a Ph.D. and you can be a nice little university professor. You can bullshit the female sophomores.

When Alberta was taking the examination for the teacher's license she met R'lene Dahlberg and brought her home for dinner. She kicked off her shoes and sat on the couch drinking wine and telling us about her life with her husband, Edward. They lived in Majorca but she returned to the States from time to time to teach and make money to keep them going in Spain. She said Edward was quite famous and I said nothing because I could remember coming across his name only once in an essay by Edmund Wilson on proletarian writers. R'lene said he'd be returning from Spain in a few months and she'd invite us over for a drink.

From the minute I met him I didn't like Edward Dahlberg, or, maybe, I was nervous about meeting a man of letters, my introduction to the social world of American literature.

The evening Alberta and I came over, he sat in a deep armchair in a corner by the window facing a semicircle of admirers. They talked about books. They asked his opinion about various writers. He waved his hand and, except for himself, dismissed everyone in the twentieth century: Hemingway wrote "baby talk," Faulkner "sludge." Joyce's *Ulysses* was "a trudge through the ordure of Dublin." He demanded everyone go home and read authors I'd never heard of: Seutonius, Anaxagoras, Sir Thomas Brown, Eusebius, the Desert Fathers, Flavius Josephus, Randolph Bourne.

R'lene introduced me. This is Frank McCourt from Ireland. He teaches high school English.

I put out my hand but he let it hang. Oh, still a high school boy, are you?

I didn't know what to say. I wanted to punch the discourteous son of a bitch, but I did nothing. He laughed and said to R'lene, Does our friend teach English to deaf mutes? In the Dahlberg world teaching was for women only.

I backed away to my chair, confused.

Dahlberg had a massive head with strands of gray hair pasted across the baldness. One eye was dead in its socket and the other moved rapidly, doing the work of two. He had a strong nose and a luscious mustache and when he smiled there was a flash of false white teeth, which clacked.

He wasn't finished. He turned the one eye on me. Does our high school boy read? And what does he read?

I searched my head for something I'd read recently, something distinguished that might please him.

I'm reading the autobiography of Sean O'Casey.

He let me suffer a moment, passed his hand over his face, grunted, Sean O'Casey. Pray, quote me a line.

My heart jumped and pounded. The semicircle of admirers

waited. Dahlberg lifted his head as if to say Yes? My mouth was dry. I could think of nothing from O'Casey that would match the grand passages Dahlberg quoted from the ancient masters. I mumbled, Well, I admire O'Casey for the natural way he writes about his life growing up in Dublin.

He let me suffer again while he smiled at his admirers. He nodded toward me. The natural way he writes, says our Irish friend. If you admire so-called natural writing you can always scrutinize the walls of a public lavatory.

The admirers laughed. My face was hot and I blurted, O'Casey fought his way out of the slums of Dublin. He was half blind. He's a . . . a . . . champion of the worker. . . . He's as good as you anytime. The whole world knows Sean O'Casey. Who ever heard of you?

He shook his head for the benefit of his admirers and they shook their heads in agreement. He called to R'lene, Tell your high school boy to leave my presence. He's not welcome here though his charming wife is welcome to stay.

I followed R'lene to the bedroom to retrieve my coat. I told her I was sorry for causing trouble and despised myself for my apology, but she kept her head down and said nothing. In the living room Dahlberg was pawing Alberta's shoulder, telling her he had no doubt she was a fine teacher and hoped she would visit again.

In silence we rode the subway to Brooklyn. I was confused and wondered why Dahlberg had to behave like that. Did he have to humiliate a stranger? And why did I put up with it?

Because I didn't have the self-confidence of an eggshell. He was sixty, I was thirty. I was like someone arrived from a wild place. I'd never be at ease in literary circles. I was out of my depth and too ignorant to belong to that squad of admirers who could lob literary names at Dahlberg.

I felt paralyzed and ashamed of myself and swore I'd never see that man again. I'd give up this dead-end teaching career that brought no respect, get a part-time job, spend my life reading in libraries, go to parties like this, quote and recite, hold my own with the likes of Dahlberg and his adoring circle. R'lene invited us back but now Dahlberg was polite and I was wary and smart enough to defer to him, to fall into the role of acolyte. He asked me always what I was reading and I kept the peace by trotting out the Greeks, Romans, the Church Fathers, Miguel de Cervantes, Burton's *Anatomy of Melancholy*, Emerson, Thoreau and, of course, Edward Dahlberg, as if I were doing nothing now but sitting on my arse all day in a deep armchair reading, reading and waiting for Alberta to serve my dinner and massage my poor neck. If the conversation turned dark and dangerous I'd quote from his books and watch his face brighten and soften. It surprised me that a man who dominated gatherings and made enemies everywhere could fall for flattery so easily. It surprised me, also, that I was clever enough to work out a strategy that would keep him from exploding in his chair. I was learning to bite my tongue and take his abuse because I thought I might profit from his learning and wisdom.

I envied him for living the life of a writer, a dream I was too timid to chance. I admired him or anyone who went his own way and stuck to his guns. Even with all my various experiences in America I still felt like someone just off the boat. When he moaned about the hard life of a writer, the daily suffering of man at desk, I wanted to say, Oh, anguish my arse, Dahlberg. All you do is sit there tapping at your typewriter a few hours in the morning and reading the rest of the day while R'lene hovers, attending to your every need. You never did a hard day's work in your life. One day teaching a hundred and seventy teenagers would send you running back to your soft literary life.

I saw him occasionally till he died in California at seventy-seven. He would invite me to dinner with instructions to bring my brach. The dictionary told me my brach was my bitch. I realized he was more interested in my brach than in me and when he suggested that we all spend a summer together driving across country I knew what he was up to, a fling along the way with Alberta. The clever man would contrive to send me on a futile errand while he uncoiled and slithered from his tree.

He called one Saturday morning to invite us to dinner and when I said we were busy that night he said, And what, my fine Irish friend, am I to do with the food I have purchased? I said, Eat it. That's all you ever do anymore anyhow.

It wasn't much of a rejoinder but it was the last word. I never heard from him again.

Every June during my eight years at McKee, the English department met in a classroom to read, evaluate, grade the New York State English Regents examination. Barely half the students at McKee passed the examination. The other half had to be helped. We tried to inflate the failure grades from high fifties to passing, the mandated sixty-five.

We could do nothing about multiple-choice questions, the answers were right or wrong, but we helped with essays on literature and general topics. Give the kid credit for being there. Sure, what the hell. He could be someplace else getting into trouble, bothering people. Three points for showing up, for selfless citizenship. Is his writing legible? Sure. Another two or three points.

Did the kid ever bother teachers in class? Well, maybe, on one occasion. Yeah, but he was probably provoked. Besides, his father is dead, a dock worker who defied the mob and wound up in the Gowanus Canal for his troubles. Give the kid another two points for having a father dead in the Gowanus. We're getting that grade up there, aren't we?

Does the student use paragraphs? Oh, yeah. Look how he indents. The kid is a master of indentation. There are definitely three paragraphs here.

Does he have topic sentences in his paragraphs? Well, you know, you could argue that the first sentence is a topic sentence. OK, give him another three points for his topic sentences. So, where are we now? Sixty-three?

Is he a nice kid? Oh, sure. Helpful in class? Yes, he cleaned erasers for his social studies teacher. Polite in the hallways? Always said good morning. Look at this, he gave his essay a title, "My Country; Right or Wrong." Now isn't that something? Pretty sophisticated, choosing an essay title. Couldn't we raise him three for choice of patriotic topic and one point for using a semicolon even if the situation calls for a colon? Is that really a semicolon or is the paper a flyport? There are kids in this school who don't even know colons exist, and don't care, and if you were to stand up there and tell them the difference between the colon and its cousin, the semicolon, they'd just ask for the pass.

Why not raise him another three points? He's a nice kid and his brother, Stan, is in Vietnam. His father got polio when he was a kid. Spends his life in a wheelchair. Oh, give the boy another point for having a father in a wheelchair and a brother in Vietnam.

So, he's up to sixty-eight. Sixty-eight is less likely to arouse suspicions in Albany, where they're supposed to be checking these tests. Unlikely they'll look at every exam with the thousands flowing in from around the state. Besides, if there are questions, we teachers will stand shoulder to shoulder to defend our marking system.

Let's go to lunch.

Mr. Bibberstein, the guidance counselor, said if I had any trouble with any kid to let him know and he'd take care of it. He said new teachers in this system were treated like dirt, or worse. You sink or swim.

I never told him about any difficulties with students. The word gets out. Yeah, man, that new teacher, McCourt, he'll send your ass to the guidance counselor and next thing he's calling your dad and you know what that means. Mr. Bibberstein joked I must be a great teacher, getting along so well with the kids I never sent one to his office. He said it must be my Irish charm. You're not much to look at but the girls love your accent. They told me, so don't waste it.

When we went on strike with the new union, the United Federation of Teachers, Mr. Bibberstein, Mr. Tolfsen and Miss Gilfillan, the art teacher, crossed the picket line. We called to them, Don't go in. Don't go in, but they went in, Miss Gilfillan weeping. The teachers who crossed the picket line were older than the ones outside. They may have been members of the old Teachers' Union, which was crushed during the McCarthy witch-hunt era. They did not want to be hounded again even though we were striking mostly for recognition as a union.

I felt sympathy for the older teachers and when the strike was over wanted to say I was sorry for the way we shouted at them. On our picket line, at least, no one called out, Scab, the way they did in other schools. Still, there was tension and division at McKee High School, and I didn't know if I could be friends anymore with the people who crossed the line. Before I became a teacher I hit the picket lines with the Hotel Workers' Union, the Teamsters and the International Longshoremens' Association, and was fired from a bank merely for talking to a union organizer. There were warnings and no one would dare to ignore them. Cross this line, pal, and we know where you live. We know where your kids go to school.

We could never say things like that from a teachers' picket line. We were professionals: teachers, college graduates. When the strike ended we gave the scabs the cold shoulder in the teachers' cafeteria. They ate together on the other side of the room. In a while they stopped coming to the cafeteria altogether and we had the place to ourselves, loyal members of the United Federation of Teachers.

Mr. Bibberstein barely nodded to me in the hallways and there were no more offers of help with difficult kids. I was surprised when he stopped me one day and barked, What's this about Barbara Sadlar?

What do you mean?

She came to my office and said you encouraged her to go to college.

That's right.

What do you mean, that's right?

I mean I suggested she go to college.

I'd like to remind you this is a vocational and technical high school, not a feeder school for colleges. These kids go into the trades, son. They're not ready for college.

I told him Barbara Sadlar was one of the brightest students in my five classes. She wrote well, read books, participated in class discussions, and if I, myself, licensed teacher, could go to college without a scrap of high school education why couldn't Barbara think of it? No one said she had to be a beautician, secretary or anything else.

Because, young man, you're giving kids ideas they shouldn't have. We're trying to be realistic here and you're coming in with your crazy half-assed ideas. I'm gonna have to talk to her and set her straight. I'd appreciate it if you backed off. Teach English and leave guidance to me. He turned to walk away but turned back again. It wouldn't have anything to do with the fact that Barbara is a good-looking blonde, would it?

I wanted to say something mean. Scab jumped into my head but I kept silent. He walked away from me and that was the last time we ever spoke. Was it the strike, or was it really Barbara?

He left a greeting card in my mailbox with a note: "A man's reach should exceed his grasp, but you better make sure they have something to grasp. Don't create impossible dreams. Regards, Fergus Bibberstein."

PART II

Donkey on a Thistle

9

In 1966, after eight years at McKee, it was time to move on. I still struggled to hold the attention of five classes every day though I was learning what was obvious: You have to make your own way in the classroom. You have to find yourself. You have to develop your own style, your own techniques. You have to tell the truth or you'll be found out. Oh, teacher man, that's not what you said last week. It isn't a matter of virtue or high morality.

So, good-bye, McKee Vocational and Technical High School. With my new master's degree I'm off to New York Community College in Brooklyn, where a friend, Professor Herbert Miller, helped me find a position as adjunct lecturer, the lowest level of teacher in the university system. I'll have five or six classes every week, not every day. I'll be in heaven with all that free time. I'll earn half the salary of the high school teacher, but the students will be mature, they'll listen and show respect. They won't throw things. They won't object and complain over work in class and homework assignments. Also, they'll call me professor and that will make me feel important. I am to teach two courses: Introduction to Literature and Basic Composition.

My students were adult, mostly under thirty, working around the city in stores, factories, offices. There was a class of thirty-three firemen working for college credit to rise in the department, all white, mostly Irish.

Almost everyone else was black or Hispanic. I could have been one of them, working by day, studying by night. Since there were no discipline problems I had to adjust and develop a kind of teaching where I didn't have to tell anyone sit down, please, and be quiet. If they were late they said sorry and took their seats. I hardly knew what to do when those first classes filed in, sat and waited for my lecture. No one asked for the lavatory pass. No one raised a hand to accuse anyone of stealing a sandwich or a book or a seat. No one tried to get me off the subject by asking me about Ireland in general or my miserable childhood in particular.

You have to get up there, man, and teach.

A footnote, ladies and gentlemen, is what you put at the bottom of the page to show the source of your information.

A hand.

Yes, Mr. Fernandez?

How come?

How come what?

I mean if I'm writing about the New York Giants why can't I just say I read it in the *Daily News,* why?

Because, Mr. Fernandez, this is a research paper and that means you have to show exactly, exactly, Mr. Fernandez, where you got your information.

I dunno, professor, I mean that seems like a lotta trouble. I'm just writing this paper about the Giants and why they're having a losing season. I mean I'm not training to be a lawyer or nothin'.

Mr. Tomas Fernandez was twenty-nine. He worked as a mechanic for New York City. He hoped an associate degree would help him get a promotion. He had a wife and three children and sometimes, in class, he fell asleep. When he snored, the other students would look at me to see what I was going to do about it. I touched his shoulder and suggested he take a break outside. He said, OK, left the room and did not return that night. He missed class the following week and when he returned said, no, he wasn't sick. He was over in New Jersey at the football game, the Giants, you know. He had to see the Giants when they were at home. Couldn't miss his Giants. He said it was too bad this class was on Monday, same night as the game when the Giants were home.

Too bad, Mr. Fernandez?

Yeah. Like, you know, I can't be in two places at one time.

But, Mr. Fernandez, this is a college. This course is required.

Yeah, says Mr. Fernandez. I understand your problem, professor.

My problem? My problem, Mr. Fernandez?

Well, like, you have to do something about me and the Giants. Right?

It's not that, Mr. Fernandez. It's just that if you don't attend class you are going to fail.

He stares at me as if trying to understand why I'm talking in this strange way. He tells me and the class how he's followed the Giants all his life and he's not going to desert them now that they're having a losing season. No one would respect him. His seven-year-old son would despise him. Even his wife, who never cared about the Giants, would lose respect for him.

Why, Mr. Fernandez?

That's easy to see, professor. All these Sundays and Mondays I spent on the Giants she waits home for me, takes care of the kids and everything, even forgives me the time of her mother's funeral when I couldn't go because the Giants were in the playoffs, man. So now if I was to give up the Giants she'd say, What was it all for, me waiting and waiting? She'd say it was all wasted. That's how she'd lose respect because there's one thing about my wife, she sticks to her guns the way I stick to the Giants, know what I mean?

Rowena from Barbados says she thinks this discussion is a waste of class time and why doesn't he grow up. Why didn't he take this class on another night besides Monday?

Because the other classes were full and I heard Mr. McCourt was a nice guy that wouldn't mind if I went to a football game after working all day. You know?

Rowena from Barbados says she doesn't know. Shit or get off the pot, mon, excuse the language. We come here after a hard day's work, too, and we don't snore in class and run off to football games. We should have a vote.

Heads nod around the room, yes to the vote. Thirty-three say Mr. Fernandez should attend class, no Giants. Mr. Fernandez votes for himself. Giants all the way.

Even though the Giants are on television that evening he's gracious enough to stay till the end of the class. He shakes my hand and assures me he has no hard feelings, that I'm really a nice guy, but we all have our blind spots.

Freddie Bell was an elegant young black man. He worked in the men's clothing department at the Abraham and Strauss Department Store. He helped me select a jacket there and that led to a different level of relationship. Yes, I'm in your class but I helped you pick out that jacket. He liked to write in a florid style using big words and rare words lifted from dictionary and thesaurus and when I wrote on his paper, "Simplify, simplify (Thoreau)," he wanted to know who was this Thoreau and why would anyone want to write like a baby?

Because, Freddie, your reader might appreciate clarity. Clarity, Freddie, clarity.

He didn't agree. His high school English teacher told him the English language was a glorious organ. Why not take advantage of this tremendous instrument? Pull out all the stops, so to speak.

Because, Freddie, what you're doing is false, forced and artificial.

That was the wrong thing to say, especially with thirty of his fellow students watching and listening. His face froze and I knew I had lost him. That would mean a hostile presence in the class the remainder of the term, a discomfiting prospect for me, still making my way in this adult-student world.

He struck back with language. His writing became more elaborate and tortured. His grades slipped from As to B minuses. At the end he asked for an explanation of the grade. He said he'd shown his essays to his old English teacher and he, the old English teacher, simply could not understand how Freddie could get less than an A plus. Look at the language. Look at the vocabulary. Look at the levels of meaning. Look at the sentence structure: varied, sophisticated, complex.

We faced each other in the hallway. He would not give up. He said he worked hard in my class looking up new words so that I wouldn't be bored with the same old words. His old English teacher said there was nothing worse than reading miles of student writing and never coming across an original thought or some fresh vocabulary. Old English teacher said Mr. McCourt should appreciate Freddie's efforts and reward him accordingly. Freddie should get credit simply for venturing into new territory, for pushing the envelope. Also, said Freddie, I work nights to make a living and pay my way through college. You know what that's like, Mr. McCourt.

I don't see what that has to do with your writing.

Also, it's not easy when you're black in this society.

Oh, Christ, Freddie. It's not easy being anything in this society. All right. You want an A? You'll get it. I don't want to be accused of bigotry.

No, I don't want it just because you're pissed off or because I'm black. I want it because I deserve it.

I turned to walk away. He called after me, Hey, Mr. McCourt, thanks. I like your class. It's weird, that class, but I figured I might even become a teacher like you.

I am teaching this course that requires a research paper. The student must demonstrate the ability to select a topic, engage in basic research, make notes on index cards so that the instructor can determine the source of the material, provide scholarly footnotes and a bibliography of primary and secondary sources.

I take my students to the library so that the pleasant enthusiastic librarian can show them how to find information, how to use the basic tools of research. They listen to her and look at one another and whisper in Spanish and French, but when she asks if they have any questions they stare, embarrassing the librarian, who so wants to be helpful.

I try to explain the simple idea of research.

First, you choose a topic.

What's that?

Think of something you're interested in, maybe a problem bothering you and people in general. You could write about capitalism, religion, abortion, children, politics, education. Some of you come from Haiti or Cuba. Two rich subjects. You could write about voodoo or the Bay of Pigs. You could look at some aspect of your country, human rights, for instance, do a little research, look at the pros and cons, think about it, come to a conclusion.

Excuse me, professor, what's pros and cons?

Pro is for, con is against.

Oh.

The Oh means they have no notion of what I am talking about. I have to backtrack, come at it from another angle. I ask them where they stand on capital punishment. The looks tell me they don't know where they stand because they don't know what I'm talking about.

Capital punishment is the execution of people by hanging, electrocution, gassing, shooting or garroting.

What's that?

A kind of strangling they have mostly in Spain.

They ask me to write it on the board. They scribble it in their notebooks and I make a mental note that if ever a class dragged I'd turn immediately to the various methods of execution.

Vivian from Haiti raises her hand. That's wrong, that executing, but I think it's OK for the other thing, the one about the babies, Oh, yeah, the abortion. They should be shot.

All right, Vivian. Why don't you write that in your research paper?

Me? Write down what I'm saying? Who cares what I'm saying? I'm nobody, professor. Nobody.

Their faces are blank. They don't understand. How could they? What's this about the other side of a story? Nobody ever told them they had a right to an opinion.

They're not shy about speaking up in class, but putting words on paper is a dangerous step, especially when you grew up with Spanish or French. Besides, they don't have time for all this. They've got kids to raise and jobs and they have to send money to their families back in Haiti and Cuba. It's easy for professors to give all these assignments but, man, there's another world out there and God only put twenty-four hours in the day.

There are ten minutes left in the hour and I tell the class they should feel free now to explore the library. No one moves. They don't even whisper anymore. They sit in their winter overcoats. They clutch book bags and wait till that exact second when the hour ends.

In the hallway I tell my friend, veteran professor Herbert Miller, of my problems with this class. He says, They work days and nights. They come to class. They sit and listen. They do their best. These people in the admissions office let them in, then expect the teacher to perform a miracle or be the hatchet man. I'm not going to be the enforcer for the front office. Research? How can these people do research papers when they still struggle to read the damn newspaper?

The class would agree with Miller. They'd nod and say, Yeah, yeah. They think they're nobody.

That was something I should have known all along: the people in my classes, adults from eighteen to sixty-two, thought their opinions did not matter. Whatever ideas they had came from the avalanche of media in our world. No one had ever told them they had a right to think for themselves.

I told them, You have a right to think for yourselves.

Silence in the classroom. I said, You don't have to swallow everything I tell you. Or what anyone tells you. You can ask questions. If I don't have the answer we can look it up in the library or discuss it here.

They look at one another. Yeah. The man is talking funny. Tells us we don't have to believe him. Hey, we came here to learn English so's we can pass. We gotta graduate.

I wanted to be the Great Liberating Teacher, to raise them from their knees after days of drudgery in offices and factories, to help them cast off their shackles, to lead them to the mountaintop, to breathe the air of freedom. Once their minds were cleared of cant they'd see me as savior.

For the people in this class life was hard enough without having an English teacher preaching about thinking and bothering them with questions.

Man, we just wanna get through this place.

The research papers turned out to be an ecstasy of plagiarism, articles on Papa Doc Duvalier and Fidel Castro lifted from encyclopedias. Vivian's paper on Touissant-L'Ouverture rambled on for seventeen pages in English and Haitian French and I gave it a B plus for the labor of copying and typing. I tried to redeem myself with a comment on the title page to the effect that Touissant thought for himself and suffered for it and I hoped Vivian might follow his example, though not to the suffering part.

When I returned the papers I tried to say positive things about them, to encourage the authors to dig into their subjects even more.

I was talking to myself. It was the last class of the year and they were looking at their watches, ignoring me. I walked to the subway, dejected and angry with myself for not having made some kind of connection with them. Four women from the class waited on the subway platform. They smiled and asked if I lived in Manhattan.

No. I go two stops in Brooklyn.

I didn't know what to say after that. No chitchat. No banter from the professor.

Vivian said, Thanks for the grade, Mr. McCourt. That's the highest I ever got in English and, you know, you're a pretty good teacher.

The others nodded and smiled, and I knew they were just being nice. When the train came in they said, See you, and hurried along the platform.

My college teaching career ended in a year. The department chairman said even though there was brisk competition for my job and applications from people with Ph.D.s, he'd stretch the rules, but if I wanted to stay I'd need to show evidence I was pursuing a degree on the doctoral level. I told him I wasn't pursuing anything.

Sorry, said the chairman.

Oh, it's all right, I said, and went searching for another high school teaching job.

Alberta said I was going nowhere in life and I congratulated her on her astuteness. She said, Cut out the sarcasm. We've been married for six years and all you do is meander from one school to another. If you don't settle down to something very soon you'll be forty and wondering where your life went. She pointed to people all around us, happily married, productive, settled, content, having children, developing mature relationships, looking to the future, going on nice vacations, joining clubs, taking up golf, growing old together, visiting relatives, dreaming of grandchildren, supporting their churches, thinking of retirement.

I agreed with her but I couldn't admit it. I gave her a sermon on life and America. I told her life was an adventure, and maybe I was living in the wrong century. I should have lived back in the days of the Conestoga wagon, when the wagon master in Western movies—John Wayne, Randolph Scott, Joel McCrea—cracked his whip and called, Move out, and the studio orchestra went into raptures, fifty violins swelling with prairie patriotism, pure wagon-train music, violins and banjos welcoming the harmonica wail, men in wagon-driver seats going, Hup, hup, hup, or men walking, leading horses and oxen, with wives up there holding reins, some wives you can see are pregnant and you know, because you've been here before, they'll have their babies in the middle of an attack by ferocious Apache, Sioux, Cheyenne. They'll get the wagons in a circle and fight off those howling braves threatening nice white mothers in labor but still, those Indians are magnificent in their feathers, on their horses, and you know the Indians will be driven off because every white man, woman, child, even the women in labor, will blaze away with rifle and revolver, will swing rolling pins and frying pans, defeat the pesky redskin so that the wagon train can move on again, so that white people will conquer this wild continent, so that the expansion of America will not be stopped by locust, drought, Rocky Mountains or whooping Apache.

I said that was the part of American history I loved. She said, Oh, Conestoga wagon, my ass, go get a job, and I snapped right back with a line from Dylan Thomas, A job is death without dignity. She said, You'll have your dignity, but you won't have me. You could see there was little hope for the future of that marriage.

The head of the Academic Department at Fashion Industries High School did not like me but there was a teacher shortage, no one wanted to teach in vocational high schools, and there I was, available and with McKee experience. He sat behind his desk, ignored my hand, told me he ran a dynamic department, rolled his shoulders like a boxer to suggest great energy and determination. He said the kids in Fashion High School were not academic hotshots but decent kids learning useful trades like tailoring and cutting, shoemaking, uphol-stery and, damn it, there was nothing wrong with that, eh? They'd be valuable members of society and I should never make the mistake of looking down my nose at kids in vocational high schools.

I told him I had just spent eight years in a vocational high school, wouldn't dream of looking down my nose at anyone.

Oh, yeah. Which school?

McKee on Staten Island.

He sniffed. Well, that doesn't have much of a reputation, does it?

I needed that job and didn't want to offend him. I told him that if I knew anything about teaching I learned it at McKee. He said, We'll see. I wanted to tell him shove his job up his arse, but that would be the end of my teaching career.

It was clear my future was not in this school. I wondered if I had a future anywhere in the school system. He said four teachers in his department were taking courses in supervision and administration and I shouldn't be surprised to see them one day in high positions in schools around the city.

We don't sit on our asses here, he said. We move on and up. And what are your long-range plans?

I don't know. I suppose I just came here to be a teacher, I said.

He shook his head, couldn't understand my lack of ambition. I wasn't dynamic enough. Because of him those four teachers taking courses were moving on and up and out. That's what he said. Why should they spend their lives in the classroom with kids when they could travel the corridors of power?

I felt brave for a moment and asked him, If everyone moved on and up and out who would teach the children?

He ignored me, allowed himself a little smile with a mouth that had no lips.

I lasted one term, September to January, before he forced me out. It may have been the matter of the shoelace and the rolled-up magazine or it may have been my lack of dynamism and ambition. Still, he praised me at a department meeting for my lesson on the parts of a sentence where I used a ballpoint pen as a visual aid.

This is the plastic tube that holds the ink. If you removed this tube from the pen what would happen?

My students look at me as if they can't believe I'm asking such a dumb-ass question. Man, you wouldn't be able to write.

OK. Now what is this I'm holding in my hand?

Again the patient look. That's a spring, man.

And what would happen if we removed the spring?

When you try to push the tube out it won't write because there's no spring to push it and keep its little nose out there where all the writing is done and then you get in a lotta trouble because you can't write your homework and the teacher's gonna think you're crazy if you come in telling him about missing springs or tubes.

Now look at what I'm writing on the board. "The spring makes the pen work." What is the subject of this sentence? In other words, what are we talking about in this sentence?

The pen.

No, no, no. There's an action word here. It's called a verb. What is it?

Oh, yeah. The spring.

No, no, no. The spring is a thing.

Yeah, yeah. The spring is a thing. Hey, man. That's poetry.

So, what does the spring do?

Makes the pen work.

Good. The spring performs the action. We're talking about the spring, right?

They look doubtful.

Suppose we say, The pen makes the spring work. Would that be right?

No. The spring makes the pen work. Anyone can see that.

So, what is the action word?

Makes.

Right. And what word uses the action word?

Spring.

So you can see how a ballpoint pen is like a sentence. It needs something to make it work. It needs action, a verb. Can you see that?

They said they could. The chairman, making notes in the back of the room, looked puzzled. At our postobservation conference he said he could understand the connection I was making between structure of pen and structure of sentence. He wasn't sure if I had succeeded in getting that across to the kids but still, it was imaginative and innovative. He was sure, ha ha, if some of his senior English teachers tried it they'd improve on it, but it was a pretty nifty idea.

When I pulled on the shoelace one morning and it broke I said, Shit.

Alberta mumbled into the pillow, What's the matter?

I broke the shoelace.

You're always breaking shoelaces.

No, I'm not always breaking shoelaces. I haven't broken a shoelace in years.

If you didn't pull on them they wouldn't break.

What the hell are you talking about? That shoelace was two years old, out in all kinds of weather, and why wouldn't it break? I pulled on it the way you try to force bureau drawers when they stick.

No, I don't force bureau drawers.

Yes, you do. You get into your Puritan Yankee rage as if the drawers were your enemy.

At least I don't break them.

No, you just yank on them so hard they're stuck forever and you have to pay a master carpenter a fortune to straighten them.

If we didn't have such cheap furniture I wouldn't have to struggle with drawers. Jesus, I should have listened to my friends who warned me against marrying Irishmen.

I could never win a domestic squabble. She would never stick to the subject, which in this case was shoelaces and bureau drawers. No, she had to drag in the Irish thing, the closing argument, the one you made before you sentenced the defendant to be hanged.

I headed for school in a rage, in no mood for teaching or cajoling, Aw, come on, Stan, sit down, Joanna, put your makeup away, please. Are you listening? Open your copy of this magazine, *Practical English,* turn to page nine, the vocabulary quiz, fill in the blank spaces and then we'll go over your answers.

They said, Yeah, yeah, yeah. Keep the teacher happy. They lifted magazine pages as if each weighed a ton. They took their time. Turning to page nine was a big deal and before they made that move they had things to discuss with their friends in front, behind, beside them. They might have to talk about what they watched on TV last night, Gawd, wasn't that scary, and did you know Miriam, yeah, the one in our drawing class, is pregnant, did you know that? Naw, I din't know that. Wow! Who's the fawder? You won't believe it. Swear you won't tell. It's that new social studies teacher. Really? I thought he was a fag. Nah, that's a big act.

Would you open the magazine to page nine?

Fifteen minutes into the class and they're still turning pages of lead. Hector, open the magazine to page nine.

He had straight black hair and a thin intensely white face. He stared straight ahead as if he hadn't heard me.

Hector. Open the magazine.

He shook his head.

I walked toward him holding a rolled-up copy of *Practical English*. Hector, the magazine. Open it.

He shook his head again. I slapped him across the face with the magazine. There was a red mark on that white cheek. He jumped up. Drop dead, he said, tears in his voice. He walked toward the door and I called after him, Sit down, Hector, but he was gone. I wanted to run after him and tell him I was sorry, but I let him go. When he cooled down a bit and I collected my wits I might be able to talk to him.

I dropped the magazine on my desk and sat there for the rest of the period staring ahead like Hector. The class made no pretense of turning to page nine. They looked at me or one another or out the window and they were quiet.

Should I talk to them, tell them how sorry I was? No, no. Teachers don't stand there confessing to mistakes. Teachers don't admit their ignorance. We waited for the bell and when they filed out, Sofia, the girl who sat next to Hector, said, You shouldna done that. You're a nice man but you shouldna, and Hector is nice, too. Hector. He got a lotta trouble and now you made it worse.

Now the class would despise me, especially the Cubans, Hector's group. There were thirteen Cubans, the largest ethnic group in the class. They considered themselves superior to any other Spanish-speaking group and every Friday wore white shirts, blue ties and black pants to make sure they weren't confused with any other group, especially the Puerto Ricans.

It was the middle of September, and if I didn't find a way of getting the Cubans back, they'd make my life a misery till the end of the term in January.

At lunch a guidance counselor brought his tray to my table. Hi. What happened with you and Hector?

I told him.

He nodded. Too bad. I wanted him in your class because of the ethnic thing.

What ethnic thing? He's Cuban, I'm Irish.

He's only half Cuban. His mother's name is Considine, but he's ashamed of it.

So why would you put him in my class?

I know it sounds like a song, but his mother was a high-class whore in Havana. He had questions about the Irish and I thought they might come up in your class. Besides, he has gender problems.

He looks like a boy to me.

Yeah, but . . . you know. There's the homosexual thing. He thinks now you hate homosexuals and he says, Fine, he's going to hate all the Irish and all his Cuban friends will hate all the Irish. No, that's not right. He has no Cuban friends. They call him *maricon* and stay away from him. His family is ashamed of him.

Oh, hell. He defied me. Wouldn't open the magazine. I don't want to be caught in a sex and ethnic war.

Melvin asked me to meet with him and Hector in the guidance office.

Hector, Mr. McCourt wants to come to an understanding with you.

I don't care what Mr. McCourt wants. I don't want to sit in class with no Irishman. They drink. Hit people for no reason.

Hector, you didn't open your magazine when I told you.

He stared at me with cold black eyes. So, you don't open your magazine and teacher slaps your face? Well, you ain't no teacher. My mother was a teacher.

Your mother was . . . I almost said it, but he was gone, second time he walked out on me. Melvin shook his head and shrugged and I knew my days at Fashion Industries High School were over. Melvin said Hector could sue me for assault and if he did my "ass was in a sling." He tried to be funny. If you wanna slap kids around go get a job in a Catholic school. Those big priests and brothers, even the nuns, are still beating up the kids. Maybe you'd be happier with them.

Of course the chairman heard about my problem with Hector. He said nothing till term's end, when he placed a letter in my mailbox saying there would not be a position for me in the coming term. He wished me well and would be pleased to give me a satisfactory rating. When I met him in the hall he said that with regard to the satisfactory rating he might have been bending the truth a little, ha ha. Still, if I kept at it I might succeed as a teacher because, in his observations, he noticed that occasionally I had hit pedagogical paydirt. He smiled and you could see he liked his little phrase. He said something about the lesson where I illustrated the parts of a sentence by breaking down a ballpoint pen. Yeah, I had hit pedagogical paydirt.

10

Alberta said they were looking for a teacher at her high school, Seward Park on the Lower East Side. The main building was overcrowded and I was assigned to an annex, an abandoned elementary school by the East River. My teenagers complained about the discomfort and indignity of squeezing their growing bodies into baby furniture.

This was a melting-pot school: Jewish, Chinese, Puerto Rican, Greek, Dominican, Russian, Italian, and I had no preparation or training for teaching English as a Second Language.

Kids want to be cool. Never mind what parents say, or adults in general. Kids want to hang out and talk street language. They want to swear eloquently. You can curse and swear and you are a man, man.

And if you're hanging out and this foxy white chick comes along the sidewalk you can look cool as shit, man, but if you don't got the words or you got some kinda crazy foreign accent she ain't gonna give you even a look and you are home, man, playing with yourself and pissed off because English is a bitch of a language that makes no sense and you'll never learn it. You're in America and you gotta get with it, man.

So, teacher man, forget your highfalutin' English literature and get down here to brass tacks. Back to c-a-t cat, man. Speak the speech and speak it slowly, slowly.

The bell rings and I'm hearing the Tower of Babel.

Excuse me.

They ignore me or they don't understand my mild request. Again. Excuse me.

A big red-haired Dominican boy catches my eye. Teacher, you wan' I should help?

He climbs up on his desk and everyone cheers because climbing on desks is strictly forbidden by the authorities and here is Red Oscar defying the authorities right there in the presence of a teacher.

Yo, says Oscar. *Mira.*

There is a chorus of *mira*s, *Mira, mira, mira, mira, mira,* till Oscar raises his hand and yells, Yo. Shaddup. Lissena teacher.

Thanks, Oscar, but would you please climb down?

A hand. So, mister. Wass you name?

I write on the board, MR. McCOURT, and pronounce it.

Hey, mister, you Jewish?

No.

Alla teachers in this school Jewish. How come you not Jewish?

I don't know.

They look surprised, even astonished, and the look travels the room. The look says, You hear that, Miguel? Teacher up there, he don't know.

It's a hot moment. Teacher confesses ignorance and the class is shocked into silence. Off with the mask, teacher man, and what a relief. No more Mister Know-It-All.

A few years earlier I could have been one of them, part of the huddled masses. This is my immigrant comfort level. I know English, but I'm not so far removed from their confusions. Rock bottom in the social hierarchy. I could drop the teacher mask, walk down the aisle, sit with them and ask them about their families, what it was like in the old country, tell them about myself, my meandering days, how I hid for years behind the mask, still hiding as a matter of fact, how I wish we could lock that door and shut out the world till they spoke enough English to make them feel so cool they can tell that foxy white chick they're ready for a little action.

Wouldn't that be pretty?

I look at this collection of kids from all continents, faces of all colors and shapes, God's plenty, this garden: Asians with hair blacker and shinier than anything ever seen in Europe; the great brown eyes of Hispanic boys and girls; shyness of some, rowdiness of others, posturing of boys, coyness of girls.

Nancy Chu asks if she can talk to me after the last class of the day. She sits at her desk and waits for the room to empty. She reminds me she's in my second-period sophomore class.

I'm here three years from China.

Your English is very good, Nancy.

Thank you. I learned English from Fred Astaire.

Fred Astaire?

I know all the songs from all his movies. My favorite is *Top Hat*. I sing his songs all the time. My parents think I'm crazy. My friends, too. All they know is rock and you can't learn English from rock. I have trouble with my parents all the time over Fred Astaire.

Well, it's unusual, Nancy.

Also, I watch you teach.

Oh.

And I wonder why you're so uptight. You know English, so you should be cool. Kids all say if they knew English they'd be so cool. Sometimes you're not uptight and the kids like that. They like it when you tell stories and sing. When I'm uptight I sing "Dancing in the Dark." You should learn that, Mr. McCourt, and sing it to the class. You don't have such a bad voice.

Nancy, I'm here to teach English. I'm not a song-and-dance man.

Could you tell me how to be an English teacher who won't be uptight?

But what will your parents say?

They think I'm crazy already and they say they're sorry they ever brought me from China, where there's no Fred Astaire. They say I'm not even Chinese anymore. They say what's the use of coming all the way from China just to be a teacher and listen to Fred Astaire. Coulda

131

been a teacher over there. You come here to make money, my parents say. Mr. McCourt, will you tell me how to be an English teacher?

I will, Nancy.

Thanks, Mr. McCourt. Do you mind if I ask questions in class?

In class she says, You were lucky you knew English when you came to America. How did you feel when you came to America?

Confused. Do you know what confused means?

The word goes around the room. They explain it to one another in their own languages and heads nod, yeah, yeah. They're surprised the man up there, the teacher, was once confused like them and he knew English and everything. So, we have something in common: confusion.

I tell them that when I came to New York I had trouble with language and the names of things. I had to learn food words: sauerkraut, cole slaw, hot dog, bagel mit a schmeer.

Then I tell them about my very first teaching experience, which had nothing to do with schools. Years before I became a teacher I worked in a hotel. Big George, a Puerto Rican cook, said five kitchen workers were trying to learn English and would pay fifty cents each if I'd teach them words, once a week, during lunch hour. Two dollars and fifty cents for an hour. At the end of the month I'd have twelve dollars and fifty cents, the most money I ever made at one time in my life. They wanted to know the names of things in the kitchen because if you don't know the names of things in English how can you move up in the world? They would hold up items and I'd name them and spell them out on sheets of paper. They laughed and shook their heads when I couldn't name that flat thing with a handle, a spatula, the first one in my life. Big George laughed with his great belly quivering and told the kitchen workers that was a spachoola.

They wanted to know how come I spoke English if I came from a foreign country that wasn't England and I had to explain how Ireland was conquered, how the English bullied us and tormented us until we spoke their language. When I talked about Ireland there were words they didn't understand and I wondered if there should be an extra charge for explaining them or could I charge only for words connected with the kitchen? No, I couldn't charge them after the way they looked sad when I talked about Ireland and the way they said, *Si, si, si,* patted my shoulder and offered me bites of their sandwiches. They understood because they were conquered, too, first by the Spaniards, then the Americans, conquered so much they didn't know who they were, didn't know if they were black or white or Indian or all three rolled into one and that's hard to explain to your kids because they want to be one thing, one thing, not three things, and that's why they were here mopping up and washing pots and pans in this greasy kitchen. Big George said, This ain't no greasy kitchen so watch yo' mouf. They said, Hell with you, and everyone laughed, even Big George, because the idea of talking like that to the biggest Puerto Rican in New York was so crazy. He laughed himself and gave everyone huge slices from a cake left over from the big lunch upstairs of the Daughters of the British Empire.

After four lessons and ten dollars there was nothing left in the kitchen for me to name till Eduardo, who planned to climb in the world, began to ask questions about food and cooking in general. How about braise? he said. How about sauté? Yeah, and marinate. I'd never heard of these words and I looked at Big George to see if he'd help but he said he wasn't telling nobody nothing long as I was hauling in the big money for being the big-ass word expert. He knew I was in over my head with these new words especially when they asked me the difference between pasta and risotto. I offered to go to the library and look them up, but they said they could do that themselves and what were they paying me for. I could have told them you can't look up something in the library if you can't read English in the first place but that didn't occur to me. I was nervous I might lose my new income, two dollars and fifty cents a week. They said they didn't mind if I slipped up that time over the spatula, they gave me the money anyway, but they weren't gonna hand over big bucks to a guy from a foreign country didn't know pasta from risotto. Two said they were sorry, they were dropping out, and three said they'd hang on, hoping I'd help with words like braise and sauté. I tried to excuse myself by claiming these were French words and surely they wouldn't expect me to know anything but English. One of the three patted my shoulder and hoped I wouldn't let them down as they wanted to rise in the world of the kitchen. They had wives and children and girlfriends all waiting for them to rise and bring home more money so I could see how much depended on me and my knowledge of words.

Big George talked in a rough way to hide how soft he was. When the five Puerto Ricans were not in the kitchen he taught me names of vegetables and fruits I'd never heard of: artichoke, asparagus, tangerine, persimmon, rutabaga. He barked the names at me and made me nervous, but I knew he wanted me to know. That's how I felt about the Puerto Ricans. I wanted them to know words and I almost forgot about the money when they were able to recite what I taught them. It made me feel superior and I thought this must be the way a teacher feels.

Then the two dropouts caused problems in the locker room where we changed and washed up. They knew the word for locker but now they wanted to know what was that thing we sat on—the bench—and what was that flat thing in the locker where you placed small items—the shelf? That was clever the way they got those words out of me free of charge. They'd point to the string in a shoe and I'd tell them it was a lace and they'd smile and say, *Gracias, gracias*. They were getting something for nothing and I didn't mind till one of the three paying Puerto Ricans said, Wha' for you tell these words for nottin' an' we pay, eh? Wha' for?

I told them these locker-room words had nothing to do with kitchens and rising in the world but they said they didn't give a shit. They were paying me and didn't see why the dropouts should get the free words. These were the last words in English they spoke in the locker room that day. The three screamed at the two in Spanish and the two screamed back at the three and there was a banging of locker doors and five middle fingers stabbing the air till Big George roared in and yelled at them in Spanish and they cut it out. I was sorry over that big row in the locker room and wanted to make up to the three paying ones. I tried to slip them free words like carpet, bulb, dustpan, broom, but they said they didn't care anymore, that I should take my dustpan and shove it up my ass and where did I say I was from?

Ireland.

Yeah, *si*. Well, I'm going back to PR. Don't like English no more. Too hard. Hurts my throat.

Big George said, Hey, Irishman. Not your fault. You hell of a good teacher. All you guys come to the kitchen for a piece of peach pie.

But we never had the pie because Big George had a heart attack and collapsed on an open flame on the stove and they said you could smell his flesh burning.

Nancy has this dream of taking her mother to a Fred Astaire movie because her mother never goes out and she's a very intelligent woman. Her mother can quote Chinese poetry, especially Li Po. You ever heard of Li Po, Mr. McCourt?

No.

She tells the class the reason her mother loves Li Po is that he died in a most beautiful way. One bright moonlit night he drank rice wine and took his boat out on a lake and he was so moved by the beauty of the moon reflected in the lake he leaned over the side to embrace it and fell into the lake and drowned.

Nancy's mother would have tears on her cheeks when she talked about this and it was her dream, if ever things got better in China, to return and take a boat out on that lake. Nancy herself had tears when she talked about how her mother said if she got very old or had a very serious illness she'd lean over the side and embrace the moon like her beloved Li Po.

When the bell rings they don't jump from their seats. They don't rush and scramble. They take their things and file out quietly and I'm sure they have moon and lake images in their heads.

In 1968, at Seward Park High School, I faced the hardest challenge of my whole teaching career. I had the usual five classes: three English as a Second Language and two regular ninth-grade English classes. One of those ninth-grade classes consisted of twenty-nine black girls from an uptown feeder school and two Puerto Rican boys who sat in a corner, minding their own business, never saying a word. If they opened their mouths, the girls would turn on them, Who axed you? All the ingredients of difficulty were wrapped up in this one group: gender clash; generation clash; culture clash; racial clash.

The girls ignored me, white guy standing up there trying to get their attention. They had stuff to talk about. There was always some adventure from last night. Boys. Boys. Boys. Serena said she didn't go out with boys. She went out with men. She had ginger hair and her skin was the color of butterscotch. She was so thin tight clothes hung loose on her. She was fifteen and the center of the class, the one who settled arguments, the one who made decisions. She told the class one day, I don't wanna be no leader. You wanna be with me? OK. You can be with me.

Some girls challenged her place in the class, tried to cross swords with her. Hey, Serena, how come you go out with old men? They can't do nothin'.

Yeah, they can. They can put five dollars in my hand every time.

They complained to me, We don't do nothin' in this class. Other classes do things.

I brought in a tape recorder. Surely they'd like to hear themselves talking. Serena took the microphone.

My sister was arrested last night. My sister is a nice person. She was only liberating two pork chops from the store. White people take pork chops an' everything all the time but they don't get arrested. I seen white women walk outa the store with steaks under their dresses. Now my sister in jail till she go to court.

She stopped, looked at me for the first time and handed back the microphone. I dunno why I'm telling you this. You just a teacher.

You just a white man. She turned away and walked to her seat. She sat primly, hands folded on the desk. She had put me in my place and the class knew it.

For the first time that term the room was quiet. They waited for me to take the next step, but I was paralyzed, standing there with the microphone in my hand, the tape running from reel to reel recording nothing.

Anyone else? I said.

They stared at me. Was that contempt?

A hand went up. Maria, the bright, well-dressed one who kept a neat notebook, had a question.

Mister, how come the other classes go on trips and we don't go nowhere? We just sit here talking into a stupid tape recorder. How come?

Yeah, yeah, said the class. How come?

Other classes go to the movies. Why can't we go to the movies?

They were looking at me, talking to me, recognizing my existence, including me in their world. If you had walked into the room at that moment you would have said, Oh, here's a teacher actually engaging with his class. Look at those bright young girls, and those two boys, gazing at their teacher. Makes you believe in public education.

So, I said, feeling like a man in charge, what movie would you like to see?

Cold Turkey, said Maria. My brother seen it up on Broadway near Times Square.

Nah, said Serena. That movie all about drugs. Cold turkey is when you just stop drugs. You don't go to no clinic an' no doctor.

Maria said her brother said nothing about drugs. Serena looked at the ceiling. Your brother goody-goody like you. Your brother don't know shit.

Next day they brought notes from their parents giving them permission to take a trip to see a movie. A dozen notes were forgeries, written in the grand manner parents are supposed to use when addressing teachers.

137

When the Puerto Rican boys brought no notes the girls objected. How come they not going to the movie? We brought notes an' everything an' we have to go to this movie an' they have the day off. How come?

To appease the girls I told the boys they'd have to write a short report on how they spent their day. The girls said, Yeah, yeah, and the boys looked sullen.

On the six-block walk to the subway, the parade of twenty-nine black girls and one white teacher attracted attention. Shopkeepers shouted at me to tell these kids keep their goddam hands off the goddam goods. Can't you control these goddam Negroes?

They ran into stores to buy candy, hot dogs and bottles of pink lemonade. They said pink lemonade was the greatest and why couldn't they have it in the school cafeteria instead of all those juices that tasted like detergent or milk.

Down the steps, into the subway. Forget the fare. Jump the turnstiles, run through gates. Man in the change booth yelled, Hey, hey, pay your fare. Pay your goddam fare. I held back, didn't want the man in the booth to know I was with that wild pack.

They ran back and forth on the subway platform. Where's the train? I don't see no train.

They pretended to push one another onto the tracks. Teacher, teacher, she tried to kill me, teacher. You see that?

People waiting for the train glared at me. A man said, Why don't they go back uptown where they belong? They don't know how to behave like human beings.

I wanted to be a brave, concerned, committed teacher, stand up to him, defend my twenty-eight rowdy black girls, Maria the exception, Maria the forger. But I was a long way from bravery, and what would I say anyway? You try it, Mister Indignant Citizen. You try taking twenty-nine black girls on the subway, all charged up with being fifteen and escaping from school for a day, all pumped up with sugar from cookies, candy and pink lemonade. Try teaching them every day when they look at you as if you were a white snowman about to melt.

I said nothing and prayed for the rumble of the F train.

On the train they squealed and pushed and fought for seats. The passengers looked hostile. Why aren't these Negro kids in school? No wonder they're ignorant.

At West Fourth Street an obese white woman waddled onto the train and stood with her back to the closing door. The girls stared at her and snickered. She stared back. What you little bitches lookin' at?

Serena had the smart, troublemaking mouth. She said, We never seen a mountain get on a train before.

Her twenty-eight classmates laughed, pretended to collapse, laughed again. Serena stared, unsmiling, at the large woman, who said, Come over here, honey, and I'll show you how a mountain can move.

I was the teacher. I had to assert myself, but how? Then I had a strange feeling. I looked at the other passengers, their frowns of disapproval, and I wanted to fight back, defend my twenty-nine.

I stood with my back to the large woman to keep Serena from coming near her.

Her classmates chanted, Go, Serena, go.

The train pulled into the Fourteenth Street station and the large woman backed out the door. You're lucky I have to get off this train, honey, or I'd have you for breakfast.

Serena sneered after her, Yeah, fatso, you really need breakfast.

She moved as if to follow the woman but I blocked the door and kept her on the train till we reached Forty-second Street. The way she looked at me gave me a feeling of satisfaction and puzzlement. If I could win her over I'd have the class. They'd say, That's Mr. McCourt, the teacher who stopped Serena from getting into a fight with a white woman on the train. He on our side. He OK.

Once they saw the pornography and sex shops along Forty-second Street it was impossible to keep them together. They hooted and giggled and postured like the half-naked figures in the shop windows.

Mr. McCourt, Mr. McCourt, can we go in?

No, no. Can't you see the signs? You have to be twenty-one. Let's go.

A policeman stood before me.

Yes. I'm their teacher.

So what are these kids doing on Forty-second Street in the middle of the day?

I blushed, embarrassed. Going to a movie.

Well, isn't that something. Going to a movie. And that's what we pay taxes for. OK, mister teacher, keep these girls moving.

All right, girls, I said. Let's go. Straight ahead to Times Square.

Maria walked beside me. She said, You know, we never came to Times Square before.

I wanted to hug her for talking to me but all I could manage was, You should come here at night to see the lights.

At the theater they rushed to the ticket office, pushing one another aside. Five lingered near me, giving me sidelong looks. What's the matter? Aren't you getting tickets?

They shuffled and looked away and said they had no money. I thought of saying, Well, why the hell did you come here? but I didn't want to spoil a budding relationship with them. Tomorrow they might let me be a teacher.

I bought the tickets, distributed them, hoped there might be a look or a thank you. Nothing. They took the tickets, ran into the lobby, straight to the concession stand, with money they'd told me they didn't have, staggered upstairs with popcorn, candy, bottles of Coke.

I followed them to the balcony, where they pushed and fought for seats and disturbed the other customers. An usher complained to me, We can't have this, and I told the girls, Please sit down and be quiet.

They ignored me. They were a tight pack of twenty-nine black girls at loose in the world, raucous, defiant, flinging bits of popcorn at one another, shouting up at the projection booth, Hey, when we gonna see the movie? We not gonna live forever.

The projectionist said, If they're not quiet I might have to call management.

I said, Yes. I want to be here when management comes. I want to see management handle them.

But the lights dimmed and the movie came on and my twenty-nine girls grew silent. The opening shot showed a perfect small American town, sweet tree-lined avenues, blond white children scooting along on little bicycles, with cheerful background music to assure us that all was well in this American paradise, and from the front row of the balcony came an agonized cry from one of my twenty-nine girls, Hey, Mr. McCourt, how come you takin' us to these honky movies?

They complained all through the movie.

The usher shone his flashlight on them and threatened them with management.

I pleaded with them. Girls. Please be quiet. Management is on its way.

They turned it into a chant:

> *Mangament on it way*
> *Mangament on it way*
> *Hi ho the daddy o*
> *Mangament on it way.*

They said management could kiss their ass and that upset the usher. He said, OK. That's it. That's i-t, it. You don't behave yourselves and you're out, o-u-t.

Oh, man. He know how to spell an' everything. OK. We be quiet.

When the movie ended and the lights came on, no one moved.

All right, I said. Let's go. It's over.

We know it's over. We not blind.

You have to go home now.

They said they were staying. They were gonna see this honky movie again.

I told them I was leaving.

OK, you leaving.

They turned away to wait for their second viewing of *Cold Turkey,* that boring honky movie.

The following week the twenty-nine girls said, Is that all we gonna do? No more trips? Just sit here every day talkin' about nouns an' you makin' us write that stuff you put on the board? That all?

A note in my mailbox announced a trip for our students to a college production of *Hamlet* on Long Island. I threw the announcement into the wastepaper basket. Twenty-nine girls who could sit through two performances of *Cold Turkey* would never appreciate *Hamlet.*

Next day, more questions.

How come all these other classes goin' on a big trip to see a play?

Well, it's a play by Shakespeare.

Yeah? So?

How could I tell them the truth, that I had such low expectations of them I thought they'd never understand a word of Shakespeare? I said it was a hard play to understand and I didn't think they'd like it.

Oh, yeah? So what's it about, this play?

It's called *Hamlet.* It's about a prince who comes home and is shocked to discover his father is dead and his mother already married to his father's brother.

I know what happened, said Serena.

The class called out, What happened? What happened?

Brother that married the mother tries to kill the prince, right?

Yes, but that comes later.

Serena gave me the look that said she was trying to be patient. 'Course it comes later. Everything comes later. If everything come at the beginning then there's nothing to come later.

Donna said, Whachoo talkin' about?

None your business. Talkin' to the teacher about the prince.

A fight was brewing. I had to stop it. I said, Hamlet was angry about his mother marrying his uncle.

They said, Wow.

Hamlet thought his uncle killed his father.

Didn't I say that already? said Serena. What's the use me sayin' something if you gonna say it, too? We still wanna know how come we not goin' to see this play? White kids gonna see this play just because this prince be white.

All right. I'll see if we can go with the other classes.

They lined up to board the bus. They told passing pedestrians and motorists they were going to Long Island to see this play about a woman who marries her dead husband's brother. The Puerto Rican boys asked if they could sit near me. They didn't want to sit with these girls who were crazy and talked nonstop about sex and everything.

As soon as the bus pulled into the street the girls were opening bags and sharing lunch. They whispered about the one who'd get a prize for hitting the bus driver with a piece of bread. They'd all contribute a dime and the winner would get two dollars and eighty cents. But he was watching in his rearview mirror and told them, Just try it. Go ahead, just try it, and your little black ass will be off this bus. The girls said, Oh, yeah, in that brave cheeky way. That's all they could say because the driver was black and they knew with him they'd get away with nothing.

At the college a man with a bullhorn announced teachers were expected to keep their classes together.

The assistant principal from my school told me they were relying on me to keep order in my class. That class had a reputation, he said.

I led them into the auditorium and stood in the aisle while they pushed and shoved and argued over seats. The Puerto Rican boys asked if they could sit far away. When Serena called them Spic and Span, the girls went into fits of giggling that didn't stop till the ghost of Hamlet's father appeared and terrified everyone. The ghost appeared on stilts draped in black and the girls oohed and aahed.

When the spotlight dimmed on him, and he disappeared into the wings, Claudia, sitting beside me, called out, Oh, he's so cute. Where he goin'? He comin' back, teacher?

Yes, he is, I said, embarrassed by whispered shushings from serious people all over the auditorium.

She applauded each time the ghost appeared, whimpered when he left. I think he's so cool. I want him back, she said.

When the play ended and the cast took their bows and there was no ghost, she stood and called to the stage, Where the ghost? I want the ghost. Where that ghost?

The other twenty-eight stood, too, and called for the ghost till an actor left the stage and the ghost reappeared immediately. The twenty-nine applauded and cheered and said they wanted to go out with him.

The ghost removed his black hat and cloak to show he was just an ordinary college student and not worth making a fuss over. The twenty-nine gasped and complained the whole play was a trick especially that phony ghost up there and they promised they'd never go to a phony play like this again not even if they had to sit in class with that Mr. McCourt and his spelling and stuff, not even if all the other classes in the school were going.

On the way home they fell asleep, all except Serena, who sat behind the bus driver. When she asked if he had any children he said he couldn't talk and drive at the same time. It was against the law but, yes, he had children and he didn't want any of them to be a bus driver. He was working to send them to good schools and if they didn't do what they were told he'd break their ass. He said you had to work harder in this country when you were black but in the end that made you stronger. When you have to push harder and climb harder you develop muscles and then no one can stop you.

Serena said she'd like to be a hairdresser but the bus driver said, You can do better than that. You wanna stand there the rest of your life fixin' hair for cranky old women? You're smart. You can go to college.

Yeah? Do you really think I can go to college?

Why not? You look intelligent enough and you talk good. So why not?

Nobody never told me that before.

Well, I'm telling you, and don't sell yourself short.

OK, said Serena.

OK, said the bus driver. He smiled at her in his rearview mirror and I suppose she smiled back at him. I couldn't see her face.

He was a bus driver and black and the way she confided in him made me think about the waste of human beings in the world.

Next day Claudia wants to know, How come everybody be pickin' on the girl?

Ophelia?

Yeah. Everybody be pickin' on that poor girl an' she not even black. How come? Guy that makes all the speeches has a sword to fight people so nobody pushes him in the river.

Hamlet?

Yeah, an' you know what?

What?

He was so mean to his mom an' he a prince an' everything. Why didn't she just get up an' slap his face? Why?

Serena, the bright one, raises her hand like an ordinary kid in an ordinary class. I stare at the hand. I'm sure she's going to ask for the lavatory pass. She says, Hamlet's mom is a queen. Queens don't act like everyone else slapping people around. You a queen you gotta have dignity.

She looks at me in that direct way that's almost a challenge, eyes wide and beautiful and unblinking, a hint of smile. This thin black fifteen-year-old knows her power. I feel myself blushing and that starts another round of giggling.

The following Monday, Serena does not return to class. The girls say she'll never be coming back on account of how her mother was arrested, For drugs an' stuff, and now Serena has to live with her grandmother in Georgia, where, they say, Black people are treated like niggers. They say Serena will never stay there. She'll be in trouble in no time talking back to white people. An' that's why she said the bad word, Mr. McCourt.

With Serena gone, the class changed, a body without a head. Maria raised her hand and asked why I talked funny. Was I married? Did I have any kids? Which did I prefer, *Hamlet* or *Cold Turkey*? Why did I become a teacher?

They were building bridges where we could travel back and forth. I answered their questions and didn't give a damn anymore about giving them too much information. How many priests had I confessed to when I was the age of these girls? I had their attention and that was all that mattered.

A month after Serena left, there were two good moments. Claudia raised her hand and said, Mr. McCourt, you really nice. The class nodded yeah yeah and the Puerto Rican boys smiled in the back of the room.

Then Maria raised her hand. Mr. McCourt, I got a letter from Serena. She said this the first letter of her life and she wouldn'ta wrote it but her grandma told her. She never met her grandma before but she loves her because she can't read or write and Serena reads the Bible to her every night. She said, this gonna kill you, Mr. McCourt, she said she gonna finish high school and go to college and teach little kids. Not big kids like us because we just a great pain but little kids that don't talk back and she say she sorry about things she did in this class and to tell you that. Someday she gonna write you a letter.

There were fireworks in my head. It was New Year's Eve and the Fourth of July a hundred times over.

11

Ten years into my teaching career, thirty-eight years old, and if I'm to assess myself I'll say, You're doing your dogged best. There are teachers who teach and don't give a fiddler's fart what their students think of them. Subject matter is king. Such teachers are powerful. They dominate their classrooms with personality backed up by the great threat: the red pen inscribing on the report card the dreaded F. Their message to their students is, I am your teacher, not your counselor, not your confidant, not your parent. I teach a subject: take it or leave it.

I often think I should be a tough, disciplined teacher, organized and focused, a John Wayne of pedagogy, another Irish schoolmaster wielding stick, strap, cane. Tough teachers deliver the goods for forty minutes. Digest this lesson, kids, and be ready to throw it up on exam day.

Sometimes I joke, Sit in that seat, kid, and be quiet, or I'll break your bloody head, and they laugh because they know. Yeah, isn't he something? When I act tough they listen politely till the spasm passes. They know.

I don't see a class as one unit sitting and listening to me. There are faces showing degrees of interest or indifference. It's the indifference that challenges me. Why is that little bastard talking to her when he could be listening to me? Excuse me, James, there's a lesson going on here.

Oh, yeah, yeah.

There are moments and looks. They may be too shy to tell you that was a good lesson but you know now from the way they leave the room and the way they look at you whether the class was a success or something to be forgotten. The approving looks warm your heart on the train home.

No matter what happened in your classroom there were rules from the officials who supervised the high schools of New York:

Children are to keep their voices down. They are not to roam rooms or hallways. There can be no learning in a noisy atmosphere.

The classroom is not to be a playground. There should be no throwing of things. If students want to ask a question or answer a question they are to raise their hands. They must not be allowed to call out. Calling out could lead to pandemonium and that would make a bad impression on Board of Education officials from Brooklyn or educators visiting from foreign parts.

Use of the lavatory pass must be kept to a minimum. Everyone knows the various ploys with the lavatory pass. A boy given the pass to go to the lavatory on the second floor is sometimes found squinting through the window of a room where a girl he has recently fallen in love with is sitting and making loving faces right back. That is not to be tolerated. Some boys and girls use the pass to meet in the basement or on the stairwell where they are up to no good and found by alert assistant principals who report them and call their parents. Others take the pass to smoke in various secret places. The bathroom pass is for the bathroom, to be used for no other purpose. Students should not stay away with the pass more than five minutes. If they do, the teacher is to inform the office of the principal, which will send a dean to inspect the lavatories and other locations to ensure there is no improper behavior.

Principals want order, routine, discipline. They prowl the hallways. They peer through the windows in classroom doors. They want to see boys and girls with heads bent over books, boys and girls writing, boys and girls with hands raised, excited, eager to answer teacher's questions.

Good teachers run a tight ship. They maintain discipline and that is crucial in a vocational high school in New York where gangs sometimes bring their problems to school. You have to keep an eye out for gangs. They could take over a whole school, and it's good-bye to learning.

Teachers learn, too. After years in the classroom, after facing thousands of teenagers, they have that sixth sense about everyone who enters the room. They see the sidelong glances. They sniff the air of a new class and they can tell if this is a pain-in-the-ass group or one they can work with. They see quiet kids who have to be drawn out and loudmouths who have to be shut up. They can tell by the way a boy sits if he's going to be cooperative or a great pain in the ass. It's a good sign when a student sits straight up, joins his hands on the desk before him, looks at the teacher and smiles. It's a bad sign if he lounges back, sticks his legs into the aisle, stares out the window, at the ceiling, over the teacher's head. Watch out for trouble.

In every class there's a pest put on earth to test you. He usually sits in the last row, where he can tilt his chair against the wall. You've already talked to the class about the danger of tilting: Chair could slip, children, and you could be hurt. Then teacher has to write a report in case parents complain or threaten to sue.

Andrew knows the tilting chair will annoy you, at least get your attention. Then he can play the little game that will catch the eyes of the girls. You'll say, Hey, Andrew.

He'll take his time. This is a showdown, man, and girls are watching.

Wha'?

That is the teenage sound you won't find in a dictionary. Wha'? Parents hear it constantly. It means, Whaddya want? Why you bothering me?

The chair, Andrew. Would you put it down, please?

I'm just sittin' minding my own business.

The chair, Andrew, has four legs. Tilting on two legs could cause an accident.

Silence in the classroom. Showdown time. This time you know you're on fairly safe ground. You feel Andrew is disliked by this group and he knows he'll get no sympathy. He's a pale thin figure, a loner. Still, the class is watching. They may not like him but if you bully him they'll turn against you. When it's boy versus teacher they choose boy. And all because of a tilted chair.

You could have let it go. No one would have noticed. So, teacher man, what's the problem? Simple. Andrew has shown his dislike for you from day one and you don't like being disliked, especially by this little shit who's disliked by the rest of the class. Andrew knows you favor the girls. Of course I favor the girls. Give me five classes with a majority of girls and I'm in heaven. Variety. Color. Games. Drama.

Andrew waits. The class waits. The chair is cocky in its tilt. Oh, the temptation to grab a leg and pull. His head would slide down the wall and everyone would laugh.

I turn away from Andrew. I don't know why I'm turning away and walking to the front of the room and I certainly don't know what I'll do or say once I reach my desk. I don't want them to think I've backed off, but I know I have to act. Andrew's head rests against the wall and he's giving me that little smile of contempt.

I don't like Andrew's tumbling red hair, the fine features. I don't like the arrogance of his delicacy. Sometimes when I've warmed up to a subject and the class is with me and I'm rolling along, delighted with myself, I look back at his cold stare and wonder if I should try to win him over or destroy him completely.

A voice in my head tells me, Make something of it. Turn it into a lesson on observation. Pretend you planned the whole thing. And I say to the class, So, what's going on here? They stare. They're puzzled.

You say, Imagine you're a newspaper reporter. You walked into this room a few minutes ago. What did you see? What did you hear? What is the story?

Michael speaks up. No story. Just Andrew being an asshole as usual.

Andrew loses his little contemptuous smile and I feel I have him on the run. I won't have to say much. Continue with the leading questions and let the class damn him. I'll wipe that smile off his face forever, the little shit, and he'll tilt no more.

I assume my reasonable, objective teacher role. A comment like that, Michael, doesn't give the reader much information.

Yeah, but who needs information like that? Is some guy from the *Daily News* gonna walk in here and write this big story about Andrew and the chair and the teacher getting all pissed off?

His girlfriend raises her hand.

Yes, Diane?

She talks to the class. Mr. McCourt is axin' us—

Asking, Diane.

She pauses. She takes her time. She says, See. Mr. McCourt, that's what's wrong with this world. People try to help people an' next thing other people are trying to correct everything they say. That's very insulting. I mean it's OK to tell Andrew put his chair down because he could crack his stupid skull, but there's no reason to be correcting the way people talk. You do that an' we never gonna open our mouths in this class. So you know what I'm gonna do? I'm gonna tell Andrew put his chair down an' not be an ass.

She's sixteen, tall and cool, and her blond hair hangs down her back in a sophisticated way that reminds me of Scandinavian actresses. I am nervous when she walks to the back of the room and stands before Andrew.

So look, Andrew. You see what's happening here. There's this big class, over thirty people in this class, and Mr. McCourt up there an' you tilting on your chair an' he tells you put it down but you just sit there with your little smile, Andrew, an' who knows what's going on in your head. You're wasting the time of everyone in this class and what's your problem? The teacher is getting paid to teach an' not tell you put your chair down like you were some kid in first grade, right? Right, Andrew?

He's still tilting but he looks at me as if to say, What's going on here? What should I do?

He tilts his chair forward till it's flat. He stands and faces Diane. See? You'll never forget me, Diane. You'll forget this whole class, you'll forget the teacher, Mr. What's-his-name, but I tilt my chair and the teacher gets uptight, and everyone in this class will remember me forever. Right, Mr. McCourt?

I wanted to drop the reasonable-teacher mask and say what was on my mind, Look, you little twerp, put the chair down or I'll throw you out the damn window so you'll be meat for pigeons.

You can't talk like that. You'd be reported to the authorities. You know your role: if the little buggers piss you off from time to time, suffer, man, suffer. No one is forcing you to stay in this miserable underpaid profession and there's nothing to keep you from going through that door to the shimmering world of powerful men, beautiful women, cocktail parties uptown, satin sheets.

Yeah, teach, and what would you do in the great world of powerful men, et cetera? Get back to work. Talk to your class. Address the problem of the tilted chair. It's not over. They're waiting.

Listen. Are you listening?

They smile. There he goes again with his old, Listen, are you listening? They call to one another in the hallways, mimicking, Listen. Are you listening? It means they like you.

I said, You saw what happened in this room. You saw Andrew tilting his chair and you saw what happened when I told him drop it. So you have material for a story, don't you? We've had conflict. Andrew versus teacher. Andrew versus the class. Andrew versus himself. Oh, yes, indeed, Andrew versus himself. You were making mental notes, weren't you? Or else you just said, Why is the teacher making such a big deal about Andrew and his chair? Or why is Andrew being such a pain in the ass? If you were reporting this there is another dimension to the incident: Andrew's motivation. Only he knows why he was tilting that chair and you are entitled to speculate. We could have over thirty speculations in this class.

* * *

Next day Andrew lingered after class. Mr. McCourt, you went to NYU, right?

I did.

Well, my mother said she knew you.

Really? I'm happy to know that someone remembered me.

I mean she knew you outside of class.

Again, Really?

She died last year. She had cancer. Her name was June.

Oh, Christ. Slow on the uptake is hardly the word for it. Late bloomer. Why didn't I guess? Why didn't I see her in his eyes?

She used to say she was going to call you but she had a bad time with the divorce and then the cancer came and when I told her I was in your class she made me promise never to tell you about her. She said you'd never want to talk to her anyway.

But I did want to talk to her. I wanted to talk to her forever. Who did she marry? Who's your father?

I don't know who my father is. She married Gus Peterson. I have to go and empty out my locker. My dad is moving to Chicago and I'm going with him and my stepmother. Isn't it funny how I have a stepfather and a stepmother and it's OK?

We shook hands and I watched him walk down the hallway. Before he went into the locker area he turned and waved and I had a moment wondering if I should let the past go that easily.

School wisdom says, Unless you can back it up, never threaten a class or an individual. And don't be such a fool as to threaten Benny "Boom Boom" Brandt, who is famous in the school for having a black belt in karate.

After an absence of four days he saunters into the classroom halfway through a lesson on foreign words in English: amen, pasta, chef, sushi, limousine and the words that start the tittering, lingerie, bidet, brassiere.

I could ignore Boom Boom, carry on with the lesson, and let him go to his seat. But I know the class is watching and thinking,

How come we have to bring in excuse notes when we're absent but Boom Boom can come in just like that and sit down? They're right and I'm with them, and I have to show I'm not soft.

Excuse me. I'm trying to be sarcastic.

He stops just inside the door. Yeah?

I play with a piece of chalk to show how cool I am. I struggle to decide between Where are you going? and Just where do you think you're going? The first sentence could sound like a simple question with a hint of teacher authority. The think in the second suggests challenge and could cause trouble. Either way, it's the tone of voice that matters. I back off a little.

Excuse me. Do you have a pass? You need a pass from the office after an absence.

This is the teacher talking. He represents authority: the office down the hall that issues passes for everything; the principal; the superintendent; the mayor; the president; God. This is not the role I want. I'm here to teach English, not to ask for passes.

Brandt says, Who's gonna stop me? He sounds almost friendly, genuinely curious, but what comes from the class is a gasp.

Oh, shit, says Ralphie Boyce.

High school teachers are urged by their superiors to discourage profanity in the classroom. Such language is disrespectful and could lead to a breakdown in law and order. I want to admonish Ralphie but can't because the words leaping around my own head are Oh, shit.

Brandt stands with his back to the door that has swung shut behind him. He seems patient.

And what is this sudden warmth I feel for this lumbering future plumber from Delancey Street, Manhattan? Is it the patient way he waits, almost gentle in his look? He seems so reasonable and thoughtful. So, why don't I drop my tough teacher act and tell him, Oh, all right. Sit down, Brandt. Forget the pass now and try to remember it next time. But I've pushed too far to turn back. His classmates are witnesses and something has to happen.

I toss the chalk into the air and catch it. Brandt watching. I step toward him. This is not my day to die, but class is waiting, and it's time to answer his question, Who's gonna stop me?

I toss the chalk, perhaps for the last time ever, and tell him, I am.

He nods as if to say, That's reasonable. You're the teacher, man.

The warm feeling is back and I have the urge to pat his shoulder, tell him forget the whole thing, just sit down, Brandt.

I toss the chalk again and miss it. It's on the floor. It is imperative that that chalk be retrieved. I bend to pick it up and there, inviting me, is Brandt's foot, offering itself. I grab it and pull. Brandt falls backward, bangs his head on the brass doorknob, slides to the floor, rests quietly as if contemplating the next move. Again there's a gasp from the class, Wow.

He rubs the back of his head. Is he preparing himself to deliver a quick punch, chop, kick?

Shit, Mr. McCourt, I didn't know you was karate.

It appears I am the winner, and the next move is mine. OK, Benny, you can sit down.

May.

What?

All the teachers say, You may sit down. Boom Boom is correcting my grammar. Am I in a madhouse?

OK. You may sit down.

So you don't want a pass or nothin'?

No. It's all right.

So we was fightin' for nothin'?

On the way to his seat Boom Boom steps on the chalk and looks at me. Was that deliberate? Should I make an issue of it? No. A voice in my head tells me, Get on with the lesson. Stop acting like a teenager. This kid could break you in two. Teacher man, get back to the lesson on foreign words in English.

Brandt acts as if nothing had ever happened between us and I feel such a wave of shame I want to apologize to the whole class and to him in particular. I berate myself for the cheapness of what I've done.

Now they admire what they think are my karate ways. I open my mouth and babble.

Imagine what the English language would be like if you removed French words. You wouldn't be able to order your chauffeur to bring around your limousine anymore. You'd have to say underwear instead of lingerie. You couldn't go to a restaurant. No more cuisine, no more gourmet, no sauce, menu, chef, perfume. You'd have to find a new word for brassiere.

Whisper, whisper. Giggle, giggle. Ooh, Mr. McCourt, what you said.

That's how to get their minds off the incident. I seem to be winning on all fronts till I look over at Brandt. His eyes seem to say, OK, Mr. McCourt. I guess you needed to look good, so it's OK with me.

He was bright enough to pass the New York State Regents' exam in English. He could have written a passable, and passing, English essay, but he chose to fail. He ignored the suggested list of topics, headed his essay, "Chirp," and wrote, three hundred and fifty times, "Chirp, chirp, chirp, chirp, chirp, chirp . . ."

I meet Boom Boom on Delancey Street after graduation and ask him what was all that about the chirp?

I dunno. I get crazy feelings and I don't care what happens. I was in that classroom and everything seemed so stupid, that monitor teacher up there warning us not to look at anyone else's paper, and there was this bird on the windowsill chirping away and I said, OK, shit, what the hell, so I put down what he was saying. When I was fourteen my dad sent me to take martial arts. The Japanese guy just let me sit on a bench outside for an hour and when I said, Yo, mister, what about the lesson? he told me go home. Home? I mean he was getting paid for the hour. He said, Go home. I said, Should I come back next week? and he said nothing. I came back next week and he said, What you want? I told him again I wanted to learn martial arts. He told me go clean the toilet. I wondered what that had to do with martial arts but I said nothing. I cleaned the toilet. He told me sit on the bench, take off my shoes and socks and look at my feet. Don't take my eyes off my feet. You ever look at your feet? I have one foot that's bigger than the other. He came out and said, Put your shoes on, no socks, and go home. It was getting easy to do what he told me. I stopped being pissed off. Sometimes I'd sit on that bench and do nothing and just go home and still pay him. I told my dad but he only made a face. It was six weeks before the Japanese guy brought me into the room for my first lesson. He made me stand with my face stuck against a wall while he kept coming at me for about fifteen minutes with some kind of sword and screaming at me. At the end of that session he said I was accepted into his school except that I had to clean the toilet before I went home that day in case I had any big ideas about myself. So I knew what was going on that day when you pulled my leg. I knew you had to save your ass and that was OK with me because I didn't need that world and you're an OK teacher and I didn't give a shit what those kids in the class thought. If you have to act like a big-ass teacher you should go home and clean the toilet.

This is the situation in the public schools of America: The farther you travel from the classroom the greater your financial and professional rewards. Get the license, teach for two or three years. Take courses in administration, supervision, guidance, and with your new certificates you can move to an office with air-conditioning, private toilets, long lunches, secretaries. You won't have to struggle with large groups of pain-in-the-arse kids. Hide out in your office, and you won't even have to see the little buggers.

But here I was thirty-eight years old, lacking ambition to climb in the school system, adrift in the American dream, facing the midlife crisis, failed teacher of high school English, but hindered by superiors, principals and their assistants, or so I thought.

I had the angst and didn't know what ailed me. Alberta said, Why don't you get your Ph.D. and rise in the world?

I said, I will.

New York University said yes, they would accept me for the doctoral program, but my wife said, Why don't you go to London or Dublin?

Are you trying to get rid of me?

She smiled.

When I was sixteen I visited Dublin with a friend on a day trip and I stood with my back to a gray stone wall to watch a parade. The gray wall belonged to Trinity College and I didn't know that was looked on as foreign territory, English and Protestant. Farther down the street iron railings and a great gate kept out the likes of me. There were statues outside of Edmund Burke and Oliver Goldsmith. Oh, I said, there he is, right up there, the man who wrote "The Deserted Village," which I had to memorize in school.

My friend from Limerick, who knew more about the world than I did, said, Take a good look at Oliver and the rest of it because your type will never step inside those gates. The archbishop said any Catholic who goes to Trinity is automatically excommunicated.

Anytime I visited Dublin after that I was drawn to Trinity. I stood by the gate admiring the elegant way the students tossed their flapping Trinity scarves over their shoulders. I admired the accents that sounded English. I coveted the beautiful Protestant girls who would never cast me a glance. They would marry their own kind, their own class of people, all Protestants with horses, and if the likes of me ever married one of them he'd be booted out of the Catholic Church with no hope of redemption.

American tourists in their bright clothes strolled in and out of the college and I wished I had the courage to walk in myself but the man at the gate might ask me what I was doing there and I wouldn't know what to say.

Six years later I returned to Ireland in my American army uniform, which I thought would bring respect. It did, till I opened my mouth. I tried to put on an American accent to go with the uniform. It didn't work. At first, waitresses would rush to lead me to a table, but when I spoke they said, Arrah, Jaysus, you're not a Yank at all, at all. You're just Irish like everyone else. Where you from? I tried to pass myself off as a GI from Alabama, but one woman in Bewley's Café on Grafton Street said, If you're from Alabama, I'm the queen of Romania. I stammered and admitted I was from Limerick and she gave up all claim to the throne of Romania. She said it was against the rules of Bewley's to be chatting up the customers, but I looked like the type that might take a drink. I bragged about how I drank beer and schnapps all over Bavaria and she said if that was the case I could buy her a sherry at McDaid's pub up the street.

I didn't think she was attractive, but it was very flattering that a waitress at Bewley's would want to have a drink with me.

I went to McDaid's Bar to wait for her. The drinkers stared at me and nudged one another over my American uniform and I felt uncomfortable. The barman stared, too, and when I asked for a pint, he said, Is it a general we have here, or what?

I didn't understand the sarcasm and when I said, No, I'm a corporal, there was a wave of laughter along the bar and I felt like the greatest fool in the world.

I was confused. I was born in America. I grew up in Ireland. I returned to America. I'm wearing the American uniform. I feel Irish. They should know I'm Irish. They should not be mocking me.

When the waitress from Bewley's arrived and sat with me against the wall and asked for a sherry there was more staring and nudging. The barman winked and said something about "another victim." He came from behind the bar and asked if I'd like another pint. Of course I'd like another pint. All the attention I was getting made my face feel hot and I knew from looking in the great mirror my eyes were fire-engine red.

The waitress said if the barman was bringing me another pint he might as well bring her another sherry after her exhausting day at Bewley's. She told me her name was Mary. She said if I was inclined to look down my nose at her because she was only a waitress I could stop right there. After all, what was I but a culchie from the country all togged out in my American uniform, putting on airs. The sherry seemed to make her talkative and the more she talked the more snickering there was in the seats along the wall. She said her job at Bewley's was temporary. She was waiting for the solicitors to settle her grandmother's will and when it was decided she'd open a little shop on Grafton Street and sell delicate garments to a better class of people.

I knew nothing about delicate garments, but I wondered about her in such a shop. She was fat, eyes buried in the folds of her face, and she had chins that hung and swung. Her body bulged everywhere. I didn't want to be with her and didn't know what to do. I could see people were laughing at me and I blurted, out of desperation, that I had to go.

What? she said.

I have to . . . I have to look at Trinity College. The inside of it. I have to go through the gate. My third pint of stout was talking.

That's a Protestant place, she said.

I don't care. I have to go through the gate.

Did you hear that? she said to the whole bar. He wants to go inside Trinity.

Aw, Jaysus, said one man, and another said, Mother o' God.

All right, General, said the barman. Go on. Go to Trinity and look inside, but make sure you go to confession on Saturday.

Did you hear that? said Mary. Confession on Saturday, but don't worry, darlin.' I'll hear your confession anytime. Come on, finish your pint and we'll go to Trinity.

Oh, God. She wants to go with me. Plump quivering Mary wants to walk down Grafton Street with me in my American army uniform. People will say, Look at the Yank. Is that the best he can do, picking up a great tub of lard like that when Dublin has the loveliest girls in the world?

I told her she shouldn't bother, but she insisted and the barman said I'd have more than one reason for confession on Saturday because, Your wan there shows no mercy.

Why didn't I show my independence? Was I to walk through the gates of Trinity the first time in my life with this babbling fat body on my arm?

I was and I did.

All the way down Grafton Street she jabbered at anyone who even looked at us, What's up with you? Didn't you ever see a Yank before? till one woman in a shawl said back to her, We did but we never saw one sink so low in the world he had to walk with the likes of you. Mary screamed if she didn't have more important business to attend to she'd tear the eyes from the shawlie's head.

I felt nervous about going through the Trinity gate. The man in uniform would surely ask what I was doing there, but he paid no attention, even when Mary said, Lovely evenin,' darlin'.

There I was, at last, standing on the cobblestones, inside the gate, not daring another step. Oliver Goldsmith walked here. Jonathan Swift walked here. All the rich Protestants down the centuries walked here. Here I was, inside the gates, and that was enough.

Mary pulled at my arm. 'Tis getting dark. Are you going to stand here all night? Come on, I'm dying for a sherry. Then we'll go to my little bedsit and who knows what will happen, who knows. She giggled and pulled me against her great soft jiggling body and I wanted to tell Dublin, No, no, she's not mine.

We walked up Nassau Street, where she stopped to admire jewelry at the Yates shop at the corner. Lovely, she said. Lovely. Oh, the day will come I'll have one of them rings on my finger.

She dropped my arm to point at a ring in the window and I ran. Away up Nassau Street I ran, barely hearing her scream that I was a dirty Limerick jackeen of a Yank.

I returned to Bewley's next day to tell her how sorry I was over my behavior. She said, Ah, that's all right. Sure you never know what's goin' to come out of you after a few sherries or pints. She said she'd be finished at six and if I liked we could go out for fish and chips and have tea later in her room. After the tea she said it was surely too late for me to walk back to my hotel off Grafton Street and it wouldn't bother her one bit if I stayed and took the bus with her in the morning. She went to the hallway lavatory and I undressed down to my underwear. She returned in a gray billowing nightdress. She dropped to her knees by the bed, blessed herself, and asked God to come between her and all harm. She told God she knew she was putting herself in the way of temptation but sure wasn't he an innocent, the boy in the bed.

She rolled in and squashed me against the wall and when I reached to pull up her nightdress she slapped my hand away. She said she didn't want to be responsible for the loss of my soul but, if I said a perfect Act of Contrition before I fell asleep, she'd feel easier in her mind. While I was saying the prayer she wriggled out of the night-dress and pulled me against her body. She whispered I must finish the prayer later and I said I would, indeed I would, as I pushed into her vast blubbery body and finished my Act of Contrition.

I was twenty-two then and now, at thirty-eight, I was applying to Trinity College. Yes, they would consider my application if I sat for the American Graduate Record Examination. I did, and astonished myself and those around me with a score in the ninety-ninth percentile in English. That meant I was up there with smart people all around the country and it gave me such a lift I went to Gage and Toll-ner's restaurant in Brooklyn, ate a sea bass with a baked potato and drank so much wine I had no memory of going home. Alberta was patient with me, did not upbraid me in the morning because, after all, I was going to Dublin to a superior university, and she wouldn't be seeing much of me in the next two years, the time Trinity gave you to write and defend a dissertation.

In the mathematics section of the GRE I had, I think, the lowest score in the world.

Alberta booked me a berth on the *Queen Elizabeth,* the ship's second-last eastward voyage on the Atlantic. We had a party on the ship because that's what you were supposed to do. We drank cham-pagne and when it was time for visitors to go ashore I kissed her and she kissed me back. I said I'd miss her and she said she'd miss me, but

I'm not sure either of us was telling the truth. I was light-headed from the champagne and when the ship pulled away from the pier I waved without knowing what I was waving at. That was my life, I thought. Waving without knowing what I was waving at. That seemed like the kind of deep observation that could be explored, but it gave me a headache and I moved on.

The ship pulled into the Hudson and headed for the Narrows. I made sure I was on deck to wave to Ellis Island. Everyone waved at the Statue, but I had a special wave for Ellis Island, the place of hope and heartbreak.

I thought of myself, little fellow nearly four years old, thirty-four years ago, waving, waving, sailing to Ireland, and here I was again, waving, and what was I doing, where was I going and what was it all about?

When you're alone and still unsteady from champagne you wander the ship, exploring. I'm on the *Queen Elizabeth* sailing to Dublin, to Trinity College, if you don't mind. Did you ever think, with your comings and goings, with all that waving, you'd be joining the enemy? Trinity College, the Protestant college, loyal always to this majesty and that majesty and what did Trinity ever contribute to the cause of freedom? But down there in your sniffling little soul you always saw them as superior, didn't you, horse Protestants with their law-dee-daw accents, their noses in the air.

Oliver St. John Gogarty was a Trinity man and even though I wrote about him, and read every word of his I could find, thinking some of his talent and style would rub off on me, it was all for nothing. I once showed my thesis to Stanley Garber, a teacher at McKee, and told him of my hopes. He shook his head and said, Look, McCourt, forget Gogarty. In the back of your brain you'll always be that little pissy-assed kid from the lanes of Limerick. Find out who the hell you are. Climb the cross and do your own suffering. No substitutions, pal.

How can you talk like that, Stanley? That stuff about the cross. You're Jewish.

That's right. Look at us. We tried to fit in with the goyim. We tried to assimilate, but they wouldn't let us. What happens then? Friction, man, and friction throws up people like Marx and Freud and Einstein and Stanley Garber. Thank God you're not assimilated, McCourt, and drop Gogarty. You are not Gogarty. You are on your own. Do you understand that? If you keeled over and died this minute the stars in their courses would still be stars in their courses and you'd be a blip. Go your own way or you'll wind up in a little house on Staten Island saying Hail Marys with a Maureen.

I couldn't think about that because here, descending that grand central staircase of the *Queen Elizabeth,* was a woman I knew. She saw me and said we should have a drink. I remembered she was a private nurse to the rich of New York and I wondered what else she was. She said she was disappointed over her friend who had changed her travel plans and here she was, the nurse, with a first-class cabin with two beds and five days of lonely travel before her. The drink loosened my tongue and I told her of my lonesomeness and how we could be company for each other on the voyage though it might be difficult with her being first class and me down below the waterline.

Oh, that would be grand, she said. She was half Irish and sometimes talked like that.

If I had been sober I might have been wiser, but I fell to temptation and forgot my own berth in the bowels of the ship.

On the third day of the crossing I slipped away for breakfast in the dining room, my first visit. The waiter said, Yes, sir? and I felt foolish telling him I didn't know where to sit.

Sir, haven't you been here before?

No.

Because he was a waiter he did not ask the obvious question. Nor did the purser, who said I'd been declared officially not aboard. The ship assumed I'd gone ashore with my friends in a fit of enthusiasm. You could see he was waiting for an explanation, but I could never tell him of my first-class-cabin experiences with the private nurse. He said, yes, there was a seat for me, and welcome to breakfast.

There were two bunks in that cabin below the waterline. My cabin mate was on his knees, praying. He looked shocked when he saw me. He was a Methodist from Idaho, sailing to Heidelberg to study theology, so I could not brag to him that I'd spent the last three nights in a first-class cabin with a private nurse from New York. I apologized for interrupting his prayer, but he said you could never interrupt his prayer as his whole life was a prayer. I thought that was a wonderful thing to say and wished my life could be a prayer. What he said gave me a pang of conscience and made me feel worthless and sinful. His name was Ted. He looked clean-cut and cheerful. He had fine-looking teeth and a Marine crew cut. His white shirt was crisp, starched, pressed. He was at ease with himself, at peace with the world. God was in his heaven, a Methodist heaven, and all was right. I felt intimidated. If his life was a prayer, what was mine? One long sin? If this ship hit an iceberg Ted would be out on the deck singing "Nearer, My God, to Thee," and I'd be searching the ship for a priest to hear my last confession.

Ted asked if I was religious, if I attended church. He said I was welcome to join him in an hour at a Methodist service, but I mumbled, I go to Mass occasionally. He said he understood. How could he? What does a Methodist know about the sufferings of a Catholic, especially an Irish Catholic? (I didn't say that, of course. I didn't want to hurt his feelings. He was so sincere.) He asked if I'd like to pray with him and I mumbled again I didn't know any Protestant prayers and, besides, I had to take a shower and change my clothes. He gave me what writers call a penetrating look and I felt he knew everything. He was only twenty-four but, already, he had faith, vision, direction. He might have heard of sin but you could see he was free of it, clean in every way.

I told Ted that after my shower I would find the Catholic chapel and attend Mass. He said, You don't need Mass. You don't need a priest. You have your faith, your Bible, two knees and a floor to pray on.

That made me feel cranky. Why can't people leave people alone? Why do people feel they have to convert the likes of me?

No, I did not want to drop to my knees and pray with the Methodist. Even worse, I didn't want to go to Mass or confession or anything else when I could go up there, walk the deck, sit in a chair and watch the horizon rise and fall.

Oh, to hell with it, I said, and took my shower, thinking of horizons. I thought horizons were better than people. They didn't bother other horizons. When I came out Ted was gone, his belongings neatly laid out on his bunk.

Up on deck the private nurse came sailing along on the arm of a short plump gray-haired man in a navy blue double-breasted blazer with a pink Ascot ballooning from his Adam's apple. She pretended she didn't see me but I stared so hard she had to give me a little nod. She passed on and I wondered if she waggled her arse deliberately to torment me.

Waggle on. I don't care.

But I cared. I felt destroyed, cast aside. After her three days with me how could that nurse go off with that old man who was at least sixty? What about the times sitting up in bed drinking bottles of white wine? What about the time I scrubbed her back in the tub? What was I to do with myself in the two days before the ship docked in Ireland? I'd have to lie on the top bunk with the Methodist praying and sighing below me. The nurse didn't care. She deliberately crossed my path on different decks to make me miserable, and when I thought about her and that old man it made me disgusted to think of his ancient wrinkled body next to hers.

The next two days it was darkness on the high seas as I stood at the rail and thought of jumping into the Atlantic Ocean, down to the bottom with all the ships that were sunk during the war, battleships, submarines, destroyers, freighters, and I wondered if an aircraft carrier was ever sunk. That got me off my misery for a while, wondering about the aircraft carriers and bodies below floating and bumping against the bulkheads, but the misery came back. When you're wandering around a ship with nothing to do but run into a nurse you spent three days with and she with the old man with the double-breasted blazer you're inclined to think little or nothing of yourself. If I jumped into the Atlantic it might give her something to think about, but it wouldn't do me any good because I'd never know.

I stood at that rail, with the ship whooshing along, thinking about my life and what a poltroon I was. (That was one of my favorite words at the time and it was apt.) Poltroon. All I did from the day I arrived in New York to this day on the *Queen Elizabeth* was meander from one thing to another: emigrate, work at dead-end jobs, drink in Germany and New York, chase women, sleep through four years at New York University, drift from one teaching job to another, marry and wish I was single, have another drink, hit a cul-de-sac in teaching, sail for Ireland with the hope that life would behave itself.

I wished I could be part of those jolly traveling groups, on land or sea, who play Ping-Pong and shuffleboard and then go off for a drink and who knows what else, but I didn't have the talent. In my head I practiced and rehearsed. Oh, hi, I'd say. How's it going? and they'd say, Fine, and by the way, won't you join us for a drink? and I'd say, Why not? with an air of insouciance. (That was another of my favorite words at the time because it was what I was aiming at, and because I liked the sound of it.) If I had a few drinks the insouciance might come. In my charming Irish way I'd be the life of the party, but I didn't want to leave the rail and the comfort of ending it all.

Thirty-eight was on my mind. Aging teacher sailing to Dublin, still a student. Is that any way for a man to live?

I forced myself onto a deck chair for a mid-Atlantic crisis meeting with myself, closed my eyes to shut out the ocean and the sight of the nurse. I couldn't block out the *click-clack* of her high heels and the American guffaw of Mr. Ancient Ascot.

If I had any kind of intelligence, beyond the mere sniffing survival skills, I would have attempted an agonizing reappraisal of my life. But I had no talent for introspection. After all those years of confession in Limerick I could examine my conscience with the best of them. This was different. Mother Church was no help here. On that deck chair I could barely venture beyond the catechism. I was beginning to understand that I did not understand, and digging into myself and my miseries made my head hurt. A thirty-eight-year-old in a mess and didn't know what to do about it. That's how ignorant I was. Now I know you're encouraged to blame everyone but yourself for everything: parents; the miserable childhood; the church; the English.

People in New York, Alberta especially, told me, You need help. I knew they were saying, You're obviously disturbed. You should see a shrink.

She insisted. She said I was impossible to live with and made an appointment for me with a psychoanalyst on East Ninety-sixth Street, shrink row. The man's name was Henry, and I got off on the wrong foot when I told him he looked like Jeeves. He said, Who's Jeeves? and he wasn't pleased when I told him about that P. G. Wodehouse character. He raised his eyebrows in a Jeevesian way and I felt like a fool. Besides, I did not know what this was all about, what I was doing in that office. I knew from psychology classes at NYU that the mind had various parts, the conscious, the unconscious, the subconscious, the ego, the id, the libido and maybe other little nooks and crannies where demons lurked. That was the extent of my knowledge, if it was knowledge at all. Then I wondered why I was paying money I could barely afford to sit opposite this man who scribbled in a notebook at chin level, stopping occasionally to stare at me as if I were a specimen.

He rarely spoke and I felt I had to fill in the silences or we'd just sit there gawking at each other. He never even said, And how do you feel about that? the way they do in the movies. When he closed his notebook I knew the session was over, and it was time for his fee. At the start he told me he would not charge me the full rate. I'd be getting the poor-teacher discount. I wanted to tell him I wasn't a charity case but I rarely said what was on my mind anyway.

His routine made me feel uncomfortable. He would come into the waiting room and stand. That was my signal to get up and walk into the consultation room. He never offered to shake hands, never passed the time of day. I wondered if it was my job to say hello or stick out my own hand and if I did how he would judge it. Would he say I was doing it out of my massive sense of inferiority? I didn't want to give him the kind of ammunition where he could decide I was a lunatic like certain ancestors in my family. I wanted to impress him with my cool demeanor, my logic and, if possible, my wit.

On the first visit he watched while I tried to decide what to do with myself. Would this be like confession? Examination of Conscience? Should I sit in that tall high chair or should I lie on the couch the way they do it in the movies? If I sat in the chair I'd have to face him for fifty minutes but if I stretched out on the couch I could look at the ceiling and avoid his eyes. I sat in the chair and he sat in his chair and I felt relieved there was no sign of disapproval on his face.

After a few visits I wanted to quit, walk over to a Third Avenue bar for the serenity of an afternoon beer. I didn't have the courage or I wasn't angry enough, yet. Week after week I sat and babbled in my chair, sometimes twice a week because, he said, I needed more frequent attention. I wanted to ask him why, but I was beginning to understand that his method was to make me figure it out for myself. If that's the case, I asked myself, Why am I paying him? Why couldn't I sit in Central Park and look at trees and squirrels and let my troubles swim to the surface? Or why couldn't I sit in a pub, have a few beers, look inward, examine my conscience? That would save hundreds of dollars. I wanted to come right out with it and say, Doctor, what's wrong with me? Why am I here? I'd like a diagnosis for all the money I'm paying you even if you're giving me the poor-teacher discount. If you put a name on my ailment I might be able to look it up and figure out a cure. I can't be coming in here week after week blathering about my life and not knowing whether I'm at the beginning or the middle or the end.

I could never talk to the man like that. I wasn't brought up like that. It wouldn't be polite and he might be offended. I wanted to look good, didn't want him to feel sorry for me. Surely he could see how reasonable and balanced I was, despite my struggle with a troubled marriage and my aimlessness in the world.

He scribbled away in his notebook and, even though he never showed it, I think he had a good time with me. I told him about my life in Ireland and in the classroom. I did my best to be lively and entertaining, to assure him all was well. I didn't want to upset him in any way. But if all was well, what was I doing there in the first place? I wanted to make him respond, one little smile, one little word to show his appreciation for my efforts. Nothing. He won. He carried the day.

Then he startled me. He said, Aha, dropped his notebook to his lap and stared at me. I was afraid to speak. What had I said to trigger this Aha?

I think you've hit paydirt, he said.

Oh, another paydirt moment. The chairman at Fashion Industries High School had complimented me on hitting paydirt with my lesson on the parts of the sentence.

All I had said before the Aha was that, outside of my high school classes, I felt shy with people. In groups I could hardly talk unless I'd had a few drinks, unlike my wife or my brother, who could march up to people and get into lively conversations. That was the paydirt.

After the Aha he said, Hmm. You might benefit from participation in a group. It might be a step forward if you interacted with other people. We have a small group here. You'd be number six.

I didn't want to be number six. I didn't know what interacting meant. Whatever it was I didn't want to do it. How could I tell him the way I felt, that this was all a waste of time and money? I had to be polite no matter what. Six weeks blathering in this chair and I felt worse than ever. When would I be able to walk up to people and chat in that easy Alberta, Malachy way?

My wife said it was a good idea even if it cost more money every week. She said I lacked certain social skills, that I was a little rough around the edges, that group work might lead to a big breakthrough.

That led to a quarrel that lasted for hours. Who was she to tell me I was rough around the edges like some mick fresh off the boat with bog mud on his brogues? I told her I was not going to spend hours with a bunch of New York loonies whining about their lives and trotting out intimate secrets. Bad enough I spent my youth whispering my sins to priests who yawned and made me promise never to sin again for fear of offending poor Jesus suffering up there on the cross for my sins. Now she and the shrink wanted me to blab again. No.

She said she was sick of hearing about my miserable little Catholic childhood. I didn't blame her. I was sick of my miserable childhood, too, the way it followed me across the Atlantic and kept nagging at me to be made public. Alberta said if I didn't continue my therapy I was in deep trouble.

Therapy? What do you mean?

That's what you're getting, and if you don't stick with it this marriage is over.

That was tempting. If I were single again I'd be free to wander Manhattan. I could have said, All right. The marriage is over, but I let it go. Even if I were free what woman in her right mind would have me anyway, a meandering rough-around-the-edges pedagogue blabbing his life away to a Jeeves on East Ninety-sixth Street? I thought of an Irish saying, "Contention is better than loneliness," and stayed where I was.

They said shocking things in that group. There was talk of sex with fathers, mothers, brothers, sisters, visiting uncles, a rabbi's wife, an Irish setter, sex with a jar of chicken livers, sex with a man who came to fix a refrigerator and stayed for days with his clothes dropped on the kitchen floor. These were things you'd reveal only to a priest, but these group people didn't mind telling their secrets to the world. I knew a bit about sex. I had read the Kama Sutra, *Lady Chatterly's Lover,* and the *One Hundred and Twenty Days of Sodom* of the Marquis de Sade, but they were only books and all in the imagination of the authors, I thought. D. H. Lawrence and the Marquis himself would have been shocked if they'd sat in this group.

We sat in a semicircle with Henry facing us, scribbling away in his notebook, occasionally nodding. Then one day there was a silence after one man talked about going to Mass and taking the communion wafer home to masturbate on it. He said that was his way of severing all connection with the Roman Catholic Church and what he did was so thrilling he often repeated that little act just for the fun. He knew there wasn't a priest in the world who would give him absolution for such an abomination.

This was my fourth session with this group and I hadn't said a word. At that moment I wanted to get up and walk out. I wasn't much of a Catholic anymore, but I would never think of using a communion wafer for my sexual enjoyment. Why didn't that man simply quit the church and go about his business?

Henry knew what I was thinking. He stopped scribbling and asked me if there was anything I wanted to say to that man and I felt my face burning. I shook my head. A red-haired woman said, Oh, come on. You've been here four times. You haven't said a word. Why should we expose ourselves so you can leave here every day all smug and silent and tell our secrets to your friends in bars?

The man with the communion story said, Yeah, I put myself on the line here, buddy, and we'd like to hear from you. What's your plan? You gonna sit on your ass and let us do the work?

Henry asked Irma, young woman to my left, what she thought of me, and I was surprised when she massaged my shoulder and said she felt power. She said she'd like to be a student in my class, that I must be a good teacher.

Did you hear that, Frank? said Henry. Power.

I knew they were waiting for me to say something. I felt I should make a contribution. I once slept with a prostitute in Germany, I said.

Oh, well, said the red-haired woman. Give him credit. He tried.

Big deal, said the communion man.

Tell us about it, said Irma.

I went to bed with her.

So? said the red-haired woman.

That's all. I went to bed with her. I paid her four marks.

Henry saved me. Time is up. See you next week.

I never went back. I thought he might telephone to see why I had dropped out, but Alberta said they were not supposed to do that. You had to make up your own mind, and if you didn't return, it meant you were sicker than ever. She said a therapist could do only so much, and if I wanted to take chances with my mental health, Your blood be upon your head.

What?

It's from the Bible.

I am leaving the office of Professor Walton, head of the English Department at Trinity College. He said, Yes, quite, to my application for admission to the doctoral program and, Yes, quite, to my dissertation topic, "Irish-American Literary Relations, 1889–1911." Why these terminal dates? In 1889 William Butler Yeats published his first book of poetry and in 1911, in Philadelphia, Abbey Theater actors were pelted with various objects after a performance of *The Playboy of the Western World*. Professor Walton said, Interesting. My dissertation mentor would be Professor Brendan Kenneally, he said, A fine young poet and scholar from County Kerry. I was now, officially, a Trinity man, exalted, dwelling in marble halls. I tried to walk out the front gate like a man accustomed to walking out that front gate. I walked very slowly so that the American tourists would notice me. Back in Minneapolis they'd tell the folks how they spotted an authentic debonair Trinity man.

When you're admitted to the doctoral program at Trinity you might as well celebrate by walking up Grafton Street to McDaid's pub where you sat long ago with Mary from Bewley's. A man at the bar said, Over from America, I suppose? How did he know? It's the clothes. You can always tell a Yank by the clothes, he said. I felt friendly, told him about Trinity, the dream come true. He turned hostile. Jaysus, it's a sad fookin' day when you have to come to

Dublin for a fookin' university. Don't they have tons of 'em in America, or is it the way they didn't want you and are you a Protestant or what?

Was he joking? I'd have to get used to the ways of Dublin men.

It was dawning on me that I was an outsider, foreigner, returned Yank and, on top of it, a Limerickman. I thought I'd come back a conquering hero, a returned Yank with college degrees, bachelor and master, man who survived nearly ten years in the high schools of New York. I made the mistake of thinking I'd fit into the warm life of Dublin pubs. I thought I'd move in a circle so bright, witty and literary that American scholars, prowling its periphery, would relay my every bon mot to academia back home and I'd be invited to lecture on the Irish literary scene to irresistible coeds at Vassar and Sarah Lawrence.

It was not to be. If there was a circle I was never part of it. I prowled the periphery.

I stayed in Dublin for two years. My first apartment was at Seaview Terrace off Ailesbury Road, where Anthony Trollope lived when he rode his horse around Ireland as a postal inspector and every morning wrote three thousand words. My landlady told me his ghost still walked and she was convinced the manuscript of a major novel was hidden in the walls of his old house. I knew the ghost of Mr. Trollope was in residence because of the way the grease would suddenly congeal around my fried eggs and rashers when he made his midnight rounds. I explored the apartment looking for that manuscript till the neighbors complained about my knocking on the walls at all hours. I floundered in Dublin. I started every day with the best intentions. I had morning coffee at Bewley's and worked at the National Library or the Trinity College library. At noon I told myself I was hungry and strolled out for a sandwich at a nearby pub: Neary's, McDaid's, the Bailey. A sandwich needs to be washed down with a pint and, as the wags said, Bird never flew on one wing. Another pint might loosen my tongue and help me chat with other customers and soon I convinced myself I was enjoying myself. When the pubs closed for the afternoon holy hour I had coffee again at Bewley's. It was all procrastination. Weeks passed and my research into Irish-American literary relations was going nowhere. I told myself I was an ignoramus who knew nothing of American literature and had a sketchy grasp of Irish literature. I would need background and that meant reading the histories of both countries. When I read Irish history I filled index cards with any reference to America. When I read American history I filled index cards with any reference to Ireland.

Reading the histories was not enough. Now I had to read the major authors and discover how they influenced or were influenced by their counterparts on the other side of the Atlantic. Of course Yeats had American connections and influences. Of course Edmund Dowden, of Trinity College, was one of the first Europeans to champion Walt Whitman, but what was I to do with all this? What was I to say? And, after all my troubles, would anyone give a fiddler's fart?

I had made other discoveries, and off I went snuffling down paths far from American Transcendentalism and the Irish Literary Revival. Here were accounts of the Irish hacking and digging and fighting and singing on the Erie Canal, on the Union Pacific Railroad and in the American Civil War itself. On opposite sides, Irishmen often fought their own brothers and cousins. It seemed that wherever there was a war the Irish fought on both sides, even in Ireland. At school in Limerick we heard repeatedly the long sad story of Ireland's sufferings under the Saxon heel, but barely a word about the Irish in America, their building and fighting and singing. Now I read about Irish music in America, the power and genius of the Irish in American politics, the exploits of the Fighting 69th, the millions who cleared a path to the Oval Office for John F. Kennedy. I read accounts of how mean Yankees discriminated against the Irish all over New England and how the Irish fought back and became mayors, governors, party bosses.

I kept a separate pile of index cards for the story of the Irish in America, a pile that grew higher than the one on literary relations. It was all enough to keep me away from the pubs at lunchtime, enough to keep me from the work I should have been doing on Irish-American literary relations.

Could I change my dissertation topic? Would Trinity allow me to present some aspect of the Irish in America, politics, music, the military, entertainment?

Professor Walton said that would not be possible in the English Department. I seemed to be straying into history and that would require approval of the History Department, which he doubted would be possible since I had no background in history. I had already spent a year at Trinity and would have only one more year to finish my dissertation on Irish-American literary relations. The professor said one must keep one's hand firmly on the helm.

How could I tell my wife in New York I'd squandered a year exploring the ditches and railbeds of Irish-American history when I should have been improving my knowledge of literature?

I hung on in Dublin making feeble attempts at shaping some kind of dissertation. If I went to a pub lunch and cleared my head with a pint surely there would be an insight, a flash of inspiration. Surely. My money went over the bar. The pint came back. Nothing else.

I sat on a bench in St. Stephen's Green coveting the office girls of Dublin. Would they run away with me to Coney Island, Far Rockaway, the Hamptons?

I watched the ducks in the pond and envied them. All they had to do in the world was quack, paddle and open their mouths for morsels. They didn't have to worry about the dissertation that was killing me. How and why did I ever get into this? Jesus! I could be in New York, grateful for my lot, teaching my five classes a day, going home, having a beer, going to a movie, reading a book, cooing to the wife and so to bed.

Oh, but no. Little snotty-nosed Frankie from the lanes of Limerick tried to rise above his station, climb the social ladder, mingle with a better class of people, the quality of Trinity College.

This is what you get, Frankie, for your paltry ambition. Why don't you run down the street and buy yourself a Trinity scarf? See if that will lift your spirits, help you write that grand original study of Irish-American literary relations, 1889 to 1911.

There is an activity called "pulling yourself together." I tried, but what was there to pull together?

The second year in Dublin dribbled away. I couldn't find my niche there. I didn't have the personality or the self-confidence to shoulder my way into a group, be one of the lads, buy my round and make the witty comments you're supposed to hear in Irish pubs.

I sat in the library and added to my mountain of index cards. Drinking added to my addleheadedness. I went for long walks around the city, up one street and down the other. I met a woman, a Protestant, and we went to bed. She fell in love with me, and I didn't know why.

I wandered the streets of Dublin looking for the door. I had a notion that in any city there was a way in for the outsider and the traveler. In New York, for me, it was schools and bars and friendship. There was no door for me in Dublin and I had to admit, finally, what ailed me: I missed New York. At first, I resisted the feeling. Go away. Leave me alone. I love Dublin. Look at the history. Every street is brimming with the past. I dreamt of Dublin when I was a child in Limerick. Yes, but, yes, but yes, as my Uncle Pa Keating would say, You're going on forty, so it's time to shit or get off the pot.

Before I left Trinity, Professor Walton glanced over the index cards and said, My, my.

In January of 1971, I returned to New York, a failing doctoral candidate. Alberta was pregnant. We had conceived the summer before, during our fortnight stay in Nantucket. I told her I could continue research at the Forty-second Street Library in New York. She was impressed with my bag of index cards, but wanted to know what purpose they served.

Every Saturday I sat in the South Reading Room of the Forty-second Street Library. I should have sat in the North Reading Room in the literature section but I found the *Lives of the Saints* in the South and they were too gripping to be ignored. Then I happened on accounts of the building of the Transcontinental Railroad, how the Irish and the Chinese, coming from opposite directions, competed, how the Irish drank and undermined their health while the Chinese smoked opium and rested, how the Irish didn't care what they ate while the Chinese nourished themselves on the food they knew and loved, how the Chinese never sang while they worked and how the Irish never stopped, for all the good it did them, the poor crazy Irish.

Alberta went on maternity leave and I took her place back at Seward. But a month after I started at Seward Park High School the principal died of a heart attack. Then I met the new principal in the elevator, the department chairman who had fired me from Fashion Industries High School. I said, Are you following me? and when his mouth tightened I knew, once again, my days were numbered.

A few weeks later I sealed my doom. In the presence of other teachers, the principal asked, So, Mr. McCourt, are you a father yet?

No, not yet.

Well, what do you want, a boy or a girl?

Oh, it's all the same to me.

Well, he said, as long as it's not a neuter.

Well, if it is, I'll train it to grow up and be a principal.

The letter that I was being "excessed" soon followed, signed by Assistant Principal (Acting) Mitchel B. Schulich.

A failed everything, I looked for my place in the world. I became an itinerant substitute teacher, drifting from school to school. High schools called me for day-to-day work to replace sick teachers. Some schools needed me when teachers were called for long spells of jury duty. I was assigned classes in English or wherever a teacher was needed: biology, art, physics, history, mathematics. Substitute teachers like me floated somewhere on the fringes of reality. I was asked daily, And who are you today?

Mrs. Katz.

Oh.

And that's what you were: Mrs. Katz or Mr. Gordon or Ms. Newman. You were never yourself. You were always Oh.

In the classroom I had no authority. Assistant principals sometimes told me what to teach, but students paid no attention and there was nothing I could do. The ones who came to class ignored me and chatted, asked for the pass, rested their heads on desks and dozed, floated paper airplanes, studied for other subjects.

I learned how to discourage them from coming to class at all: If you want an empty classroom all you have to do is stand at the classroom door and scowl. They'll decide you're mean and run. Only Chinese came to class. They must have been warned by their parents. They sat in the back and studied, resisting my subtle hints that they disappear, too. Principals and their assistants looked displeased when they saw me sitting at the teacher's desk reading the paper or a book in a near-empty room. They said I should be teaching. That's what I was hired for. I would gladly teach, I said, but this is a physics class and my license is in English. They knew it was a silly question, but they were supervisors and had to ask, Where are the kids? Everyone in every school knew the rule: When you see a substitute teacher, run, baby, run.

PART III

Coming Alive
in Room 205

12

A year after I returned from Dublin, our old friend R'lene Dahlberg introduced me to Roger Goodman, head of the English Department at Stuyvesant High School. He asked if I would be interested in covering the classes of Mr. Joe Curran for a month or so while he convalesced from something. Stuyvesant was said to be the top high school in the city, the Harvard of high schools, alma mater of various Nobel Prize winners, of James Cagney himself, a school where, as soon as a boy or girl was admitted, doors opened to the best universities in the country. Thirteen thousand candidates sat every year for the Stuyvesant admissions test and the school skimmed off the top seven hundred.

Now I taught where I could never have been one of the seven hundred.

When Joe Curran returned after a few months Roger Goodman offered me a permanent position. He said the kids liked me, that I was a vital, engaging teacher, that I'd be a valuable addition to the English Department. I was embarrassed by this praise but I said yes and thank you. I promised myself I'd stay only two years. Teachers all over the city vied for jobs at Stuyvesant High School, but I wanted to be out in the world. At the end of a school day you leave with a head filled with adolescent noises, their worries, their dreams. They follow you to dinner, to the movies, to the bathroom, to the bed.

You try to put them out of your mind. Go away. Go away. I'm reading a book, the paper, the writing on the wall. Go away.

I wanted to be doing something adult and significant, going to meetings, dictating to my secretary, sitting with glamorous people at long mahogany boardroom tables, flying to conventions, unwinding in trendy bars, sliding into bed with luscious women, entertaining them before and after with witty pillow talk, commuting to Connecticut.

When my daughter was born in 1971 my fantasies faded before her sweet reality and I began to feel at home in the world. Every morning I gave Maggie her bottle, changed her diaper, dipped her bottom in warm soapy water in the kitchen sink, resisted the morning newspaper because of the time it would consume, stood with the rush-hour crowd on the train from Brooklyn to Manhattan, walked along Fifteenth Street to Stuyvesant, made my way through a crowd of waiting students to the front door, pushed in, said good morning to the guard, punched in at the time clock, took a pile of papers from my mailbox, said good morning to teachers punching in, opened the door to my empty classroom, room 205, opened windows with the long pole, sat and looked over the empty desks, relaxed for the few minutes before my first class, thought of my daughter gurgling that morning in the kitchen sink, watched dust dancing in the shaft of sunlight piercing the room, took the attendance book from a drawer and spread it on the desk, erased from the blackboard grammar notes from last night's French lesson in the adult evening school, opened the classroom door, said hi to the surge of students in the first class.

Roger Goodman said it was important to teach diagramming. He loved the structure and Euclidian beauty of it. I said, Oh, because I knew nothing about diagramming. He told me these things at lunch in the Gas House Bar and Restaurant around the corner from the school.

Roger was short and bald, his baldness offset by rich bushy black-and-gray eyebrows and a short beard, which lent him a twinkling impishness.

He lunched with teachers. That made him unusual among assistant principals, who reminded me of the Cabots and Lodges.

In Boston, the home of the bean and the cod,
Where Cabots speak only to Lodges
And Lodges speak only to God.

Some afternoons Roger came to the Gas House to drink with us. He had no affectations, always cheerful, always encouraging, a supervisor you could feel comfortable with. He put on no airs, no intellectual pretensions, and mocked bureaucratic gobbledygook. I don't think he could have uttered "pedagogical strategizing" without chuckling.

He trusted me. He seemed to think I could teach on any of the four levels of high school: freshman, sophomore, junior, senior. He even asked what I'd like to teach and took me to the room where books were organized by grade. It was dazzling to see them ranged on shelves reaching to the twenty-foot ceilings and stacked on carts for delivery to classrooms. There were anthologies of English, American and world literature, piles of *The Scarlet Letter, The Catcher in the Rye, The Painted Bird, Moby-Dick, Arrowsmith, Intruder in the Dust, Lie Down in Darkness, Introduction to Poetry* by X. F. Kennedy. There were dictionaries, collections of poetry, short stories, plays, textbooks on journalism and grammar.

Take whatever you want, said Roger, and if there's anything else you'd like we can order it. Take your time. Think about it tonight. Let's go to the Gas House for lunch.

School, books, lunch. It was all one to Roger. He did not change hats. At day's end when teachers lined up to punch out and rush home he'd waggle his eyebrows and invite you around the corner for a stirrup cup, one for the road. For the long journey to his apartment at the far end of Brooklyn a man needed sustenance. He would sometimes drive me home, on three-martini days a drive slow and deliberate. Perched on the cushion that elevated his short body he would hold the steering wheel as if guiding a tugboat. Next day he'd confess he didn't remember much about the drive.

In my years of teaching this was the first time I felt free in the classroom. I could teach whatever I liked. If outsiders stuck their heads in the door it didn't matter. When Roger came for a rare observation he wrote enthusiastic positive reports. He broke down my resistance to anyone in the world a step or two above me. I told him what I was doing in my classes and all I got was encouragement. Sometimes he'd slip in a word or two about the necessity of teaching diagramming and I'd promise to try it. After a while it was a joke.

I tried but failed. I made lines vertical, horizontal, slanting, and then I stood, adrift at the blackboard, till a Chinese student volunteered to take over and teach the teacher what the teacher should have known.

My students were patient, but I could tell from the looks they exchanged, and the traffic in notes passing back and forth, that I was in a grammar wilderness. At Stuyvesant they had to know grammar for their classes in Spanish, French, German, Hebrew, Italian, Latin.

Roger understood. He said, Maybe diagramming is not your strong point. He said some people just don't have it. R'lene Dahlberg had it. Joe Curran certainly had it. After all, he was a graduate of Boston Latin, a school two and a half centuries older than Stuyvesant and, he claimed, more prestigious. Teaching at Stuyvesant for him was a step down in the world. He could diagram in Greek and Latin and probably French and German. That's the kind of training you get at Boston Latin. Jesse Lowenthal had it, too, but of course he would. He was the oldest teacher in the department with his elegant three-piece suit, the gold watch chain looping across his waistcoat front, his gold-rimmed spectacles, his old-world manners, his scholarship, Jesse who did not want to retire but, when he did, planned to spend his days studying Greek and drifting into the next life with Homer on his lips. It pleased Roger to know he had in his department a solid core of teachers who could be relied on to diagram at a moment's notice.

Roger said it was sad Joe Curran had such a drinking problem. Otherwise he could have entertained Jesse with miles of Homer from memory and, if Jesse was up to it, Virgil and Horace, and the one Joe favored out of his own great anger, Juvenal himself.

In the teachers' cafeteria Joe told me, Read your Juvenal so you'll understand what's going on in this miserable fookin' country.

Roger said it was sad about Jesse. Here he is in his twilight years with Christ only knows how many years of teaching under his belt. He doesn't have the same energy for five classes a day. He asked to have his load reduced to four but no, oh no, the principal says no, the superintendent says no, all the way up the bureaucracy they say no, and Jesse says good-bye. Hello Homer. Hello Ithaca. Hello Troy. That's Jesse. We're going to lose a great teacher and, boy, could he diagram. What he did with a sentence and a piece of chalk would stun you. Beautiful.

If you asked the boys and girls of Stuyvesant High School to write three hundred and fifty words on any subject they might respond with five hundred. They had words to spare.

If you asked all the students in your five classes to write three hundred and fifty words each then you had 175 multiplied by 350 and that was 43,750 words you had to read, correct, evaluate and grade on evenings and weekends. That's if you were wise enough to give them only one assignment per week. You had to correct misspellings, faulty grammar, poor structure, transitions, sloppiness in general. You had to make suggestions on content and write a general comment explaining your grade. You reminded them there was no extra credit for papers adorned with ketchup, mayonnaise, coffee, Coke, tears, grease, dandruff. You suggested strongly they write their papers at desk or table and not on train, bus, escalator or in the hubbub of Joe's Original Pizza joint around the corner.

If you gave each paper a bare five minutes you'd spend, on this one set of papers, fourteen hours and thirty-five minutes. That would amount to more than two teaching days, and the end of the weekend.

You hesitate to assign book reports. They are longer and rich in plagiarism.

Every day I carried home books and papers in a fake brown

leather bag. My intention was to settle into a comfortable chair and read the papers, but after a day of five classes and 175 teenagers I was not inclined to prolong that day with their work. It could wait, damn it. I deserved a glass of wine or a cup of tea. I'd get to the papers later. Yes, a nice cup of tea and a read of the paper or a walk around the neighborhood or a few minutes with my little daughter when she told me about her school and the things she did with her friend Claire. Also, I ought to scan a newspaper in order to keep up with the world. An English teacher should know what's going on. You never knew when one of your students might bring up something about foreign policy or a new Off-Broadway play. You wouldn't want to be caught up there in front of the room with your mouth going and nothing coming out.

That's the life of the high school English teacher.

The bag sat on the floor in a corner by the kitchen, never far from sight or mind, an animal, a dog waiting for attention. Its eyes followed me. I didn't want to hide it in a closet for fear I might forget completely there were papers to read and correct.

There was no point in trying to read them before dinner. I'd wait till later, help with the dishes, put my daughter to bed, get down to work. Get that bag, man. Sit on the couch where you can spread things out, put some music on the phonograph or turn on the radio. Nothing distracting. Some acoustic syrup. Music to grade papers by. Settle yourself on the couch.

Rest your head a minute before you tackle the first paper on your lap, "My Stepfather the Jerk." More teen angst. Close your eyes a moment. Ah . . . drift, teacher, drift . . . You're floating. A slight snore wakes you. Papers on the floor. Back to work. Scan the paper. Well-written. Focused. Organized. Bitter. Oh, the things this girl says about her stepfather, that he's a bit too familiar with her. Invites her to movies and dinner when her mother works overtime. And there's the way he looks at her. Mother says, Oh, that's nice, but there's something about her eyes, and then the silence. Writer wonders what she should do. Is she asking me, the teacher? And should I do something? Am I to respond, help her out of her dilemma? If there is a dilemma. Stick my nose into family matters where it doesn't belong? She could be making it up. What if I say something and it gets back to stepfather or mother? I could read and evaluate this paper objectively, congratulate the writer on the clarity and development of her theme. That's what I'm there for, isn't it? I'm not supposed to get involved in every little family squabble, especially in Stuyvesant High School, where they like to "let it all hang out." Teachers tell me half these kids are in therapy and the other half should join them. I'm not a social worker or a therapist. Is this a cry for help or another teenage fantasy? No, no, too many problems in these classes. Kids in other schools were never like this. They didn't turn the class into group therapy. Stuyvesant is different. I could give this paper to a guidance counselor. Here, Sam, you take care of this. If I didn't, and it came out later that the stepfather abused the girl and the world knew I'd let it slip by, important people in the school system would summon me to their offices: assistant principals, principals, superintendents. They would want explanations. How could you, experienced teacher, let this happen? My name might even blaze across page three of the tabloids.

Make a few marks with the red pen. Give her a 98. The writing is terrific, but there are spelling errors. Congratulate her on writing that is honest and mature, and tell her, Janice, you have great promise and I hope to see more of your work in the coming weeks.

They have ideas I want to dissipate, about the private lives of teachers. I tell them, In your head choose one of your teachers. Don't tell anyone the name. Don't write it down. Now speculate. When that teacher leaves the school every day what does he—or she—do? Where does he go?

You know. After school, teacher goes directly home. Carries a bag filled with papers to be read and marked. Might have a cup of tea with spouse. Oh, no. Teacher would never have a glass of wine. That's not how teachers live. They don't go out. Maybe a movie on the weekend. They have dinner. They put their kids to bed. They watch the news before they settle in for the night to read those papers. At eleven it's time for another cup of tea or a glass of warm milk to help them sleep. Then they put on pajamas, kiss the spouse and drift off.

Teachers' pajamas are always cotton. What would a teacher be doing in silk pajamas? And, no, they never sleep naked. If you suggest nudity students look shocked. Man, can you imagine some teachers in this school naked? That always triggers a big laugh and I wonder if they're sitting there imagining me naked.

What is the last thing teachers think about before sleeping?

Before they drift off, all those teachers, snug and warm in their cotton pajamas, think only of what they might teach tomorrow. Teachers are good, proper, professional, conscientious, and they'd never throw a leg over the other one in the bed. Below the belly button the teacher is dead.

In 1974, my third year at Stuyvesant High School, I am invited to be the new Creative Writing instructor. Roger Goodman says, You can do it.

I know nothing about writing or the teaching of it. Roger says don't worry. Across this country there are hundreds of teachers and professors teaching writing and most have never published a word.

And look at you, says Bill Ince, Roger's successor. You've had pieces published here and there. I tell him a few pieces in *The Village Voice, Newsday* and a defunct magazine in Dublin hardly qualifies me to teach writing. It will be common knowledge soon that in the matter of teaching writing I don't know my arse from my elbow. But I remember a remark of my mother's: God help us, but sometimes you have to chance your arm.

I can never bring myself to say I teach creative writing or poetry or literature, especially since I am always learning myself. Instead I say I conduct a course, or I run a class.

I have the usual five classes a day, three "regular" English, two

Creative Writing. I have a homeroom of thirty-seven students, with the clerical work that entails. Each term I am given a different Building Assignment: patrolling hallways and stairwells; checking boys' lavatories for smoking; substituting for absent teachers; watching for drug traffic; discouraging high jinks of any kind; supervising student cafeterias; supervising the school lobby to ensure that everyone, coming or going, has an official pass. Where three thousand bright teenagers are gathered under one roof you can't be too careful. They are always up to something. It's their job.

They moaned when I announced we were going to read *A Tale of Two Cities*. Why couldn't they read *The Lord of the Rings, Dune,* science fiction in general? Why couldn't they . . . ?

Enough. I ranted at them about the French Revolution, the desperation of people drained by tyranny and poverty. I was one with the downtrodden French and having a grand time with my righteous indignation. To the barricades, *mes enfants*.

They gave me the look, the one that says, Here we go again. Another teacher with a bug up his ass.

Not that you care, I jeered. Even now there are billions of people who don't slide out of their warm white sheets every morning to relieve themselves in warm white bathrooms. There are billions who know nothing about hot and cold running water, bars of perfumed soap, shampoo, conditioner, great luxurious towels with naps thick as your skulls.

Their faces said, Oh, let the man talk. You can't win when teachers are like that. Nothing you can do about it. Talk back and he gets out the old red pen and makes the little red mark that drops your grade. Then your dad says, What's this? and you have to explain teacher has a bug up his ass about the poor or something. Your dad doesn't believe you and you're grounded for a million years. So, best thing is to keep your mouth shut. With parents and teachers you can't go wrong with the shut mouth. Just listen to him.

You'll go home today to your comfortable apartments and houses, head for the refrigerator, open the door, survey contents, find nothing that will please you, ask Mom if you can send out for pizza even though you'll have dinner in an hour. She says, Sure, honey, because you have a hard life going to school every day and putting up with teachers who want you to read Dickens and why shouldn't you have a little reward.

Even during the rant I knew they were seeing me as another great predictable two-faced pain in the arse. Did they know I was enjoying it? Teacher as demagogue. It wasn't their fault if they were bourgeois and comfortable and wasn't I carrying on that old Irish tradition of begrudgery? So, back off, Mac.

In the front, under my nose, Sylvia raises her hand. She's black, petite and stylish.

Mr. McCourt.

Yes.

Mr. McCourt.

What?

You're losing it, Mr. McCourt. Chill. Relax. Where's that big old Irish smile?

I was about to bark that the sufferings of the French poor that triggered the revolution were not a smiling matter, but the class drowned me out with laughter and applause for Sylvia.

Yeah, Sylvia. You go, girl.

She smiled up at me. Oh, those great brown eyes. I felt weak and foolish. I slid to my chair and let them joke the rest of the period about how they'd mend their ways. They'd be worthy of Charles Dickens. They'd start by giving up the afternoon pizza. The money they saved they'd send to descendants of the poor people in the French Revolution. Or they'd give it to the homeless on First Avenue, especially the man who was insulted if you offered him less than five dollars.

When the class ended Ben Chan lingered in the room. Mr. McCourt, could I talk to you?

He knew what I was saying about poverty. The kids in this class didn't understand anything. But it wasn't their fault and I shouldn't get mad. He was twelve when he came to this country four years ago. He knew no English but he studied hard and learned enough English and mathematics to pass the Stuyvesant High School entrance exam. He was happy to be here and his whole family was so proud of him. People back in China were proud of him. He competed against fourteen thousand kids to get into this school. His father worked six days a week, twelve hours a day, in a restaurant in Chinatown. His mother worked in a downtown sweatshop. Every night she cooked dinner for the whole family, five children, her husband, herself. Then she helped them get their clothes ready for the next day. Every month she had younger ones try on the clothes of the older kids to see if they'd fit. She said when everyone was grown and none of the clothes fit anymore, she'd keep them for the next family from China or she'd send them right over there. Americans could never understand the excitement in a Chinese family when something came from America. His mother made sure the children sat at the kitchen table and did their homework. He could never call his parents silly names like Mom or Dad. That would be so disrespectful. They learned English words every day so that they could talk to teachers and keep up with the children. Ben said everyone in his family respected everyone else and they'd never laugh at a teacher talking about the poor people of France because it could just as easily be China or even Chinatown right here in New York.

I told him the story of his family was impressive and moving and wouldn't it be a tribute to his mother if he were to write it and read it to the class?

Oh, no, he could never do that. Never.

Why not? Surely the kids in this class would learn something and appreciate what they have.

He said, no, he could never write or talk to anyone else about his family because his father and mother would be ashamed.

Ben, I feel honored you told me about your family.

Oh, I just wanted to tell you something I wouldn't tell anyone else in case you were feeling bad after that class.

Thanks, Ben.

Thank you, Mr. McCourt, and don't worry about Sylvia. She really likes you.

Next day Sylvia stayed after class. Mr. McCourt, about yesterday. I didn't mean to be mean.

I know, Sylvia. You were trying to help.

The class didn't mean to be mean, either. They just hear grown-ups and teachers yelling at them all the time. But I knew what you were talking about. I have to go through all kinds of stuff when I go down my street every day in Brooklyn.

What stuff?

Well, it's like this. I live in Bedford-Stuyvesant. You know Bed-Stuy?

Yes. Black neighborhood.

So there is nobody on my street ever gonna go to college. Whoops.

What's the matter?

I said gonna. If my mom heard me say gonna she'd make me write "going to" a hundred times. Then she'd make me say it another hundred times. So, what I'm saying is, when I walk to my house there are kids out there jeering at me. Oh, here she come. Here come whitey. Hey, Doc, you scrape yourself an' you find that honky skin? They call me Doc because I wanna, want to, be a doctor. 'Course I feel sorry for the poor French, but we have our own troubles in Bed-Stuy.

What kind of doctor will you be?

Pediatrician or psychiatrist. I want to get to the kids before the streets get to them and tell them they're no good because I see kids in my neighborhood afraid to show how smart they are and the next thing is they're acting stupid in vacant lots and burned-out buildings. You know there's a lotta, lot of, smart kids in poor neighborhoods.

Mr. McCourt, will you tell us one of those Irish stories tomorrow?

For you, Doctor Sylvia, I would recite an epic. This stuck in my memory like a rock, forever. When I was fourteen, growing up in Ireland, I had a job delivering telegrams. One day I delivered a telegram to a place called the Good Shepherd Convent, a community of nuns and lay women who made lace and ran a laundry. There were stories in Limerick that the lay women in the laundry were bad women known for leading men astray. Telegram boys were not allowed to use the front door, so I went to a side door. The telegram I was delivering required an answer, so the nun answering the door told me step inside, that far and no farther, and wait. She put down on her chair a piece of lace she was working on and when she disappeared down the hallway I peered at the design, a little lace cherub hovering over a shamrock. I don't know where I found the courage to speak, but when she returned I told her, That's a lovely piece of lace, sister.

That's right, boy, and remember this: The hands that fashioned this lace never touched flesh of man.

The nun glared at me as if she hated me. Priests were always preaching love on Sundays, but this nun probably missed the sermon, and I told myself if I ever had a telegram again for the Good Shepherd Convent, I'd slip it under the door and run.

Sylvia said, That nun. Why was she so mean? What was her problem? What's wrong with touching flesh of man? Jesus was a man. She's like that mean priest in James Joyce going on about hell. You believe all that stuff, Mr. McCourt?

I don't know what I believe except that I wasn't put on this earth to be Catholic or Irish or vegetarian or anything. That's all I know, Sylvia.

When I discussed *A Portrait of the Artist as a Young Man* with my classes I discovered they were ignorant of the Seven Deadly Sins. Blank looks around the room. I wrote on the blackboard: Pride, Greed, Lust, Anger, Gluttony, Envy, Sloth. If you don't know them, how can you enjoy yourselves?

So, like, Mr. McCourt, what does this have to do with creative writing?

Everything. You don't have to be poor and Catholic and Irish to be miserable, but it gives you something to write about and an excuse for drinking. Wait. I take that back. Delete the part about the drinking.

When my marriage collapsed I was forty-nine, Maggie eight. I was broke and slept in a series of friends' apartments in Brooklyn and Manhattan. Teaching forced me to forget my troubles. I could cry into my beer at the Gas House or the Lion's Head Bar, but in the classroom I had to get on with business.

In a while I would borrow money from the Teachers' Pension Fund to rent and furnish an apartment. Till then, Yonk Kling invited me to stay in the apartment he rented on Hicks Street near Atlantic Avenue.

Yonk was an artist and restorer in his sixties. He came from the Bronx, where his father was a politically radical doctor. Any revolutionary or anarchist passing through New York was welcome to a dinner and a bed at Dr. Kling's. Yonk went through World War II working in Graves Registration. After a battle he searched the area for bodies or parts of bodies. He told me he never wanted to fight but this was worse, and he often felt like asking for a transfer to the infantry where you just shot your man and moved on. You didn't have to finger the dog tags of the dead or look in their wallets at pictures of wives and kids.

Yonk still had nightmares and his best cure or defense was a generous shot of brandy, something he always kept in his bedroom. I could gauge the frequency of the nightmares by the level in the bottle.

He painted in his room. He moved from bed to chair to easel and everything was part of everything else. When he woke he would lie in bed, smoke a cigarette, study the canvas he'd worked on the day before. He brought his mug of coffee from the kitchen to the bedroom, where he sat on a chair and continued looking at the canvas. He would dab at the work from time to time to correct or erase something. He never finished his coffee. There were half-filled mugs all over the apartment. When the coffee turned cold it curdled and developed a ring halfway down the cup.

There was one scene he painted over and over on canvases of various sizes: a group of women in bright pastel head scarves and long flowing silky dresses stood on a beach looking out to sea. I asked him if someone had drowned or were they waiting for something? He shook his head. He didn't know. How could he? He had just put those women there and he wasn't going to interfere with them. That's what he disliked about certain artists and writers. They interfered and pointed to everything as if you couldn't see or read for yourself. Not Van Gogh. Look at Van Gogh. There's the bridge, the sunflower, the room, the face, the shoes. Come to your own conclusion. Van Gogh ain't telling you.

He had two other subjects: racehorses and dancing Hasidim. He showed horses coming round the bend. That's where the horse's body is most fluid, he said. Anyone can paint a horse out of the gate or heading for the finish line. That's just straight horse from nostril to tail, but coming round the bend, man, they're tilting and straining and sideswiping, adjusting to the bend, finding a slot for the stretch.

The Hasidim were wild: six men in black costume, black hats and long black coats, hair and beards flying out. You could almost hear the high clarinet wail and the fiddle chirp and soar.

Yonk said he didn't give a damn about religion himself, Judaism or anything else, but if you could dance your way to God like the men in his picture then he was right with them.

At the Aqueduct track I watched him watching. He seemed to be the only one at the track interested in what he called the laggard nags, the ones who trailed in at the end of the field. He ignored horses being led into the winner's enclosure. Winning was winning but losing made you dig deep. Before I knew Yonk I saw nothing but groups of horses being pointed in one direction and running their hearts out till one of them won. I looked through his eyes at a different Aqueduct. I knew nothing about art or the mind of the artist but I knew he took horse and rider images home in his head.

At dusk he'd invite me for a brandy in his corner room, where we looked down Atlantic Avenue toward the waterfront. Trucks grunted up the avenue, wheezing and hissing when they changed gears at the red traffic light while the ambulances of Long Island College Hospital screamed day and night. We could see the blinking red neon sign for Montero's Bar, a gathering place for seamen off freighters and container ships and the ladies of the night who made them welcome to Brooklyn.

Pilar Montero and her husband, Joe, owned the bar and building on Atlantic Avenue. She had a vacant apartment over the bar that I could have for two hundred and fifty dollars a month. She could give me a bed, some tables and chairs and, I know you'll be happy up there, Frankie. She said she liked me because of the time I said I preferred Spanish bagpipes to Irish bagpipes and I wasn't like the rest of the Irishers, who wanted to fight fight fight, all they ever wanted to do.

The apartment looked out on Atlantic Avenue. Outside my window, the MONTERO BAR neon sign blazed on and off, turning my front room from scarlet to black to scarlet while on the jukebox downstairs the Village People sang and pounded "YMCA."

I could never tell my classes how I lived over one of the last waterfront bars in Brooklyn, how every night I struggled to drown out the sounds of rowdy sailors, how I stuffed cotton wool in my ears to muffle the shrieking and laughing of women who offered shore love, how the pounding of the jukebox in the bar below, the Village People singing "YMCA," jolted me nightly in my bed.

13

At the start of each term I told the new students of creative writing, We're in this together. I don't know about you, but I'm serious about this class and sure of one thing: at the end of the term, one person in this room will have learned something, and that person, my little friends, will be me.

I thought that was clever, the way I presented myself as the most eager of all, elevating myself above the masses, the lazy, the opportunists, the indifferent.

English was a required subject, but Creative Writing was an elective. You could take or leave it. They took it. They flocked to my classes. The room was packed. They sat on windowsills. One teacher, Pam Sheldon, said, Why don't they just let him teach in Yankee Stadium? That's how popular I was.

What was this enthusiasm for "creative writing"? Did the boys and girls suddenly want to express themselves? Was it my masterly teaching, my charisma, my Irish charm? The old faith and begorrah factor?

Or had the word spread that this McCourt just rambled on and then disbursed high marks as easily as peanuts?

I didn't want to be known as an easy marker. I would have to toughen my image. Tighten up. Organize. Focus. Other teachers were spoken of in awe and fear. Up on the fifth floor, Phil Fisher taught mathematics and terrified all who came before him. The stories came down. If you struggled with the subject or showed little interest, he roared, Every time you open your mouth you add to the sum total of human ignorance, or Every time you open your mouth you detract from the sum total of human wisdom. He could not understand how any human brain could find difficulty with advanced calculus or trigonometry. He wondered why the stupid little bastards could not apprehend the elegant simplicity of it all.

At the end of the term, his stupid little bastards flaunted passing grades from him and bragged of their achievement. You could not be indifferent to Phil Fisher.

Ed Marcantonio was the chairman of the Mathematics Department. He taught in a room across the hall from mine. He taught the same courses as Phil Fisher, but his classes were oases of reason and serious purpose. A problem was presented and for forty minutes he led or urged the class toward an elegant solution. When the bell rang his students, satisfied, floated serene in the hallways, and when they passed Ed's course they knew they had earned it.

Adolescents don't always want to be set afloat on seas of speculation and uncertainty. It satisfies them to know that Tirana is the capital of Albania. They don't like it when Mr. McCourt says, Why was Hamlet mean to his mother, or why didn't he kill the king when he had the chance? It's all right to spend the rest of the period going round and round discussing this, but you'd like to know the answer before the goddam bell rings. Not with McCourt, man. He's asking questions, throwing out suggestions, causing confusion, and you know the warning bell is about to ring and you get this feeling in your gut, Come on, come on, what's the answer? and he keeps saying, What do you think? What do you think? and the bell rings and you're out in the hallway knowing nothing and you look at other kids from the class pointing to their heads and wondering where this guy is coming from. You see the kids from Marcantonio's class sailing down the hall with that peaceful expression that says, We got the answer. We got the solution. Once, just once, you wish McCourt had the answer to something, but no, he throws everything back at you. Maybe that's how they do it in Ireland, but somebody should tell him this is America and we like answers here. Or maybe he doesn't have the answers himself and that's why he throws everything back to the class.

I wanted to teach with Fisher passion and Marcantonio mastery. It was flattering to know that hundreds wanted to be in my classes, but I wondered about their reasons. I didn't want to be taken for granted. Oh, McCourt's class is just bullshit. All we do is talk. The old yack, yack, yack. If you don't get an A in his class, man, you're just plain stoopid.

Yonk Kling was having an afternoon brandy at Montero's. He told me I looked like shit.

Thanks, Yonk.

Have a brandy.

I can't. I have a million papers to correct. I'll have a glass of Rioja, Pilar.

Good for you, Frankie. You like the Spanish bagpipes. You like the Rioja. You find a nice Spanish girl. Keep you in bed all weekend.

I sat up on the bar stool and told Yonk my story. I think I'm too easy. There's no respect for easy teachers. One teacher at Stuyvesant was called Something for Nothing. I want to make them earn their grades. Have respect. They're signing up for my classes by the hundreds. That bothers me, the idea those kids might be saying I'm easy. One mother came to the school and pleaded with me to let her daughter into my class. Mom was divorced and offered to spend a weekend with me in a resort of my choice. I said no.

Yonk shook his head and said that sometimes I was not too bright, that there was an element of the tight ass in my character and if I didn't loosen up I'd slide into a miserable middle age. Christ, man. You could have spread joy. A weekend with the mother, a bright writing future for her little girl. What's the matter with you?

There wouldn't be any respect.

Oh, the hell with respect. Have another Rioja. No. Pilar, give him some of that Spanish brandy on me.

All right, but I have to go easy, Yonk. All these papers. One hundred and seventy papers, each three hundred and fifty words if I'm lucky, five hundred if I'm not. I'm buried.

He said I deserved two brandies, and he didn't know how I did it. He said, All you teachers. I dunno how you do it. If I ever became a teacher I'd have one thing to say to those little bastards: Shut up. Just shut up. Tell me this. Did you let the little girl into your class?

Yes.

And the mother's offer still stands?

I suppose so.

And you're sitting here drinking Spanish brandy when you could be off in the resort of your choice losing your teacher integrity?

After fifteen years in four different high schools—McKee, Fashion Industries, Seward Park, Stuyvesant—and the college in Brooklyn, I'm developing the instincts of a dog. When new classes come in September and February I can sniff their chemical composition. I watch the way they look and they watch the way I look. I can pick out types: the eager, willing ones; the cool; the show-me; the indifferent; the hostile; the opportunists here because they've heard I'm an easy marker; the lovers here simply to be near the beloved.

In this school you have to get their attention, challenge them. There they sit, row after row, bright intelligent faces looking up at me, expectant, ready to let me prove myself. Before Stuyvesant, I was more taskmaster than teacher. I wasted class time in routine and discipline: telling them to take their seats, open their notebooks, fielding requests for the pass, dealing with their complaints. Now there was no more rowdy behavior.

No more complaints about pushing or being pushed. No sandwiches in flight. No excuses for not teaching.

If you don't perform you'll lose their respect. Busywork is an insult. They know when you're blathering or killing time.

Broadway audiences meet actors halfway with politeness and applause. They've paid high prices for their tickets. They cluster at stage doors and ask for autographs. Public high school teachers perform five times a day. Their audiences disappear when bells ring and they're asked for autographs only on yearbooks at graduation.

You can fool some of the kids some of the time, but they know when you're wearing the mask, and you know they know. They force you into truth. If you contradict yourself they'll call out, Hey, that's not what you said last week. You face years of experience and their collective truth, and if you insist on hiding behind the teacher mask you lose them. Even if they lie to themselves and the world they look for honesty in the teacher.

At Stuyvesant I decided to admit it when I didn't have answers. I just don't know, friends. No, I've never read the Venerable Bede. I'm hazy on Transcendentalism. John Donne and Gerard Manley Hopkins can be tough going. I'm weak on the Louisiana Purchase. I've glanced at Schopenhauer and fallen asleep over Kant. Don't even mention mathematics. I used to know the meaning of condign but now it escapes me. I'm strong on usufruct. I'm sorry, I couldn't finish *The Faerie Queen*. I'll try again someday after I sort out the Metaphysicals.

I won't use ignorance as an excuse. I won't take refuge behind the gaps in my education. I will lay out a program of self-improvement to make me a better teacher: disciplined, traditional, scholarly, resourceful, ready with answers. I will dip into history, art, philosophy, archaeology. I'll sweep through the pageant of English language and literature from the Angles and Saxons and Jutes to the Normans, the Elizabethans, the Neoclassicists, the Romantics, the Victorians, the Edwardians, the War Poets, the Structuralists, the Modernists, the Postmodernists. I'll take an idea and trace its history from a cave in France to that room in Philadelphia where Franklin and the rest hammered out the Constitution of the U.S.A. I'll show off a bit, I suppose, and there might be sneering, but who can begrudge the ill-paid teacher a moment to prove a little learning is a dangerous thing?

The students never stopped trying to divert me from traditional English, but I was on to their tricks. I still told stories, but I was learning how to connect them with the likes of the Wife of Bath, Tom Sawyer, Holden Caulfield, Romeo and his reincarnation in *West Side Story*. English teachers are always being told, You gotta make it relevant.

I was finding my voice and my own style of teaching. I was learning to be comfortable in the classroom. Like Roger Goodman, my new chairman, Bill Ince, gave me free rein to try out ideas about writing and literature, to create my own classroom atmosphere, to do whatever I liked without bureaucratic interference, and my students were mature and tolerant enough to let me find my own way without the help of the mask or the red pen.

There are two basic ways of capturing the attention of the American teenager: sex and food. You have to be careful with sex. Word goes back to the parents and you're called on the carpet to explain why you're allowing your writing students to read stories about sex. You point out that it was done in good taste, in the spirit of romance rather than biology. That is not enough.

Kenny DiFalco called from the back of the room to ask if I'd like a marzipan. He held up something white and said he'd made it himself. I told him in my proper teacher way it was against the rules to eat or drink in class and what was marzipan anyway. Taste it, he said. It was delicious. There was a chorus of requests for marzipans, but Kenny said he'd run out of them. Tomorrow he'd bring in thirty-six marzipans, which, of course, he'd make himself. Then Tommy Esposito said he'd bring various bits and pieces from his father's restaurant. They might be leftovers but he'd make sure they were nice and hot. That started a chorus of offers. A Korean girl said she'd bring in something her mother made, kimchee, a hot cabbage that could take the roof off your mouth. Kenny said if all this food was coming in we should forget class, meet tomorrow in Stuyvesant Square next door and lay everything out on the grass. He said also we should remember to bring plastic utensils and napkins. Tommy said no, he'd never eat his father's meatballs with plastic. He was willing to bring in thirty-six forks and didn't mind one bit if we used them for other dishes. He suggested also that Mr. McCourt be excused from bringing anything. It's hard enough teaching kids without having to feed them, too.

Next day people walking in the park stopped to see what we were doing. A doctor from Beth Israel Hospital said he'd never seen such an array of food. When he was offered bits and sips he rolled his eyes and hummed with pleasure till he tasted the kimchee and had to beg for a cold drink for his burnt palate.

Instead of laying the dishes out on the grass we spread them along park benches. There were Jewish dishes (kreplach, matzos, gefilte fish), Italian (lasagna, Tommy's meatballs, ravioli, risotto), Chinese, Korean, a huge thirty-six-person meatloaf made with beef, veal, potatoes, onions. A police car cruised by. The cops wanted to know what was going on. You're not supposed to have fairs in the park without city permission. I explained this was a lesson in vocabulary and look at what my students were learning. The cops said they'd never had a vocabulary lesson like this in Catholic school, everything looked delicious, and I said they should step out of the car and try something. When the Beth Israel doctor warned them to watch out for the kimchee they said bring it on, there wasn't a hot food in Vietnam and Thailand they hadn't tried. They spooned it in and yelped and called for something cold. Before they drove away, they asked how often we planned to have these vocabulary lessons.

The homeless shuffled and edged their way into the group and we gave them the little that was left over. One spat out a marzipan, saying, What kinda crap is this? I might be homeless, but you don't have to insult me.

I stood on a park bench to announce my new idea. I had to compete with student chatter, the mumbling and complaining of the homeless, the remarks of the curious public, the hoot and honk of Second Avenue traffic.

Listen. Are you listening? Tomorrow I'd like you to bring to class a cookbook. Yes. A cookbook. What? You don't have a cookbook?

Well, then, I'd like to plan a visit to the family that doesn't own a cookbook. We'll take up a collection for you. Don't forget, tomorrow the cookbook.

Mr. McCourt, why do we have to bring cookbooks?

I don't know yet. Maybe I'll know tomorrow. There's something in my head that might become an idea.

Mr. McCourt, don't get mad, but sometimes you're like weird.

They brought the cookbooks. They said, What does this have to do with learning how to write?

You'll see. Open your book to any page. If you've already been through the book and have a favorite recipe open to that. David, read yours.

What?

Read your recipe.

Out loud? Right here in class?

Yes. Come on, David. It's not pornography. We don't have all day. We have to get through dozens of recipes.

But, Mr. McCourt, I never read a recipe in my life. I never read a cookbook in my life. I never even cooked an egg.

Good, David. Today your palate comes to life. Today your vocabulary expands. Today you become a gourmet.

A hand. What's a gourmet?

Another hand. A gourmet is a person who appreciates good food and wine and the finer things in life.

A chorus of O-o-o-hs travels around the room and there are smiles and admiring glances for James, who is the last one you'd ever expect to know anything beyond hot dogs and french fries.

David reads a recipe for coq au vin. His voice is flat and tentative but his interest seems to grow as he goes through the recipe, discovering ingredients he's never heard of.

David, I want you and the class to note the time and date and the fact that in room 205 of Stuyvesant High School you recited to your peers the first recipe of your life. Only God knows where this will lead you. I want all of you to remember that this is probably the first time in history a class in creative writing or English sat together and read cookbook recipes. David, you will note the absence of wild applause. You read that recipe as if you were reading a page of the New York telephone directory. But don't despair. You were in virgin territory and when we return for your next reading I'm sure you'll give the recipe full value. Anyone else?

There is a forest of hands. I call on Brian. I know it's a mistake and I know the negative comment is coming. He's another little twerp like Andrew of the Tilted Chair, but I'm the teacher rising above it, mature and ready to put my ego aside.

Yes, Brian.

He looks at Penny in the seat beside him. He's gay, she's lesbian. They don't hide it. They never knew a closet. He's short and fat. She's tall and thin and she holds her head as if to say, You wanna make something of it? I don't want to make something of it. Why have they joined forces against me? I know they dislike me and why can't I accept that simple fact? You can't be liked by every one of the hundreds of kids you have every year. There are teachers like Phil Fisher who don't give a damn about being liked or disliked. He'd say, I am teaching calculus, you hopeless blockheads. If you don't pay attention and if you don't study, you'll fail and if you fail you'll wind up teaching arithmetic to schizophrenics. If all the kids in the class despised him Phil would despise them in turn and pound advanced calculus into their heads till they could recite it in their sleep.

Yes, Brian?

Oh, he's a cool one, this Brian. There's another little smile for Penny. He's going to turn me into shish kebab. He takes his time.

I don't know, Mr. aw McCourt, how could I go home and aw tell my parents we're sitting around in a junior class at Stuyvesant High School reading aw recipes from cookbooks? Other classes are reading aw American literature but we have to sit here reading recipes like we were aw retards.

I feel irritated. I'd like to demolish Brian with a cutting remark, but James of the gourmet definition takes charge. Could I say something? He looks at Brian. All you ever do is sit there criticizing. Tell me this: Are you glued to your seat?

Of course I'm not glued to my seat.

Do you know where the program office is?

Yeah.

So, if you don't like what we do here, why don't you get your ass off that chair and go to the program office and change your class? Nobody's keeping you here. Right, Mr. McCourt? Transfer, says James. Get outta here. Go read *Moby-Dick,* if you're strong enough.

Susan Gilman never raises her hand. Everything is too urgent. No use telling her calling out is against the rules. She brushes that aside. Who cares? She wants you to know she's discovered your game. I know why you want us to read these recipes out loud like this.

You do?

Because they look like poetry on the page and some of them read like poetry. I mean they're even better than poetry because you can taste them. And, wow, the Italian recipes are pure music.

Maureen McSherry chimes in. The other thing I like about the recipes is you can read them the way they are without pain-in-the-ass English teachers digging for the deeper meaning.

All right, Maureen, we'll get back to that sometime.

What?

The pain-in-the-ass English teachers digging for meaning.

Michael Carr says he has his flute with him and if anyone would like to recite or sing a recipe he'll play with them. Brian looks skeptical. He says, Are you kidding? Play your flute with a recipe? Are we going crazy in this class? Susan tells him can it and offers to read a recipe for lasagna with Michael backing her up. While she reads a recipe for Swedish meatballs he plays "Hava Negila," a melody that has nothing to do with Swedish meatballs, and the class goes from giggling to serious listening to applause and congratulations. James says they should take it on the road and call themselves The Meatballs or The Recipes and offers to be their agent as he is going into accounting. When Maureen reads a recipe for Irish soda bread Michael plays "The Irish Washerwoman" to a tapping and a clacking around the room.

The class is alive. They tell one another this is wild, the very idea of reading recipes, reciting recipes, singing recipes with Michael adjusting his flute to French, English, Spanish, Jewish, Irish, Chinese recipes. What if someone walked in? Those Japanese educators who come and stand in the back of the room and watch teachers teach. How would the principal explain Susan and Michael and the Meatball Concerto?

Brian casts a damper on the proceedings. He asks if he can have a pass to the program office to see if he can get a transfer on account of how he is learning nothing in this class. I mean, if the taxpayers heard how we were wasting our high school years chanting recipes you'd be out of a job, Mr. McCourt. Nothing personal, he says.

He turns to Penny for support but she's rehearsing a paella recipe from another student's cookbook. She shakes her head at Brian and when she's finished with the recipe tells him if he leaves this class he's crazy. Crazy. Her mother has a recipe for lamb stew that is out of this world and when Penny brings it in tomorrow she'd like Michael to be prepared with his flute. Oh, if she could bring her mother to class. Her mother always sings when she makes that lamb stew in the kitchen and wouldn't it be something if Penny could just read out that recipe with her mother singing and Michael playing that beautiful flute. Wouldn't that be something!

Brian blushes and says he plays the oboe and would love to play with Michael when Penny does her lamb-stew recipe tomorrow. She puts her hand on his arm and says, Yeah, we'll do it tomorrow.

On the A train to Brooklyn I feel uneasy over the direction this class is taking, especially since my other classes are asking why can't they go to the park with all kinds of food and why can't they have recipe readings with music? How can all this be justified to the authorities who keep an eye on the curriculum?

Mr. McCourt, what the hell is going on in this room? You've got these kids reading cookbooks, for Christ's sakes. And singing recipes? Are you kidding us? Could you kindly explain what this has to do with the teaching of English? Where are your lessons on literature, English or American or anything else? These kids, as you know very well, are preparing for the best colleges in the country and is this how you want to send them into the world? Reading recipes? Chanting recipes? Singing recipes? How about choreographing Irish stew or the classic Western omelet, with appropriate music, of course? Why not forget English and college preparation altogether and turn the classroom into a kitchen with demonstration lessons on cooking? Why don't we create a Stuyvesant High School Recipe Chorus and give concerts around town and internationally to benefit these kids who wasted their time in your class, McCourt, and didn't get into college and now flip dough in pizza joints or wash dishes in second-rate French bistros uptown? That's what it's going to come to. These kids might be able to sing a recipe for pâté de something or other but they'll never sit in Ivy League classrooms.

It's too late. I can't walk in tomorrow and tell them it's all over, forget the cookbooks, no more recipes. Put your flute away, Michael. Silence your mother, Penny. Sorry about the oboe, Brian.

Except for Brian's little moment of rebellion, hadn't we had three days of complete class participation? And, most of all, teacher man, didn't you enjoy yourself?

Or were you just a bloody fool, allowing yourself once again to be diverted from Mark Twain and F. Scott Fitzgerald in junior classes and Wordsworth and Coleridge in senior classes? Shouldn't you insist they bring textbooks daily so they can go a-dipping and a-hunting for deeper meanings?

Yes, yes, but not now, not now.

Are the kids on to you? Playing you along with the recipes and the music? *Mea culpa* time. Are you, under it all, a fraud? Playing along with the way they're playing you along? You can imagine what they're saying in the teachers' lounge: The Irishman has his classes completely duped. All they do is—man, you won't believe this—all they do is read cookbooks. Yeah. Forget Milton and Swift and Hawthorne and Melville. F'Christ's sakes, they're reading the *Joy of Cooking* and Fanny Farmer and Betty Crocker and singing recipes. Jesus! You can hardly hear yourself down the hall with the din of oboes and flutes and chanted recipes coming from his goddam room. Who does he think he's fooling?

Maybe you could find a way of enjoying yourself less. You were always ingenious at making yourself miserable and you don't want to lose the touch. Maybe you could try again to teach diagramming or grub for deeper meanings? You could inflict *Beowulf* and the *Chronicles* on your suffering adolescents. What about your grand program of self-improvement, Mr. Polymath? Look at your life outside the school. You belong nowhere. Periphery man. You have no wife, and a child you rarely see. No vision, no plan, no goal. Just amble to the crypt, man. Fade and leave no legacy but memories of a man who turned his classroom into a playground, a rap session and a group-therapy forum.

Why not? What the hell. What are schools for anyway? I ask you, is it the task of the teacher to supply canon fodder for the military-industrial complex? Are we shaping packages for the corporate assembly line?

Ooh, aren't we getting solemn, and where did I leave my soapbox?

Look at me: wandering late bloomer, floundering old fart, discovering in my forties what my students knew in their teens. Let there be no caterwauling. Sing no sad songs for me. No weeping at the bar.

I am called before the court, accused of leading a double life. To wit: that in the classroom I enjoy myself and deny my students a proper education while I toss nightly on my celibate cot and wonder, God help us, what it's all about.

I must congratulate myself, in passing, for never having lost the ability to examine my conscience, never having lost the gift of finding myself wanting and defective. Why fear the criticism of others when you, yourself, are first out of the critical gate? If self-denigration is the race I am the winner, even before the starting gun. Collect the bets.

Fear? That's it, Francis. The little slum boy still fears loss of job. Fears he'll be cast into the outer darkness and deafened by the weeping, the wailing, the gnashing. Brave, imaginative teacher encourages teenagers to sing recipes but wonders when the axe will fall, when Japanese visitors will shake their heads and report him to Washington. Japanese visitors will instantly detect in my classroom signs of America's degeneracy and wonder how they could have lost the war.

And if the axe falls?

A pox on the axe.

Friday the agenda was packed. In the room four guitarists plucked at strings, the new cooperative Brian practiced his oboe, Michael trilled on his flute, Zach rapped out culinary themes on the small bongo drums between his knees, two boys played harmonicas. Susan Gilman stood ready to monopolize the period with a recipe that ran for multiple columns, required forty-seven different steps and called for ingredients not seen in the average American household. She said it was pure poetry and Michael was so excited he was ready to compose a piece for woodwind, strings, bongo drums and Susan's voice. Pam is gonna do a Peking duck recipe in Cantonese and her brother from another class is playing this strange-looking instrument no one in this class ever saw before.

I try to inject a little teaching. I say, If you're an observant writer you'll recognize the significance of this event. For the first time in history a Chinese recipe is to be read with background music. You have to be alert to historic moments. The writer is always saying, What's going on here? Always. You can bet your last dime that nowhere in history, Chinese or otherwise, will you find a moment like this.

I attend to the historic event. Write the items on the blackboard. We'll start with Pam and her duck, then Leslie with English trifle, Larry with eggs Benedict, Vicky with stuffed pork chops.

Guitars, oboes, flutes, harmonicas, bongo drums are warming up. Readers are silently rehearsing recipes.

Shy Pam nods to her brother and the Peking duck recital begins. It's a long recipe, with Pam singing in a high wail and her brother plucking the strings of his instrument, so long a recipe that the other musicians begin to join in, one at a time, and by the time Pam has finished reading, the instruments are in full ensemble challenging Pam to octaves so high and rhythms so urgent that Assistant Principal Murray Kahn rushes from his office fearing the worst and when he looks through the window and sees this performance in progress he can't resist coming in, his eyes wider than wide, till Pam's voice grows softer and softer, the musicians fade, and the duck is done.

At the end, class critics suggested Pam should have performed last. They said her duck recipe and the Chinese music were so dramatic everything else sounded anemic. Also, they said, words and music were often mismatched. It was a big mistake using bongo drums to back English trifle. You need the delicacy and sensitivity of the violin or maybe the harpsichord and it really puzzled them that anyone would link bongos and English trifle. And speaking of violins, Michael was just perfect backing the eggs Benedict reading, and they really dug the bongo-and-harmonica combination for stuffed pork chops. There was something about pork chops that demanded the harmonica and it was amazing now how you could think of a food and an instrument to go with it. Man, this experience called for a new kind of thinking. They said kids in other classes wished they could read recipes instead of Alfred Lord Tennyson and Thomas Carlyle. Other English teachers were teaching solid stuff, analyzing poetry, assigning research papers and giving lessons on the correct use of footnotes and bibliography.

Thinking of those other English teachers and the solid stuff makes me uneasy again. They're following the curriculum, preparing the kids for higher education and the great world beyond. We're not here to enjoy ourselves, teacher man.

This is Stuyvesant High School, the jewel in the crown of the

New York educational system. These kids are the brightest of the bright. In a year they'll be sitting at the feet of distinguished professors at the best universities in the country. They'll be taking notes, copying words that will require looking up. No farting around with cookbooks and visits to the park. There will be direction and focus and serious scholarship and whatever became of that teacher we had back in Stuyvesant, you know the one.

14

On Monday I'll make the announcement. There will be groans and muted catcalls and whispered comments about my mother but I have to get back on track like all those other conscientious teachers. I will remind my students that the mission of this school is to prepare them for the best colleges and universities so that they can graduate someday and make solid contributions to the welfare and progress of this country, for if this country falters and fails what hope is there for the rest of the world? You bear a heavy responsibility as you go forth and it would be criminal of me, the teacher, to waste your young lives with the reading of recipes no matter how much you enjoy the activity.

I know we're all having a good time reading recipes with background music but that is not why we were put on earth. We have to move on. That is the American way.

Mr. McCourt, why shouldn't we read recipes? Isn't a recipe for meat loaf as important as these poems that no one can understand anyway? Isn't it? You can live without poetry but you can't live without food.

I tried to balance Walt Whitman and Robert Frost with meat loaf and recipes in general but rambled into a mumble.

They groan again when I announce I am going to recite my favorite poem. That pisses me off and I tell them, You are pissing me off. A shocked silence. Teacher using bad language. Never mind. Recite the poem.

Little Bo Peep has lost her sheep
And doesn't know where to find them.
Leave them alone and they will come home
Wagging their tails behind them.

Hey, what's going on here? That's not a poem. This is high school and he's giving us Mother Goose? Is he pulling our leg? Playing little games with us?

I recite the poem again and encourage them to waste no time in digging for the deeper meaning.

Aw, come on. Is this a joke? Man, this is high school.

On the surface the poem, or nursery rhyme, seems simple, a plain story of a little girl who has lost her sheep, but are you listening? This is significant. She has learned to leave them alone. Bo Peep is cool. She trusts her sheep. She doesn't go bothering them as they nibble away in pasture, glen, vale and hillside. They need their grass, their roughage, and the occasional draught of water from a tinkling mountain stream. Also, they have little lambs who need time for bonding with their mothers after they've frolicked all day with their peers. They don't need the world barging in and destroying the mood. They might be sheep, they might be lambs, they might be ewes, they might be rams, but they're entitled to a little communal happiness before they are transformed into the mutton we devour, the wool we wear.

Aw, God, Mr. McCourt, did you have to end it like that? Why couldn't you just leave them out there, sheep and lambs, all loving and enjoying themselves? We eat them, we wear them. It's not right.

There are vegetarians and vegans in the class who thank God right here and now they have nothing to do with exploiting these poor animals and could we get back to Bo Peep? They'd like to know if I'm trying to make some kind of point.

No, I'm not trying to make some kind of point except to say I like this poem because of its simple message.

What's that?

That people should stop bothering people. Little Bo Peep backs off. She could stay up all night, waiting and whimpering by the door, but she knows better. She trusts her sheep. She leaves them alone and they come home, and you can imagine the joyful reunion, a lot of merry bleating and frolicking and deep expressions of satisfaction from the rams as they settle in for the night while Bo Peep knits by the fire happy in the knowledge that in her daily rounds, caring for the sheep and their offspring, she has bothered nobody.

In my English classes at Stuyvesant High School the students agreed that nothing on television or out of Hollywood could equal, in violence and horror, the story of Hansel and Gretel. Jonathan Greenberg spoke out. How can we subject children to the story of some asshole of a father who is so dominated by his new wife he's willing to lose his kids in the woods and let them starve to death? How can we tell children how Hansel and Gretel were locked up by that witch who wanted to fatten and cook them? And is there anything more horrible than the scene where they push her into the fire? She's a mean old cannibal of a witch and deserves what she got but wouldn't all this give a kid nightmares?

Lisa Berg said these stories have been around for hundreds of years. We all grew up with them and enjoyed them and survived them, so what is the big deal.

Rose Kane agreed with Jonathan. When she was little, she had nightmares over Hansel and Gretel and maybe that was because she herself had a new stepmother who was a bitch on wheels. A real bitch who wouldn't think twice of losing her and her sister in Central Park or some distant station in the New York subway system. After she heard the Hansel and Gretel story from her first-grade teacher she refused to go anywhere with her stepmother unless her father was with them. That would infuriate her father so much he'd threaten her with all kinds of punishment. You go with your stepmother, Rose, or you're grounded forever. Which, of course, proved he was completely dominated by the stepmother, who had a carbuncle on her chin like all the stepmothers in fairy tales, a carbuncle with little sprouting hairs that she was always plucking.

Everyone in the class seemed to have an opinion on the Hansel and Gretel story and the main question was, Would you tell this story to your children? I suggested that the pros and the antis separate and sit on opposite sides of the room and it was remarkable to see that the class was split down the middle. I suggested also that there should be a moderator for this discussion but passions were running high, no one was neutral on the matter, and I'd have to take the job myself.

It was minutes before I could calm the hullabaloo in the room. The anti–Hansel and Gretel side said their children could be damaged so badly it would lead to huge costs in psychotherapy. Oh, bullshit, said the pro side. Come off it. No one is in therapy because of fairy tales. Every kid in America and Europe grew up with these stories.

The antis brought up the violence in Little Red Riding Hood, the wolf swallowing the grandmother without even chewing her, and the meanness of the stepmother in Cinderella. You wonder how a kid could survive hearing or reading any of this.

Lisa Berg said something so remarkable it caused a sudden silence in the room. She said kids have stuff in their heads so dark and deep it's beyond our comprehension.

Wow, someone said.

They knew Lisa had hit on something. They weren't so far removed from childhood themselves, although they wouldn't like to hear you say it, and you could sense in that silence a drifting back to a childhood dreamland.

Next day we sang fragments from my childhood. There was no point to the activity, no deeper meaning. No test loomed to infect our singing. I felt twinges of guilt but I enjoyed myself and from the way they sang, those Jewish, Korean, Chinese, American kids, I assumed they enjoyed themselves, too. They knew the basic nursery rhymes. Now they had melodies to go with them.

Old Mother Hubbard Hubbard
Went to the cupboard cupboard
To get her poor doggie a bone a bone
When she got there there
The cupboard was bare bare
And so the poor doggie got none.

Observation report I would have written if I were Assistant Deputy Superintendent of Pedagogy at the Board of Education, 110 Livingston Street, Brooklyn, New York, 11201:

Dear Mr. McCourt:

When I entered your classroom on March 2 your students were singing, rather loudly and disturbingly, I may say, a medley of nursery rhymes. You led them from rhyme to rhyme with no pauses for elucidation, exploration, justification, analysis. Indeed, there seemed to be no context at all for this activity, no purpose.

A teacher of your experience might surely have noted the number of students attired in outerwear, the number lounging in their seats with legs stuck into the aisles. No one seemed to have a notebook, nor instructions for its use. You realize the notebook is the basic tool of any high school student of English and the teacher who neglects that tool is derelict in his or her duty.

Regrettably, there was nothing on the chalkboard to indicate the nature of the day's lesson. That may explain why the notebooks lay unused in the students' bags.

Within my rights as an Assistant Deputy Superintendent of Pedagogy I queried some of your students when the session ended as to whatever learnings they might have carried away that day. They were vague to the point of head scratching, completely at a loss as to the point of this singing activity. One said he had enjoyed himself and that is a valid comment but, surely, that is not the purpose of a high school education.

I fear I will have to pass on my observations to the Deputy

Superintendent of Pedagogy, who, no doubt, will inform the
Superintendent of Pedagogy herself. You may be summoned for a
hearing at the Board of Education. If so you may be accompanied
by a union representative and/or a lawyer.

Sincerely,

Montague Wilkinson III

All right, the bell has rung. Once again you are mine. Open your books. Turn to this poem, "My Papa's Waltz," by Theodore Roethke. If you don't have a book, look over someone's shoulder. No one in this class will begrudge you an over-the-shoulder look. Stanley, would you read the poem aloud? Thanks.

My Papa's Waltz, by Theodore Roethke

The whiskey on your breath
Could make a small boy dizzy;
But I hung on like death:
Such waltzing was not easy.

We romped until the pans
Slid from the kitchen shelf;
My mother's countenance
Could not unfrown itself.

The hand that held my wrist
Was battered on one knuckle;
At every step you missed
My right ear scraped a buckle.

You beat time on my head
With a palm caked by dirt,
Then waltzed me off to bed
Still clinging to your shirt.

Thanks again, Stanley. Take a few minutes to look over the poem again. Let it sink in. So, when you read the poem, what happened?

What do you mean, What happened?

You read the poem. Something happened, something moved in your head, in your body, in your lunch box. Or nothing happened. You're not required to respond to every stimulus in the universe. You're not weather vanes.

Mr. McCourt, what are you talking about?

I'm saying you don't have to respond to everything a teacher or anyone else sets before you.

They look dubious. Oh, yeah. Tell that to some of the teachers around here. They take everything personally.

Mr. McCourt, do you want us to talk about what the poem means?

I'd like you to talk about whatever you'd like to talk about in the general neighborhood of this poem. Bring in your grandmother if you like. Don't worry about the "real" meaning of the poem. Even the poet won't know that. When you read it something happened, or nothing happened. Would you raise your hand if nothing happened? All right, no hands. So, something happened in your head or your heart or your bowels. You're a writer. What happens when you hear music? Chamber music? Rock? You see a couple arguing on the street. You look at a child rebelling against his mother. You see a homeless man begging. You see a politician giving a speech. You ask someone to go out with you. You observe the response of the other person. Because you're a writer, you ask yourself always always always, What's happening, baby?

Well, like, this poem is about a father dancing with his kid and it's not pleasant because the father is drunk and insensitive.

Brad?

If it's not pleasant, why does he hang on like death?

Monica?

There's a lot going on here. The kid is dragged around the kitchen. He could be a rag doll for all the papa cares.

Brad again?

There's a giveaway word here, romped. That's a happy word, right? I mean he could've said danced or something ordinary, but he says romped and, like you're always telling us, a word can change the atmosphere of a sentence or a paragraph. So, romped creates a happy atmosphere.

Jonathan?

You can tell me I'm out of order, Mr. McCourt, but did your father ever dance you around the kitchen?

He never danced us around the kitchen, but he got us out of bed late at night and made us sing patriotic Irish songs and promise to die for Ireland.

Yeah, I figured this poem had something to do with your childhood.

That's partly true, but I asked you to read this because it captures a moment, a mood, and there might be, forgive me for this, there might be a deeper meaning. Some of you want the worth of your money. What about the mother? Sheila?

What's going on in this poem is very simple. This guy has a hard job, coal miner or something. Comes home with a battered knuckle, hands caked with dirt. The wife sits over there mad as hell but she's used to it. She knows it's going to happen once a week when he gets paid. Like your dad. Right, Mr. McCourt? The kid loves his father because you're always drawn to the crazy one. Doesn't matter that the mother keeps the house going. Kid takes that for granted. So when the dad comes home, oh, he's all charged up from the drink and gets the kid all excited.

What happens when the poem finishes? David?

The dad waltzes him off to bed. The mom puts the pans back on the kitchen shelf. Next day is Sunday and the dad gets up feeling lousy. The mom makes breakfast but won't talk to anyone and the kid is caught between. He's only about nine because he's only tall enough to scrape his ear on the buckle. The mother would like to walk out and get a divorce because she's sick of the drinking and the

222

lousy life but she can't because she's stuck in the middle of West Virginia and there's no escape when you don't have money.

Jonathan?

What I like about this poem is, there it is, a simple story. Or, no. Wait a minute. It isn't that simple. There's a lot going on, and there's a before and after. If you were to make a movie of this poem you'd have a hard job directing it. Would you have the kid in the opening scene where the mother and the kid are waiting for the father? Or would you just show the opening lines where the kid is wincing over the whiskey? How would you tell the kid to hang on? Reaching up to hang on the shirt? How would you get the mother's countenance without making her look mean? You'd have to decide what kind of guy this dad is when he's sober because if he's like this all the time you wouldn't even want to make a movie about him. What I don't like is how he beats time on the kid's head with a dirty hand, which, of course, is proof he works hard.

Ann?

I dunno. There's a lot in here after you talk about it. Why can't we just leave it alone? Just take the story and feel sorry for the kid and the mother with her countenance and, maybe, the dad, and not analyze it to death.

David?

We're not analyzing. We're just responding. If you go to a movie you come out talking about it, don't you?

Sometimes, but this is a poem and you know what English teachers do to poems. Analyze, analyze, analyze. Dig for the deeper meaning. That's what turned me against poetry. Someone should dig a grave and bury the deeper meaning.

I asked you only what happened when you read the poem. If nothing happened it's not a crime. When I hear heavy metal, the eyes glaze. Some of you could probably explain it to me and I'd try to listen to that music with some understanding, but I just don't care. You don't have to respond to every stimulus. If "My Papa's Waltz" leaves you cold, then it leaves you cold.

That's one thing, Mr. McCourt, but we have to be careful. If you say something negative about anything, English teachers take it personally and get mad. My sister got in trouble with an English professor at Cornell over the way she interpreted one of Shakespeare's sonnets. He said she was off the mark entirely, and she said a sonnet can be read a hundred different ways, otherwise why would you see a thousand Shakespeare criticism books on the library shelves, and he got pissed off and told her to see him in his office. This time he was nice to her and she backed off and said maybe he was right and went out to dinner with him in Ithaca and I got pissed off at her for giving in like that. Now we only say hello to each other.

Why don't you write about that, Ann? It's an unusual story, you and your sister not talking because of a Shakespeare sonnet.

I could, but I'd have to get into the whole sonnet thing, what he said, what she said, and, since I hate getting into deeper meanings, and she's not talking to me anyway, I don't have the entire story.

David?

Make it up. There are three characters here, Ann and her sister and the professor, and there's the sonnet that's causing all the trouble. You could have a hell of a time with that sonnet. You could change the names, get away from the sonnet, say it's a big fight about "My Papa's Waltz," and next thing is you have a story they want to turn into a movie.

Jonathan?

No offense to Ann but I can't think of anything more boring than a story about a college student arguing with a professor over a sonnet. I mean, Jesus, excuse the language, this world is falling to pieces, people starving, et cetera, and these people have nothing else to do but argue over a poem. I'd never buy that story and I wouldn't go to the movie if they let me take my whole family for free.

Mr. McCourt.

Yes, Ann?

Tell Jonathan he can kiss my ass.

Sorry, Ann. That's a message you'll have to deliver yourself.

There's the bell but, remember, you don't have to respond to every stimulus.

Whenever a lesson sagged, whenever their minds wandered, when too many asked for the pass, I fell back on the "dinner interrogation." Government officials or concerned superiors might have asked, Is this a valid educational activity?

Yes, it is, ladies and gentlemen, because this is a writing class and everything is grist to our mill.

Also, the interrogation made me feel like a prosecutor playing with a witness. If the class was amused I took credit. I was at center stage: Master Teacher, Interrogator, Puppeteer, Conductor.

James, what did you have for dinner last night?

He looks surprised. What?

Dinner, James. What did you have for dinner last night?

He seems to be searching his memory.

James, it's less than twenty-four hours ago.

Oh, yeah. Chicken.

Where did it come from?

What do you mean?

Did someone buy it, James, or did it fly in the window?

My mother.

So your mother does the shopping?

Well, yeah, except like sometimes we run out of milk or something and she sends my sister to the store. My sister always complains.

Does your mother work?

Yeah, she's a legal secretary.

How old is your sister?

Fourteen.

And you?

Sixteen.

So your mother works and does the shopping and your sister is two years younger than you and has to run to the store. You are never sent to the store?

No.

So who cooks the chicken?

My mother.

And what are you doing while your sister runs to the store and your mother is knocking herself out in the kitchen?

I'm like in my room.

Doing what?

Catching up with my homework or, you know, listening to music.

And what is your father doing while your mother cooks the chicken?

He's like in the living room watching the news on TV. He has to keep up with things because he's a broker.

Who helps your mother in the kitchen?

Sometimes my sister helps.

Not you, not your father?

We don't know how to cook.

But someone has to set the table.

My sister.

Haven't you ever set the table?

Yeah, once when my sister went to the hospital with her appendix but it was no good because I didn't know where to put things and my mom got mad and told me get out of the kitchen.

All right. Who puts the food on the table?

Mr. McCourt, I dunno why you keep asking me these questions when you know what I'm gonna say. My mom puts the food on the table.

What did you have with the chicken last night?

We had, like, you know, salad.

What else?

We had baked potatoes, me and my dad. My mom and sister won't eat them because they're on a diet and the potato is a killer.

And what about the table setting? Did you have a tablecloth?

Are you kidding? We had straw place mats.

What happened during the dinner?

What do you mean?

Did you talk? Was there fine music to dine by?

My dad kept listening to the TV and my mom got mad at him for not paying attention to his dinner after all the trouble she went to.

Oh, conflict at the dinner table. Didn't you all discuss the events of the day? Didn't you talk about school?

Naw. Then Mom started clearing the table because my dad went back to watch the TV. My mom got mad again because my sister said she didn't want her chicken. She said it was making her fat, the chicken. Mr. McCourt, why are we doing this? Why you asking all these questions? It's so boring.

Turn it back to the class. What do you think? This is a writing class. Did you learn anything about James and his family? Is there a story there? Jessica?

My mom would never put up with that crap. James and his dad get treated like kings. The mom and the sister do everything and they just hang out and get their dinner served up to them. I'd like to know who cleans up and washes the dishes. No, I don't have to ask: the mom, the sister.

Hands are waving, all girls. I can see they want to attack James. Wait, wait, ladies. Before you zero in on James, I'd like to know if each of you is a paragon of virtue around the house, always helpful, always thoughtful. Before we go on tell me this: how many of you, after eating last night, thanked your mother, kissed her, and complimented her on the dinner. Sheila?

That'd be phoney. The mothers know we appreciate what they do.

A dissenting voice. No, they don't. If James thanked his mother she'd faint.

I played to the crowd till Daniel took the wind out of my sails.

Daniel, what did you have for dinner last night?

Veal medallions in a kind of white-wine sauce.

What did you have with the veal medallions in white wine?

Asparagus and a small tossed salad with vinaigrette.

Any appetizer?

No. Just the dinner. My mother thinks they ruin the appetite.

So, your mother cooked the veal medallions?

No, the maid.

Oh, the maid. And what was your mother doing?

She was with my father.

So the maid cooked the dinner and, I suppose, served it?

That's right.

And you dined alone?

Yes.

At a vast highly polished mahogany table, I suppose?

That's right.

With a crystal chandelier?

Yes.

Really?

Yes.

Did you have music in the background?

Yes.

Mozart, I suppose? To go with the table and the chandelier.

No. Telemann.

And then?

I listened to Telemann for twenty minutes. He's one of my father's favorites. When the piece ended I called my father.

And where was he, if you don't mind my asking?

He's in Sloan-Kettering Hospital with lung cancer and my mother is with him all the time because he's expected to die.

Oh, Daniel, I'm sorry. You should have told me instead of letting me put you through the dinner interrogation.

It doesn't matter. He's going to die anyway.

It was quiet in the classroom. What could I say now to Daniel? I had played my little game: clever and amusing teacher-interrogator, and Daniel had been patient. Details of his elegant solitary dinner filled the classroom. His father was here. We waited by a bed with Daniel's mother. We'd remember forever the veal medallions, the maid, the chandelier, and Daniel alone at the polished mahogany table while his father died.

I tell my classes that on Mondays they should bring in *The New York Times* so we can read Mimi Sheraton's restaurant reviews.

They look at one another and shrug in the New York way. Raise your eyebrows. Lift your hands, palms out, elbows against your ribs. This shows patience, resignation, wonder.

Why are you asking us to read restaurant reviews?

You might enjoy them and, of course, broaden and deepen your vocabulary. That's what you are to tell important visitors from Japan and other places.

Man, oh, man, next you'll be asking us to bring in obituaries.

That's a good idea, Myron. You could learn a lot from reading obituaries. Would you prefer that to Mimi Sheraton? You could bring in some juicy obituaries.

Mr. McCourt, let's stick to recipes and restaurant reviews.

OK, Myron.

We look into the structure of a Mimi Sheraton review. She gives us the ambience of the restaurant and the quality of service, or lack of it. She reports on each stage of a meal: appetizers, entrees, desserts, coffee, wine. She writes a summarizing final paragraph in which she justifies the stars she is awarding or not awarding. That is the structure. Yes, Barbara?

I think this review is one of the meanest things I've ever read. I had this image of blood dripping from the paper in her typewriter or whatever she writes on.

If you paid high prices in a restaurant like this, Barbara, wouldn't you like to be warned by someone like Mimi Sheraton?

I try to focus on the review, use of language, details, but they want to know if she eats out every night of her life and how does she do it?

They said you'd have to feel sorry for someone with a job like that where you can't just stay at home and have a hamburger or a bowl of cereal with a banana in it. She probably goes home nights and tells her husband she never wants to look at chicken or pork chops again in her life. The husband himself never has the pleasure of preparing a little collation to perk her up after a long day as she's probably had enough food already to keep her going for a week. Imagine the dilemma of the husbands and wives of all these food critics. Husband can never invite wife out to dinner just for the sake of going out to dinner where you don't have to glide things over your palate to figure out what spices were used or what was in that sauce. Who would want to eat with a woman who knows everything about food and wine? You'd be watching to see what kind of face she made at the first mouthful. No, she might have this glamorous job that pays loads of money but you'd get tired of the same old routine of having to eat the best of everything and can you imagine what it does to your insides anyway.

Then, for the first time in my life, I used a word I'd never used before. I said, Nevertheless, and repeated it. Nevertheless, I'm going to make Mimi Sheratons out of all of you.

I asked them to write about the school cafeteria or neighborhood restaurants. No one wrote positive reviews of the school cafeteria. Three ended their essays with the same sentence, It sucks. There were rave reviews of local pizzerias and the vendor who sold hot dogs and pretzels on First Avenue. One pizzeria proprietor told students he'd like to meet me and thank me for calling attention to his business and bringing honor to his profession. It was a hell of a thing to think of this teacher with an Irish name encouraging his students to appreciate the finer things in life. Anytime I wanted a pizza, not just a slice but a whole one, the door was wide open and I could have on that pizza anything I wanted, even if he had to send out to a delicatessen for extra toppings he might not have.

I challenged them on the smugness and meanness of their school cafeteria reviews. All right, I said, the ambience is bleak. Mimi would agree with you. The cafeteria could be mistaken for a subway station or an army mess hall. You complain about the service. The women dishing out the food are too brusque. They don't smile enough. Aw, gee. That hurts your feelings. They simply dump the food, whatever it is, on a tray. Well, what do you expect? Put yourself into some dead-end job and we'll see if you come out smiling.

I tell myself, Stop. No preaching. You did that years ago with your rant on the French Revolution. If they want to say it sucks, let them. Isn't this a free country?

I ask them what they mean when they say the food sucks. You're writers. How about raising the level of your vocabulary? What would Mimi say?

Aw, God, Mr. McCourt, does it have to be Mimi, Mimi every time we write about food?

Well, what do you mean by it sucks?

You know. You know.

What?

Like, you can't eat that stuff.

Why not?

Tastes like crap or it has no taste at all.

How do you know what crap tastes like?

You know, Mr. McCourt, you're a nice guy but you can be exasperating.

You know, Jack, what Ben Jonson said?

No, Mr. McCourt, I don't know what Ben Jonson said.

He said, Language reveals the man. Speak that I may see thee.

Oh, is that what Ben Jonson said?

That's what Ben Jonson said.

Pretty clever, Mr. McCourt. He should have dinner with Mimi.

15

On Open School Day the kids are dismissed at noon and the parents come swarming in from one to three and again in the evening from seven to nine. At the end of the day you meet teachers punching out at the time clock and they're weary from talking to hundreds of parents. There are three thousand kids in this school and that should add up to six thousand parents, but this is New York, where divorce is a major sport and kids have to sort out who's who and what's what and when will it happen. Three thousand kids could have ten thousand parents and stepparents who are certain their sons and daughters are the brightest of the bright. This is Stuyvesant High School, where, the minute students step inside, doors swing open to the best universities and colleges in the country and if you don't succeed it's your own damn fault. The moms and dads are cool, confident, cheerful, self-assured when they're not worried, concerned, despairing, uncertain, suspicious. They have high expectations and nothing less than success will satisfy them. They turn out in such numbers every teacher needs a student monitor to manage the flow. They are anxious about their child's standing in the class. Would I say Stanley is above average? Because they think he's getting lazy and hanging out with the wrong people. They hear things about Stuyvesant Square, things about drugs, you know, and that's enough to make you lose sleep. Is he doing his work? Do you notice any changes in his behavior and attitudes?

Stanley's parents are going through a bitter divorce and no wonder Stanley is screwed up. The mother keeps the classic six-room apartment on the Upper West Side while Dad is in some hovel in the arse end of the Bronx. They've agreed to split Stanley down the middle, three and a half days every week with each of them. Stanley is good at mathematics but even he doesn't know how to divide himself like that. He's good-humored about it. He turns his dilemma into some kind of algebraic equation: If a equals $3\frac{1}{2}$ and b equals $3\frac{1}{2}$, then what is Stanley? His math teacher, Mr. Winokur, gives Stanley a grade of 100 for even thinking along such lines. In the meantime, my monitor on Open School Night is Maureen McSherry and she tells me Stanley's battling father and mother are sitting in my classroom waiting to see me and, Maureen adds, there must be half a dozen battling couples who won't sit together while I talk about their little darlings.

Maureen has given them numbers like the ones you get in a bakery and my heart is sinking because there seems to be no end to the flow of parents coming into the room. As soon as you're finished with one, another arrives. They fill all the seats: three are perched like kids on the back windowsill, whispering, and half a dozen stand along the back wall. I wish I could tell Maureen to call a halt but you can't in a school like Stuyvesant where the parents know their rights and are never at a loss for words. Maureen whispers, Watch out. Here comes Stanley's mother, Rhonda. She'll have you for breakfast.

Rhonda reeks of nicotine. She sits and leans toward me and tells me not to believe a word of what that son-of-a-bitch, Stanley's father, tells me. She can't even bear to say the bastard's name and feels sorry for poor Stanley that he's stuck with this prick for a father figure and how is Stanley doing anyway?

Oh, fine. He's a pretty good writer and popular with the other kids.

Well, that's a miracle considering what he's going through with jerko Dad running around with every bit of skirt he can pick up. I do my best the times I have Stanley but he can't concentrate three and a half days a week knowing the next three and a half he's in that hovel in the Bronx. What's happening is that he's started to stay over at other kids' houses. That's what he tells me but I happen to know he's got this girlfriend whose parents are completely permissive and I have my suspicions.

I'm afraid I don't know anything about that. I'm just his teacher and it's impossible to get into the private lives of one hundred and seventy-five kids every semester.

Rhonda's voice carried and the waiting parents were shifting in their seats, rolling their eyes, restless. Maureen told me I'd have to watch the clock, give each parent no more than two minutes, even Stanley's father, who would demand equal time. He said, Hi, I'm Ben. Stanley's dad. Look, I heard what she said, the therapist. I wouldn't send a dog to her. He laughed and shook his head. But let's not get into that. I got this problem with Stanley now. After all this education, after me saving for his college education for years, he wants to screw the whole thing up. You know what he wants to do? Go to some conservatory in New England and study classical guitar. Tell me, what kinda money is there in playing classical guitar? I told him . . . but look, I won't take up your time, Mr. McCord.

McCourt.

Yeah. I won't take up your time, but I told him, Over my dead body. We agreed from day one he'd be an accountant. Never any doubt about that. I mean what am I working for? I'm a CPA myself and if you have any little problems I'd be glad to help out. No, sir. No classical guitar. I tell him, Go get your accountancy degree and play your guitar in your spare time. He breaks down. He cries. He threatens to live with his mother and I wouldn't wish that on a Nazi. So, I wonder if you could have a word with him? I know he likes your class, likes playing recipes and whatever you're doing here.

I'd like to help but I'm not a guidance counselor. I'm an English teacher.

Oh, yeah? Well, from what Stanley tells me about this class, the last thing you do here is teach English. No offense but I don't know what cooking has to do with English. Thanks anyway and how is he doing?

He's doing well.

The bell rings and Maureen, who is not shy, announces that time is up but she'd be glad to take names and phone numbers of anyone who would like to come in for a fifteen-minute conference on school days. She passes around a sheet of paper, which remains blank. They want my attention here and now. Christ, they've waited half the night while these other loonies babbled on about their messed-up kids and no wonder they're a mess, the parents they have. The frustrated ones follow me down the hall asking how is Adam doing, Sergei, Juan, Naomi? What kind of school is this where you can't get the attention of a teacher for a minute and what am I paying taxes for?

At nine, teachers punching out at the time clock are talking about going round the corner for a drink at the Gas House. We sit at a table in the back and order pitchers of beer. We're dry from talk talk talk. Jesus, what a night. I tell R'lene Dahlberg and Connie Collier and Bill Tuohy that in all my years at Stuyvesant only one parent, a mother, asked if her son was enjoying school. I said yes. He seemed to be enjoying himself. She smiled, stood up, said, Thank you, and left. One parent in all those years.

All they care about is success and money, money, money, says Connie. They have expectations for their kids, high hopes, and we're like workers on an assembly line sticking a little part in here, another little part in there till the finished product comes out at the end all ready to perform for parent and corporation.

A group of parents wandered into the Gas House. One came over to me. This is nice, she said. You have time to guzzle beer but you can't spare a minute for a parent who waited half an hour to see you.

I told her I was sorry.

She said, Yeah, and joined her group at another table. I felt so weighed down by that evening of parents I drank too much and stayed in bed next morning. Why didn't I just tell that mother to kiss my royal Irish arse?

*　*　*

235

In my class Bob Stein never sat at a desk. It could have been his bulk but I think he found comfort perched on the deep capacious windowsill in the back of the room. As soon as he was settled he smiled and waved. Good morning, Mr. McCourt. Isn't this a great day?

Through all the seasons of the school year he wore a white shirt open at the neck, the white collar lapped over the gray collar of his double-breasted jacket. He told the class that the jacket once belonged to Orson Welles and if he ever met Welles they'd have something to talk about. If it weren't for the jacket, he wouldn't know what to say to Orson Welles as his interests were completely different from the actor's.

He wore short pants that were long pants cut off at the knees and, no, they did not match the jacket so there was no connection with Orson Welles.

He wore gray socks so heavy they lumped in woolen piles over his yellow construction boots.

He carried no bag, no books, no notebooks, no pen. He joked that it was partly my fault because of the excited way I once talked about Thoreau and how you should simplify, simplify, simplify and get rid of possessions.

When there was a written assignment or a test in class he asked me if by any chance he could borrow a pen and some paper.

Bob, this is a writing class. It requires certain materials.

He assured me everything would be all right and advised me not to worry. He told me from the windowsill the snow was appearing on my head and I should enjoy the years left to me.

No, no, he told the class. Don't laugh.

But they were already in hysterics and so loud I had to wait to hear him again. He said that in a year from now I'd just look back at this moment and wonder why I wasted my time and emotions on his lack of pen and paper.

I had to play the part of stern teacher. Bob, you could fail this class if you don't participate.

Mr. McCourt, I can't believe you're telling me this, you of all people with your miserable childhood and everything, Mr. McCourt. But it's OK. If you fail me I'll take the course again. No big hurry. What's a year or two one way or the other? For you, maybe, it's a big thing but I'm only seventeen. All the time in the world, Mr. McCourt, even if you fail me.

He asked the class if anyone would like to help him out with pen and paper. There were ten offers but he took the one closest so that he wouldn't have to climb down from his windowsill. He said, See, Mr. McCourt? See how nice people are. Long as they carry these big bags you and I will never have to worry about supplies.

Yes, yes, Bob, but how is that going to help you next week when we have the big test on *Gilgamesh*?

What's that, Mr. McCourt?

It's in the world-literature book, Bob.

Oh, yeah. I remember that book. Big book. I have it at home and my dad's reading the Bible parts an' all. My dad's a rabbi, you know. He was so happy you gave us that book with all the prophets an' everything and he said you must be a great teacher an' he's coming to see you on Open School Night. I told him you were a great teacher except you have this thing about pens and paper.

Cut it out, Bob. You haven't even looked at the book.

He urged me again not to worry as his father, the rabbi, often talked about the book and he, Bob, would be sure to find out all about Gilgamesh and anything else that would make the teacher happy.

Again the class erupted, embracing one another, high fiving.

I wanted to erupt, too, but I had to maintain teacher dignity.

Across the room, over the giggling and gasping and laughing, I called, Bob, Bob. It would make me happy if you read the world-literature book yourself and left your poor father in peace.

He said he'd love to read the book cover to cover but it did not fit into his plans.

And what are your plans, Bob?

I'm going to be a farmer.

He smiled and waved the pen and paper so kindly donated by

Jonathan Greenberg and said he was sorry for disrupting the class and maybe we should start writing what I wanted them to write at the start of the period, which was quickly passing. He, Bob, was ready and suggested the class quiet down so Mr. McCourt could get on with his work. He told them teaching is the hardest work in the world and he should know because, once in summer camp, he tried to teach a bunch of small kids about things that grow in the ground but they wouldn't listen to him, just ran around chasing bugs till he got mad and said he'd kick their asses and that was the end of his teaching career, so have a little concern for Mr. McCourt. But before we got down to business he'd like to explain he had nothing against world literature except that now he read nothing but publications from the Department of Agriculture and magazines that had to do with farming. He said there's more to farming than meets the eye, but that's another subject, and he could see I wanted to get on with my lesson and what was that lesson, Mr. McCourt?

What was I to do with this large boy on the windowsill, a Jewish Future Farmer of America? Jonathan Greenberg raised his hand and asked what was it about farming that didn't meet the eye?

Bob looked gloomy for a moment. It's my dad, he said. He's having trouble with the corn and the pigs. He says Jews don't eat corn on the cob. He says you can go up one street and down the other in Williamsburg and Crown Heights and look in Jewish windows at dinnertime and you'll never see anyone chewing on corn on the cob. It just isn't a Jewish thing. Gets in the beard. Show me a Jew eating corn on the cob and I'll show you one who has lost the faith. That's my dad talking. But the last straw was pigs. I told my dad I like them. I'm not planning to eat them or anything but I'd like to raise them and sell them to the goyim. What's wrong with that? They're really pleasant little animals and they can be very affectionate. I told my dad I'll be married and have kids and they'll like the little piglets. He nearly went crazy and my mom had to go lie down. Maybe I shouldn't have told them but they taught me to tell the truth and it'll come out in the end anyway.

The bell rang. Bob climbed off the windowsill and returned pen and paper to Jonathan. He said his father the rabbi would be in to see me on Open School Night next week and he was sorry about the disruption.

The rabbi sat by my desk, heaved up his hands and said, Oy. I thought he was joking but the way he dropped his chin to his chest and shook his head told me this was not a happy rabbi. He said, Bob, how's he doing? He had a German accent.

Fine, I said.

He's killing us, breaking our hearts. Did he tell you? He wants to be a farmer.

It's a healthy life, Mr. Stein.

It's a scandal. We're not paying for him to go to college so he can raise pigs and corn. Fingers will be pointed on our street. It's gonna kill my wife. We told him he wants to go that way he's gonna pay for himself and that's final. He says don't worry. Big government programs have scholarships for kids who want to be farmers and he knows all about that. House full of books and stuff from Washington and some college in Ohio. So we're losing him, Mr. McCoot. Our son is dead. We can't have a son living with pigs every day.

I'm sorry, Mr. Stein.

Six years later I met Bob on Lower Broadway. It was a January day but he was attired as usual in short pants and Orson Welles jacket. He said, Hi, Mr. McCourt. Great day, isn't it?

It's freezing, Bob.

Oh, that's OK.

He told me he was already working for a farmer in Ohio, but he couldn't go through with the pig thing, that would destroy his parents. I told him that was a good and loving decision.

He paused and looked at me. Mr. McCourt, you never liked me, did you?

Never liked you, Bob? Are you joking? It was a joy to have you in my class. Jonathan said you drove the gloom from the room.

Tell him, McCourt, tell him the truth. Tell him how he brightened your days, how you told your friends about him, what an original he was, how you admired his style, his good humor, his honesty, his courage, how you would have given your soul for a son like him. And tell him how beautiful he was and is in every way, how you loved him then and love him now. Tell him.

I did, and he was speechless and I didn't give a tinker's damn what people thought on Lower Broadway when they saw us in a long warm embrace, the high school teacher and the large Jewish Future Farmer of America.

Ken was a Korean boy who hated his father. He told the class how he had to take piano lessons even though they had no piano. His father made him practice scales on the kitchen table till they could afford a piano and if his father suspected he wasn't practicing properly he whacked him across the fingers with a spatula. His six-year-old sister, too. When they got a real piano and she played "Chopsticks" he dragged her off the piano stool, into her room, tore a pile of her clothes from drawers, stuffed them into a pillowcase, dragged her down the hallway so that she could see him throwing her clothes into the incinerator.

That would teach her to practice properly.

When Ken was in elementary school he had to join the Boy Scouts and amass merit badges, more than anyone in his troop. Then, in high school, the father insisted he achieve Eagle Scout because that would look good when Ken applied to Harvard. Ken did not want to spend time trying to be an Eagle Scout but he had no choice. Harvard was on the horizon. Also, he was required by his father to excel in the martial arts, to rise from belt to belt till he reached black.

In everything he obeyed till it came to choice of college. His father told him he was to concentrate on applying to two universities, Harvard and M.I.T. Even back in Korea everyone knew that's where you go.

Ken said no. He was applying to Stanford in California. He wanted to live on the other side of the continent, as far from his father as possible. His father said no. He would not allow that. Ken said if he didn't go to Stanford he wasn't going to college at all. The father moved toward him in the kitchen and threatened him. Ken, martial arts expert, said, Just try it, Dad, and Dad backed off. Dad could have said, All right. Do what you like, but what would his neighbors say? What would they say in his church? Imagine having a son graduating from Stuyvesant High School and refusing to go to college. Dad would be disgraced. His friends were proudly sending their children to Harvard and M.I.T. and if Ken had any regard for the reputation of his family he'd forget Stanford.

He wrote me from Stanford. He liked the sunshine out there. College life was easier than Stuyvesant High School, less pressure, less competition. He had just had a letter from his mother, who said he was to concentrate on his studies and participate in no extracurricular activities, no sports, no clubs, nothing, and unless he had straight As in his courses he was not to come home for Christmas. He said, in the letter, that would suit him fine. He didn't want to come home for Christmas anyway. He came home only to see his sister.

He appeared at my classroom door a few days before Christmas and told me I had helped him get through the last year of high school. At one time he had a dream of going into a dark alleyway with his father and only one of them would come out. He'd be the one, of course, but out there in Stanford he began to think about his father and what it was like coming from Korea, working day and night selling fruit and vegetables when he knew barely enough English to get through the day, hanging on, desperate for his children to get the education he never had in Korea, that you couldn't even dream of in Korea, and then, in an English class at Stanford, when Ken was called on by the professor to talk about a favorite poem, what popped up in his memory was "My Papa's Waltz" and, Jesus, it was too much, he broke down and wept in front of all those people, and the professor was terrific, put his arm around Ken's shoulder and led him down the hallway to his office till he could recover. He stayed an hour in the professor's office, talking and crying, the professor saying it was OK, he had a father he thought was a mean son-of-a-bitch Polish Jew, forgetting that that mean son-of-a-bitch survived Auschwitz and made his way to California and raised the professor and two other kids, ran a delicatessen in Santa Barbara, every organ in his body threatening to collapse, undermined in the camp. The professor said their two fathers would have a lot to talk about but that would never happen. The Korean grocer and the Polish-Jewish delicatessen man could never find the words that come so easily in a university. Ken said a huge weight was lifted in the professor's office. Or you could say all kinds of poison had flowed out of his system. Something like that. Now he was going to buy his father a tie for Christmas and flowers for his mother. Yeah, it was crazy buying her flowers since they sold them in the store, but there was a big difference between the flowers you bought from the Korean corner grocery and the flowers you bought from a real florist. He kept thinking of one remark of the professor's, that the world should let the Polish-Jewish father and the Korean father sit in the sun with their wives, if they were lucky enough to have them. Ken laughed over how excited the professor became. Just let them sit in the goddam sun. But the world won't let them because there's nothing more dangerous than letting old farts sit in the sun. They might be thinking. Same thing with kids. Keep 'em busy or they might start thinking.

16

I'm learning. The mick from the lanes of Limerick letting the envy hang out. I'm dealing with first- and second-generation immigrants, like myself, but I've also got the middle classes and the upper middle classes and I'm sneering. I don't want to sneer but old habits die hard. It's the resentment. Not even anger. Just resentment. I shake my head over the things that concern them, that middle-class stuff, it's too hot, it's too cold and this is not the toothpaste I like. Here am I after three decades in America still happy to be able to turn on the electric light or reach for a towel after the shower. I'm reading a man named Krishnamurti and what I like about him is that he doesn't hold himself up as a guru like some of these characters who come storming out of India with tin cups that collect millions. He refuses to be guru or wise man or anything else. He tells you, suggests, that in the long run, baby, you're on your own. There's a chilling essay by Thoreau called "Walking," where he says when you go out the door for a walk you should be so free, so unencumbered, you need never return to the starting place. You just keep walking because you're free. I had the kids read this essay and they said, Oh, no, they could never do that. Just walk away? You kiddin'? Which is strange because when I talked to them about Kerouac and Ginsberg hitting the road, they thought it was wonderful. All that freedom. Marijuana and women and wine for three thousand miles. When I talk to those kids I'm talking to myself. What we have in common is urgency. Christ, I'm middle-aged and making discoveries the average intelligent American knew at twenty. The mask is mostly off and I can breathe.

The kids are opening up in their writing and classroom discussions and I'm getting a written tour of American family life from East Side town houses to Chinatown tenements. It's a pageant of the settled and the new and everywhere there are dragons and demons.

Phyllis wrote an account of how her family gathered the night Neil Armstrong landed on the moon, how they shuttled between the living room television and the bedroom where her father lay dying. Back and forth. Concerned with the father, not wanting to miss the moon landing. Phyllis said she was with her father when her mother called to come and see Armstrong set foot on the moon. She ran to the living room, everyone cheering and hugging till she felt this urgency, the old urgency, and ran to the bedroom to find her father dead. She didn't scream, she didn't cry, and her problem was how to return to the happy people in the living room to tell them Dad was gone.

She cried now, standing in front of the classroom. She could have stepped back to her seat in the front row and I hoped she would because I didn't know what to do. I went to her. I put my left arm around her. But that wasn't enough. I pulled her to me, embraced her with both arms, let her sob into my shoulder. Faces around the room were wet with tears till someone called, Right on, Phyllis, and one or two clapped and the whole class clapped and cheered and Phyllis turned to smile at them with her wet face and when I led her to her seat she turned and touched my cheek and I thought, This isn't earthshaking, this touch on the cheek, but I'll never forget it: Phyllis, her dead father, Armstrong on the moon.

Listen. Are you listening? You're not listening. I am talking to those of you in this class who might be interested in writing.

Every moment of your life, you're writing. Even in your dreams you're writing. When you walk the halls in this school you meet various people and you write furiously in your head. There's the principal. You have to make a decision, a greeting decision. Will you nod? Will you smile? Will you say, Good morning, Mr. Baumel? or will you simply say, Hi? You see someone you dislike. Furious writing again in your head. Decision to be made. Turn your ahead away? Stare as you pass? Nod? Hiss a Hi? You see someone you like and you say, Hi, in a warm melting way, a Hi that conjures up splash of oars, soaring violins, eyes shining in the moonlight. There are so many ways of saying Hi. Hiss it, trill it, bark it, sing it, bellow it, laugh it, cough it. A simple stroll in the hallway calls for paragraphs, sentences in your head, decisions galore.

I'll do this as a male because women, for me, still remain the great mystery. I could tell you stories. Are you listening? There's a girl in this school you've fallen in love with. You happen to know she's broken up with someone else so the field is clear. You'd like to go out with her. Oh, the writing now sizzles in your head. You might be one of those cool characters who could saunter up to Helen of Troy and ask her what she's doing after the siege, that you know a nice lamb-and-ouzo place in the ruins of Ilium. The cool character, the charmer, doesn't have to prepare much of a script. The rest of us are writing. You call her to see if she'll go out with you on Saturday night. You're nervous. Rejection will lead you to the edge of the cliff, the overdose. You tell her, on the phone, you're in her physics class. She says, doubtfully, Oh, yeah. You ask if she's busy Saturday night. She's busy. She has something planned, but you suspect she's lying. A girl cannot admit she has nothing to do on Saturday night. It would be un-American. She has to put on the act. God, what would the world say? You, writing in your head, ask about the following Saturday night and all the other Saturdays stretching into infinity. You'll settle for anything, you poor little schmuck, anything as long as you can see her before you start collecting Social Security. She plays her little game, tells you call her again next week and she'll see. Yeah, she'll see. She sits home on Saturday night watching TV with her mother and Aunt Edna, who never shuts up. You sit home Saturday night with your mother and father, who never say anything. You go to bed and dream that next week, oh, God, next week, she might say yes and if she does you have it all planned, that cute little Italian restaurant on Columbus Avenue with the red and white checked tablecloth and the Chianti bottles holding those dripping white candles.

Dreaming, wishing, planning: it's all writing, but the difference between you and the man on the street is that you are looking at it, friends, getting it set in your head, realizing the significance of the insignificant, getting it on paper. You might be in the throes of love or grief but you are ruthless in observation. You are your material. You are writers and one thing is certain: no matter what happens on Saturday night, or any other night, you'll never be bored again. Never. Nothing human is alien to you. Hold your applause and pass up your homework.

Mr. McCourt, you're lucky. You had that miserable childhood so you have something to write about. What are we gonna write about? All we do is get born, go to school, go on vacation, go to college, fall in love or something, graduate and go into some kind of profession, get married, have the two point three kids you're always talking about, send the kids to school, get divorced like fifty percent of the population, get fat, get the first heart attack, retire, die.

Jonathan, that is the most miserable scenario of American life I've heard in a high school classroom. But you've supplied the ingredients for the great American novel. You've encapsulated the novels of Theodore Dreiser, Sinclair Lewis, F. Scott Fitzgerald.

They said I must be joking.

I said, You know the ingredients of the McCourt life. You have your ingredients, too, what you'll use if you write about your life. List your ingredients in your notebook. Cherish them. This is urgent. Jewish. Middle class. *New York Times*. Classical music on radio. Harvard on the horizon. Chinese. Korean. Italian. Spanish. A foreign-language newspaper on the kitchen table. Ethnic music pouring out of the radio. Parents dream of trips to the Old Country. Grandmother, sitting silent in a corner of the living room, remembers glimpses of cemeteries in Queens. Thousands of headstones and crosses. Begs: Please, please, don't put me there. Take me to China. Please. So, sit with your grandmother. Let her tell her story. All the grandmothers and grandfathers have stories and if you let them die without taking down their stories you are criminal. Your punishment is banishment from the school cafeteria.

Yeah. Haw, haw.

Parents and grandparents are suspicious of this sudden interest in their lives. Why you asking me so many questions? My life is nobody's business, and what I did I did.

What did you do?

Nobody's business. Is it that teacher again? Stickin' his nose in?

No, Grandma. I just thought you'd want to tell me about your life so I can tell my kids and they can tell their kids and you won't be forgotten.

You tell that teacher mind his own business. All these Americans the same, always asking questions. We got privacy in this family.

But, Grandma, this teacher is Irish.

Oh, yeah? Well, they're the worst, always talking and singing about green things or getting shot and hung.

Others come in with stories of how they ask the elders one question about the past and the dam bursts and the old people won't stop talking, going on till bedtime and beyond, expressing heartache and tears, yearnings for the Old Country, declaring love for America. Family relationships are rearranged. Grandpa isn't taken for granted by sixteen-year-old Milton anymore.

In World War II Grandpa had adventures you wouldn't believe. Like he fell in love with the daughter of an SS officer and nearly got killed for it. Grandpa escaped and had to hide in the whaddya-call-it of a cow in a garbage dump.

The hide?

Yeah. The only reason the hide was there was it was already half eaten by rats and he had to fight them off. Three days in the hide fighting off the rats till a Catholic priest saw him and hid him under his church till the Americans came a year later. All these years Grandpa sits in the corner and I never talked to him and he never talked to me. His English still isn't good but that's no excuse. Now I have him on my tape recorder and my parents, my parents for Christ's sakes, are saying, Why bother?

Clarence was black, bright and diffident. He sat in the back of the room with three other black kids and never contributed to a class discussion. He and his friends had secret jokes and that annoyed me, that black cabal. At the same time I thought if I were black that is just where I'd be, in the back in a little ghetto of my own, mocking white teacher behind my hand.

David was black, bright and not a bit diffident. He sat over by the great windows with his white friends who followed him in and out of the classroom. When I asked the class a question his hand would go up and if he gave the wrong answer he'd shake his head in exasperation and say, Oh, spit. They tried to imitate him but no one could say, Oh, spit, like David. No one could create merriment like David. Students changed their programs just to be in a class with him. When he read his stories and essays on Fridays, they howled. Last Monday morning I got out of bed. Or didn't get out of bed. I only dreamed I was getting out of bed and I couldn't swear to you now that I was in or out of bed or dreaming about it or could I be dreaming about dreaming about it. This is all Mr. Lipper's fault because he was going on in the philosophy class about the Chinese thing where a man dreams about being a butterfly or was it a butterfly dreaming about being a man. Or a butterfly. Oh, spit.

Everyone laughed, but not Clarence. His three friends laughed, though they looked a bit sheepish. I asked him if he'd like to read today. He shook his head. I told him this was a writing class where everyone was expected to contribute and if he was reluctant to read himself maybe someone else would read what he had written. His indifference irritated me. I wanted one big happy class of Davids saying, Oh, spit.

That day I had cafeteria patrol. Clarence sat against a wall with a group of black kids. They were laughing at his impersonation of Hitler: a hot dog clasped between lip and nose as a mustache; a bowl on his head; a salute and a Seig Heil with raised arm. The cafeteria Clarence was not the classroom Clarence.

David watched from another table, quiet, unsmiling.

After lunch I asked Clarence if he'd read someday. No, he had nothing to say.

Nothing?

Well, I could never be like David.

You don't have to be like David.

You wouldn't like it. The only stories I know are street stories. Things happen on my street.

So, write something about your street.

Can't. Bad language and all that.

Clarence, tell me one word you know that I haven't heard. One word, Clarence.

But I thought we were to use proper English.

Use any English you like as long as you get it on paper.

The following Friday he was ready. Other readers stood when they read, but he wanted to sit. He reminded me there would be street language and did I mind?

I said, Nothing human is alien to me, and then told him I couldn't remember what Russian writer I was quoting.

He said, Oh, and started his account of how the mothers on his street dealt with a drug dealer. They warned him to get off the street but he told them he had to make a living and they should go to hell. Six mothers grabbed him one night and took him to a vacant lot. What they did to him there Clarence couldn't say but there were rumors. He couldn't repeat the rumors even if he was allowed and the language would be too raw for Stuyvesant students. All he could say was that one of the mothers called the ambulance so the guy wouldn't die in the vacant lot. The cops came around, of course, but nobody knew anything and the cops understood. That's the way it was on Clarence's street.

Silence. Wow, wild cheers, applause. Clarence sat back in the chair and looked at David, whose clapping was the most enthusiastic of all. David didn't say, Oh, spit. He knew this was Clarence's moment.

They wanted to know who was that weird guy at the classroom door. He was chalk white, cadaverous and stoned. He could have called me Frank but Good afternoon, Mr. McCourt, showed respect for the teacher.

I stepped into the hallway for one of our brief occasional conferences where he explained he happened to be in this neighborhood and was thinking about me and wondering how I was doing. Also, he happened to be caught short for the necessities and wondered if I might have any spare change about me. He appreciated past kindnesses and even though he saw little possibility of repayment he would always remember me warmly. It was such a pleasure to visit me here and to see the youth of America, these beautiful children, in such capable and generous hands. He said thanks and he might see me soon at Montero's Bar in Brooklyn, a few blocks from his apartment. In a few minutes the ten dollars I slipped him would be passed to a Stuyvesant Square drug dealer.

That's Huncke, I told them. Pick up any history of recent American writing or the Beat Generation and in the index you'll find Huncke, Herbert.

Alcohol is not his habit but he'll kindly allow you to buy him a drink at Montero's. His voice is deep, gentle and musical. He never forgets his manners and you'd rarely think of him as Huncke the Junkie. He respects law and obeys none of it.

He's done jail time for pickpocketing, robbery, possession of drugs, selling drugs. He's a hustler, a con man, a male prostitute, a charmer, a writer. He is given credit for coining the term Beat Generation. He uses people till he exhausts their patience and money and they tell him, Enough, Huncke. Out, out already. He understands and never carries grudges. It's all the same to him. I know he's using me, but he knew everyone in the Beat movement and I like listening to him talk about Burroughs, Corso, Kerouac, Allen Ginsberg. R'lene Dahlberg told me that Ginsberg once compared Huncke to St. Francis of Assisi. Yes, he's a criminal, an outlaw, but he steals only to sustain his drug habit and makes no profit out of his activities. Also, he's sensitive about what he takes. He will never take a piece of jewelry that looks like an heirloom. He knows if he leaves one thing a victim cherishes it will generate all kinds of good will and ease the pain of losing the other stuff. That will also bring him good luck. He confesses to every crime but murder, even tried suicide in R'lene's house in Majorca. Giving him the occasional ten dollars brings a kind of guarantee he won't break into my apartment though he tells me he's a bit over the hill for second-story work these days and usually has to hire a helper if he hears of good pickings. There's no shortage of willing boys on the Lower East Side. No more climbing fire escapes and rain pipes for Herbert Huncke. There are other ways of penetrating the fastnesses of the affluent, he says.

Such as?

You won't believe how many queer doormen and maintenance workers there are on Park and Fifth. If I made the right deals, arrangements for this body to meet that body, they'd wave me in and I could practically take a nap in some of those apartments. In the old days, when I was young, I'd peddle myself and I did very nicely, thank you. I was surprised once by this big insurance executive and ready to face a year in jail but he called down the hall to his wife, who brought martinis, and we all wound up in the bed in a beautiful menage. Oh, those were the days. We weren't gay then, just queer.

Next day there is a protest note on my desk signed, "A Mother." She doesn't want to give her name lest I hold this against her daughter, who came home and told the family about this despicable character, Honky, who is, from what her daughter told her, hardly a figure to inspire the youth of America. She realizes, does the mother, that this person exists on the fringes of American society, and couldn't I find more worthwhile figures to hold up as examples of "the good and the true"? People like Elinor Glynn or John P. Marquand.

I can't respond to this note, can't even mention it in class for fear of embarrassing the daughter. I understand the mother's fears but, if this is a class in writing with a nod to literature, what are the limits for the teacher? If a boy or girl writes a story about sex should I allow it to be read in class? After years with thousands of teenagers, listening to them and reading their work, I know their parents have an exaggerated idea of their innocence. The thousands have been my tutors.

Without mentioning Huncke I circle the subject. Look at the lives of Marlowe, Nash, Swift, Villon, Beaudelaire, Rimbaud, not to mention those disgraceful characters Byron and Shelley, down to Hemingway's loose ways with women and wine and Faulkner drinking himself to death down there in Oxford, Mississippi. You might think about Anne Sexton killing herself, Sylvia Plath likewise, and John Berryman jumping off a bridge.

Oh, aren't I the connoisseur of the dark.

For Christ's sake, McCourt, stop bothering the kids. Back off. Leave them alone and they will come home, and if their tails are not wagging it's due to the numbing effect of an English teacher's blather.

Serious students raise their hands and ask how I will evaluate them for their report cards. After all, I don't give them the usual tests: no multiple choice; no matching columns; no fill-in-the-blank spaces; no true or false. Concerned parents are asking questions.

I tell the serious students, Evaluate yourselves.

What? How can we evaluate ourselves?

You do it all the time. We all do it. Constant process of self-evaluation. Examination of conscience, boys and girls. You say to yourself, honestly, Did I learn anything from reading recipes as poetry, discussing Little Bo Peep as if it were a verse from T. S. Eliot, getting inside "My Papa's Waltz," listening to James and Daniel telling the inside story of their dinner, feasting in Stuyvesant Square, reading Mimi Sheraton. I say to you if you learned nothing from the above it means you were asleep during the tremendous violin playing of Michael and Pam's epic ode to duck or, and this is possible, friends, I am a lousy teacher.

They cheer. Yeah, that's it. You are a lousy teacher, and we all laugh because it is partly true and because they are free to say it and because I can take the joke.

Serious students are not satisfied. They argue that in other classes the teacher tells you what you are supposed to know. The teacher teaches it and you are supposed to learn it. Then the teacher gives you an examination and you get the grade you deserve.

Serious students say it is satisfying when you know in advance what you are supposed to know so that you can set about knowing it. They say, In this class you never know what you're supposed to know, so how can you study and how can you possibly evaluate yourself? In this class you never know what's going to pop up from day to day. The big puzzle at the end of the term is how does the teacher arrive at a grade?

I'll tell you how I arrive at a grade. First, how was your attendance? Even if you sat quietly in the back and thought about the discussions and the readings, you surely learned something. Second, did you participate? Did you get up there and read on Fridays? Anything. Stories, essays, poetry, plays. Third, did you comment on the work of your classmates? Fourth, and this is up to you, can you reflect on this experience and ask yourself what you learned? Fifth, did you just sit there and dream? If you did, give yourself credit.

This is where teacher turns serious and asks the Big Question: What is education, anyway? What are we doing in this school? You can say you're trying to graduate so that you can go to college and prepare for a career. But, fellow students, it's more than that. I've had to ask myself what the hell I'm doing in the classroom. I've worked out an equation for myself. On the left side of the blackboard I print a capital F, on the right side another capital F. I draw an arrow from left to right, from FEAR to FREEDOM.

I don't think anyone achieves complete freedom, but what I am trying to do with you is drive fear into a corner.

17

Time's winged chariot is hurrying near followed closely by the Hound of Heaven. You're getting older, and aren't you a two-faced blathering mick, prodding and encouraging kids to write when you know your own writer dream is dying. Console yourself with this: One day one of your gifted students will win a National Book Award or a Pulitzer and invite you to the event, and in a brilliant acceptance speech, allow as how he or she owes it all to you. You'll be asked to stand. You'll acknowledge the cheers of the multitudes. This will be your moment in the sun, your reward for thousands of lessons taught, millions of words read. Your prizewinner embraces you, and you fade into the streets of New York, little old Mr. Chips, toiling the stairs of his tenement, a crust in the cupboard, a jorum of water in the ice-box, a bulb of modest wattage dangling over the celibate cot.

The great American drama is the clash of adolescence with middle age. My hormones beg for a quiet clearing in the woods, theirs are brassy, throbbing, demanding.

Today they do not want to be bothered by teachers or parents.

Nor do I want to be bothered by them. I don't want to see or hear them. I have squandered my best years in the company of squawking adolescents. In the time I've spent in classrooms I could have read thousands of books. I could have roamed the Forty-second Street Library, up one side and down the other. I wish the kids would disappear. I'm not in the mood.

Other days I'm desperate to get into the classroom. I wait, impatient, in the hallway. I paw the ground. Come on, Mr. Ritterman. Hurry up. Finish your damn math lesson. There are things I want to say to this class.

A young substitute teacher sat beside me in the teachers' cafeteria. She was to start her regular teaching career in September and could I offer her any advice?

Find what you love and do it. That's what it boils down to. I admit I didn't always love teaching. I was out of my depth. You're on your own in the classroom, one man or woman facing five classes every day, five classes of teenagers. One unit of energy against one hundred and seventy-five units of energy, one hundred and seventy-five ticking bombs, and you have to find ways of saving your own life. They may like you, they may even love you, but they are young and it is the business of the young to push the old off the planet. I know I'm exaggerating but it's like a boxer going into the ring or a bullfighter into the arena. You can be knocked out or gored and that's the end of your teaching career. But if you hang on you learn the tricks. It's hard but you have to make yourself comfortable in the classroom. You have to be selfish. The airlines tell you if oxygen fails you are to put on your mask first, even if your instinct is to save the child.

The classroom is a place of high drama. You'll never know what you've done to, or for, the hundreds coming and going. You see them leaving the classroom: dreamy, flat, sneering, admiring, smiling, puzzled. After a few years you develop antennae. You can tell when you've reached them or alienated them. It's chemistry. It's psychology. It's animal instinct. You are with the kids and, as long as you want to be a teacher, there's no escape. Don't expect help from the people who've escaped the classroom, the higher-ups. They're busy going to lunch and thinking higher thoughts. It's you and the kids. So, there's the bell. See you later. Find what you love and do it.

It was April and sunny outside and I wondered how many Aprils I had left, how many sunny days. I was beginning to feel I had nothing left to say to the high school students of New York about writing or anything else. My voice began to trail away. I thought I wanted to be out in the world before I was out of the world. Who was I to talk about writing when I had never written a book never mind published one? All my talk, all my scribbling in notebooks amounted to nothing. And didn't they wonder about that? Didn't they say, How come he talks so much about writing when he never did it?

It was time to retire, live on the teacher's pension that was less than princely. I'll catch up on the books I missed in the last thirty years. I'll spend hours at the Forty-second Street Library, the place I love most in New York, walk the streets, have a beer at the Lion's Head, talk to Deacy, Duggan, Hamill, learn the guitar and a hundred songs to go with it, take my daughter, Maggie, for dinner in the Village, scribble in my notebooks. Something might come.

I'll get by.

When Guy Lind was a sophomore he brought an umbrella to school on a snowy slushy day. He met a friend on the second floor who also had an umbrella. They began to fence with their umbrellas till the friend slipped and the tip of his umbrella pierced through Guy's eye and left him paralyzed on one side.

They took him to Beth Israel Hospital across the street and that started a long journey from city to city and country to country. They even took him to Israel, where the fighting keeps them up to date on trauma and treatment.

Guy returned to school in a wheelchair and wearing a black eye patch. After a while he made his way through the corridors with the help of a walking stick. Eventually he discarded the stick and you wouldn't know of his accident except for the black eye patch and an arm that lay useless on the desk.

Here was Guy in my last class listening to Rachel Blaustein on the other side of the room. She was talking about a poetry class she took with Mrs. Kocela. She enjoyed the class and the way Mrs. Kocela taught poetry but it was really a waste of time for her. What was there to write about when everything in her life was perfect: her parents happy and successful; Rachel the only child and headed for Harvard; Rachel with perfect health?

I told her she could add beauty to her catalogue of perfection.

She smiled, but the question remained, What was there to write about?

Someone said, I wish I had your troubles, Rachel. She smiled again.

Guy told of his experiences in the past two years. For all he went through he wouldn't want to change anything. In hospital after hospital he met people shattered, sick, suffering in silence. He said all this put his accident in a different perspective. It took him out of himself. No, he wouldn't change a thing.

This is their last high school class, and mine. There are tears and expressions of wonder that Guy is sending us on our way with a story that reminds us to count our blessings.

The bell rings and they sprinkle me with confetti. I am told to have a good life. I wish them the same. I walk, color speckled, along the hallway.

Someone calls, Hey, Mr. McCourt, you should write a book.

18

I'll try.

P.S.

Ideas,
interviews
& features . . .

About the author

Read on

A Hell of a Second Act

Louise Tucker talks to Frank McCourt

How did the experience of writing *Teacher Man* differ from that of writing *Angela's Ashes* and *'Tis*?
Teacher Man was much harder to write. I think that, perhaps, I was more self-conscious now that I was a big shot, bestselling author. And the stuff did not flow that easily. I was dealing with thirty years of teaching and thousands of students and there was a heavy process of selection.

You end *Teacher Man* saying 'I'll try'. Now that you have tried, and succeeded, how do you feel about that man on the threshold of his 'second act'?
The main thing is I'm a late bloomer and that means I'm having a hell of a second act.

You spent years teaching creative writing and yet not writing. Did you find that frustrating?
All through my teaching years I tried to write. I filled notebooks with ideas and even nibbled at *Angela's Ashes* material but I never sustained anything.

Some argue that writing cannot be taught, that MAs and MFAs are a waste of time. Do you think such courses are helpful?
I was a 'creative writing' teacher at Stuyvesant High School – but for God's sake don't tell anyone as I don't have much faith in such courses. The aspiring writer would be better off out there suffering.

Teaching is in some ways good training for the life of a writer now, in that it is as much about performance as it is about sitting at a desk. Do you enjoy the public side of being a writer as much as the private?
I enjoy most of the public stuff. At this stage of my life I'm simply recycling my teaching career. The 'private part' of writing is hard – especially with *Teacher Man*.

In Chapter Four you tell your students about your experiences of 'real work'. Do you think it helped you, in both professions, to have experienced a much harder way of earning a living?
I'm glad I worked on the docks and at various other jobs. It gives you different perspectives on life and, most of all, material. Such experiences help ground one.

One parent in thirty years asks if her child is enjoying school. Enjoyment, a colleague points out, is not the priority for most parents but what, as far as you're concerned, should a school's purpose be?
I think a school should work like hell to help young people with their 'potential' – whatever that is. It should be a liberating rather than a narrowing place where curiosity is encouraged and fostered. Oh, I could go on.

You describe teaching as the 'downstairs maid of professions'. Why do you think ▶

❛ I was a "creative writing" teacher at Stuyvesant High School – but for God's sake don't tell anyone as I don't have much faith in such courses. The aspiring writer would be better off out there suffering. ❜

A Hell of a Second Act *(continued)*

◄ **that many parents, pupils and social commentators have so little respect for it?**
People in general look down on teachers the way they regard members of their family: they think they know what teaching is all about when the fact is they don't have a clue, any more than they know what surgery is all about. Teachers, in my examples, are people who failed in other areas, but that doesn't take away from those who are gifted, hard-working and committed. Also, many people think teaching is easy. Oh, you simply walk into a classroom and blather and the kids sit and listen. Hell, no.

You frequently mention that 'no one is forcing you to stay in this miserable underpaid profession'. Why did you stay for thirty years?
I think I stayed because I didn't want to admit I couldn't do it and because, the more I did it, the more I liked the job – profession – and the challenge of getting through to the kids.

Is failing to finish your doctorate ever a regret?
If I had earned that doctorate I would have wound up teaching in a college. I might have become a pompous academic and there would have been no *Angela's Ashes*.

Often you mention that the 'farther you travel from the classroom, the greater the financial and professional rewards'. Were you ever tempted?
No, never. Again I would have become a pompous ass with an office.

❝ I think a school should work like hell to help young people with their "potential" – whatever that is. It should be a liberating rather than a narrowing place where curiosity is encouraged and fostered. ❞

4

If you could choose one moment, one student, that epitomized what teaching meant to you, what or who would it be?
I'd choose a negative moment. I barked at a girl who merely questioned the grade I'd given her and I was so mean about it I shocked myself. I learned never to do that again. From the negative came the positive.

What do you miss most about the job? And least?
What I miss most is the exuberance and excitement of the classroom. What I miss least is the claustrophobic atmosphere created by bureaucrats and politicians.

Are you still in touch with any of your students?
I meet former students everywhere. One, Susan Gilman, was recently on the *New York Times*' bestseller list with a memoir, *Hypocrite in a Pouffy White Dress*. She said she owes it all to me. I agreed with her.

The parents called you a fraud for telling stories but the students loved you: how did such conflicting opinions help or hinder your teaching?
I paid little attention to parents. Their ideas of education conflicted with mine. I don't mean that in any disrespectful way but they worried mostly about grades and I didn't really give a fiddler's fart.

How has teaching changed since you left? Are there any changes that you mourn?
Teachers now have to deal with a tsunami ▶

> ❝ People in general look down on teachers the way they regard members of their family: they think they know what teaching is all about when the fact is they don't have a clue. ❞

Author photo © Jerry Bauer

LIFE
at a Glance

BORN

Manhattan

EDUCATED

Leamy's National School, Limerick; New York University

CAREER

Telegram boy, letter-writer, Easons delivery boy, houseman at the Biltmore Hotel, US Army, warehouseman, Blue Cross insurance clerk, teacher

LIVES

Connecticut, USA, with his wife Ellen
Family: One daughter and three grandchildren

A Hell of a Second Act *(continued)*

◀ of technology that would have driven me out of my mind. I would have had to bar all mobile phones, iPods, etc, from my classroom – and that would have been a great problem.

Writing is essentially solitary; teaching social. Do you believe that you weren't ready for the quiet solitude required to write when you were younger?
When I was younger I wanted the fame and attention that come with publishing so I would have been more interested in the superficial than in the hard grind of private work.

'You are your material,' you tell your students and this has been the case for you. Do you think you have exhausted yours now?
Yes, I'm finished with Frank McCourt memoir stuff – unless I draw on it to write a novel. ■

The Most Important Books and Authors in My Life

P.G. Wodehouse, Charles Dickens and Mark Twain

These three writers opened up the idea to me that you can write natural, that you don't have to write like Trollope or Thackeray. I suppose in the long run the influence on me has been mainly English because of the Victorian society we grew up in and the books and newspapers that were available. Also with these three writers you can look at any page and know that nobody else could have written it: that style fascinates me.

The Four Just Men
Edgar Wallace

In a way I grew up in a Victorian age so we never read James Joyce – it wasn't that he was banned or anything, it just wasn't available – but I read a lot of authors that are now forgotten, like Wallace who was a mystery writer. This is his most famous novel: the characters were like four Robin Hoods who deal with bad guys and I wanted to grow up and be like them.

Mrs Dalloway
Virginia Woolf

Next to Wodehouse on the shelf in the public library in Limerick was this woman Virginia Woolf and that's how I discovered *Mrs Dalloway*. I've read it ten times now. I tried to read her others and I wasn't ready for them but I swallowed this. ▶

The Most Important Books and Authors in My Life *(continued)*

◄ *Lives of the Poets*
Samuel Johnson

When I went to the States I went into a bar on my second day and the barman, the owner, told me, 'Get out of here, go up to the library and read Samuel Johnson.' This man knew more about Samuel Johnson than any professor. 'Don't come back,' he said, 'don't come back until you've read the *Lives of the Poets*.' So I went and read the *Lives of the Poets*, three volumes, and discovered the most glorious place in Manhattan, the main library on 42nd Street. I couldn't believe it when I went there: the world was opened up to me.

Dubliners and *A Portrait of the Artist as a Young Man*
James Joyce

When I was drafted I rediscovered that strange thing called Irish literature, through a librarian who urged me to read Joyce. But I had no notion of what he was doing!

Juno and the Paycock, The Plough and the Stars and *Shadow of a Gunman*
Sean O'Casey

O'Casey was the other Irish writer who made a big impression on me. I had heard his plays on English radio when I was a kid listening to the woman next door's set and I especially liked them but then I discovered his autobiographies in the library in New York. There are four of them, and although the writing's a bit too rich for me, like having three desserts, the subject matter was appealing because he grew up in a poor family and he was one of those strange creatures, a Protestant in Dublin. Through him I discovered Frank O'Connor and Sean O'Faolain, two of the greatest Irish short-story writers.

Studs Lonigan
James T. Farrell

When I was in the army in New Jersey I discovered this book about a character growing up in Chicago, the usual American story about the streets, the slums and Irish-American Catholicism, and that introduced me to Irish-American literature. I started reading in the encyclopedia about Irish-American literature and discovered Eugene O'Neill. I went to see one of his plays, *The Iceman Cometh*, which knocked me out of the seat.

Evelyn Waugh, Graham Greene and David Lodge

Faith fascinates me, especially when brilliant, intelligent, witty, charming Englishmen like Waugh and Greene turn to the Catholic Church. I've looked at Waugh's letters and memoirs and I think he did it out of pure snobbery, realizing that the Catholic Church puts on the best show in town. Greene got into it because of a marriage but then he never shook it off and struggled with it the rest of his life. I read a lot of David Lodge now because in a lighter way he tangles ▶

The Most Important Books and Authors in My Life *(continued)*

◀ with the stuff that Greene and Waugh struggled with as he's also a committed Catholic. I don't think I have faith myself, but maybe I'm going after it. ■

A Writing Life

When do you write?
In the morning.

Where do you write?
Wherever I am.

Why do you write?
Because I can't help it.

Pen or computer?
Pen but now computer because of my poor
maimed hands!

Silence or music?
Silence.

How do you start a book?
I make coffee.

And finish?
I never know. When my head begins to get
dull I stop.

**Do you have any writing rituals or
superstitions?**
No.

Which living writer do you most admire?
Tom Wolfe.

What or who inspires you?
Time is running out, that's what inspires me.

If you weren't a writer what job would you do?
Musician, the piano. I don't know how to play
it but I would learn it. ▶

A Writing Life *(continued)*

◄ **What's your guilty reading pleasure? Favourite trashy read?**
Newspapers, they're trash. ■

Have You Read?

Angela's Ashes

Frank McCourt's first book tells the story of his childhood until his departure for America. Witty and harrowing in equal measure, it takes the reader into the world of a poor and hungry small boy in the slums of Limerick and narrates both his struggle to survive and his dreams of escape.

....

'Tis

In the sequel to *Angela's Ashes,* Frank arrives in New York where, far from his family, he must negotiate a world of strangers to create his own life. From the meat-packing district to the classroom, every forward and backward step, in the world of love and professions, is his own responsibility. He is free to do what he wants, but is freedom what he wants?

If You Loved This,
You Might Like . . .

Books and films about teaching seem to fall into two distinct categories: the English public-school tale of unfulfilled promise and self-sacrifice and the inner-city high-school experience in which a determined and perhaps deluded young teacher strives to make a difference. Perhaps these are the only narrative-worthy tales to be found in education; or perhaps this tells us that whereas staff may lose their dreams by working in schools, some pupils are lucky enough to find theirs. Interestingly, many prominent stories about education have been televised or filmed: so watching it is obviously not as painful as experiencing it . . .

The Blackboard Jungle
Evan Hunter

Evan Hunter is better known as Ed McBain, famous for many books and screenplays including the 87th Precinct crime thrillers. This, his first novel, brought him instant success. Set in fifties' New York, it tells the story of Richard Dadier, a middle-class teacher who is assigned to a tough inner-city high school. Determined to make a difference, despite resistance and mockery from both pupils and established staff, he finds that teaching is the least of his problems when faced with confrontational pupils and threats.

Made into an equally successful film in 1955, in which Sidney Poitier stars as Gregory Miller, a clever but streetwise boy torn between the chance to better himself and impressing his peers, it helped launch the Rock and Roll era when its theme tune, 'Rock Around the Clock', reached the number one slot. Interestingly, it was X-rated when released in the UK in 1955.

The Browning Version
Terence Rattigan

On the last day of term at a boys' public school, a new teacher arrives to familiarize himself with his workplace. His predecessor, Andrew Crocker-Harris, is retiring and, it seems, no one will miss him. A bitter scholar whose work and marriage have not turned out as he hoped, Crocker-Harris seems to be disliked by both pupils and staff. But an unexpected act of kindness forces him to reconsider his life and relationships as he prepares to leave. Rattigan's play was made into a film starring Michael Redgrave in 1951.

Goodbye Mr Chips

James Hilton's novel was made into a much more famous film in 1939, starring Robert Donat and Greer Garson. Hilton's story, of a much-loved teacher looking back on his life and love as he faces retirement, is said to be based on his classics master, W. H. Balgarnie, who taught for over 50 years at a private school in Cambridge, England.

In 1969 another film of the same name was made, but in this instance the shy retiring Mr Chips falls for a showgirl. Interestingly the screenplay was by Terence Rattigan and Michael Redgrave played the headmaster. Evidently the field of actors ▶

If You Loved This,
You Might Like . . . *(continued)*

◄ and writers interested in education was rather narrow!

***

To Serve Them All Our Days
R. F. Delderfield
Once again the English public school serves as the backdrop for a novel about a teacher's life in the interwar years in England. However, Delderfield's main character is a little different. David Powlett-Jones is a Welsh miner's son and a scholarship boy. Having been invalided out of the trenches, he ends up in the sort of school which he could never have attended and must struggle to make a place for himself in a country which is trying to do the same.

WATCH . . .

Dead Poets Society
Unashamedly sentimental but nonetheless enjoyable story of an extraordinary teacher's ability to inspire and motivate his pupils. Robin Williams plays new English teacher John Keating who encourages his classes to question the status quo and 'seize the day'. Again, the fascination with 1950s boarding schools continues, though this one is in the USA. ■